Recalling the Wild

Recalling the Wild

Naturalism and the Closing of the American West

MARY LAWLOR

RUTGERS UNIVERSITY PRESS
New Brunswick, New Jersey, and London

Library of Congress Cataloging-in-Publication Data

Lawlor, Mary, 1949–
Recalling the wild : naturalism and the closing of the American West / Mary
Lawlor.
    p.   cm.
Includes bibliographical references (p.) and index.
ISBN 0-8135-2829-1 (alk. paper) — ISBN 0-8135-2830-5 (paper : alk. paper)
1. American fiction—20th century—History and criticism.   2. West (U.S.)—In
literature.   3. American fiction—19th century—History and criticism.
4. American fiction—West (U.S.)—History and criticism.   5. Historical fiction,
American—History and criticism.   6. Literature and history—West (U.S.)—
History.   7. Western stories—History and criticism.   8. Frontier and pioneer
life in literature.   9. Wilderness areas in literature.   10. Naturalism in literature. 11. Closure (Rhetoric).   I. Title.

PS374.W4 L39 2000
813'.52093278—dc21   99-056541

British Cataloging-in-Publication data for this book is available from the British
Library

Manufactured in the United States of America

To my mother, Frances Lawlor,
and to the memory of my father, John Lawlor,
and my sister, Elizabeth Davis

Contents

Preface

M<small>Y INTERESTS IN THE</small> American West and in literary naturalism have certain biographical antecedents. I grew up in a military family and in a cold war climate saturated in the ideology and the ethics of an idealized West. But my father's tales of "Air Cav" adventures and the atmosphere of military bravado that prevailed on the bases where we lived stood in marked contrast to the regimented order of landscapes dominated by barracks, guard posts, drill fields, and hangars.. This contrast constituted, perhaps, a preview of the dichotomies between Western romanticism and naturalism that I write about in this book.

Another, later phase of my life might also have fostered this interest. I went to high school in northern California and to college in Paris. I was in the French capital during the spring of 1968, when student and labor movements joined forces in a memorable uprising. Poststructuralism and postmodernism, which offered theoretical frameworks for the Parisian movements, soon found their way across the Atlantic and across America to the rebellious regions of California, where they collided head-on with the romanticisms of what Thomas Pynchon calls "the olden hippy days."

This familiar collision between Western romanticism of the sixties and a French paradigm skeptical of claims to innocence, originality, and autonomy alerted me, perhaps, to the earlier clash of Western romanticism with French naturalism. The naturalism of the 1890s, like poststructuralism in the 1960s and 1970s, served notice that no place— no single city, state, or country—could be a simple source of freedom or of new beginnings. Rather than inviting inspiration and regeneration, California, no less than France, came to be understood in both generations as the locus of seemingly ineluctable repetitions—of political, commercial, and artistic tendencies that went a long way to shape the person as well as the culture.

My hope is that by elucidating the earlier collision—when the apparently ineradicable American myth was doused in the cold waters of Gallic critical theory—I can help clarify some of our contemporary confusions and accommodations.

Some sections of the book have been published previously in different form. An earlier version of the discussion of Daniel Boone in chapter 1 appeared as "The Fictions of Daniel Boone," in Eric Heyne's collection *Desert, Garden, Margin, Range: Literature on the American Frontier*. The analysis of Frank Norris's short stories in chapter 5 had an earlier avatar as "'Life' and 'Literature' in Frank Norris's Cowboy Tales," published in *Prairie Winds*. Sections of the discussions of Norris's naturalism appeared in "Placing Source in *Greed* and *McTeague*" in *Intertextuality in Literature and Film: Selected Papers from the 13th Florida State University Conference on Literature and Film*, edited by Elaine D. Cancalon and Antoine Spacagna; and in "Naturalism in the Cinema: Erich von Stroheim's Reading of *McTeague*" in *Frank Norris Studies*.

I would like to thank many other people who have helped in the production of *Recalling the Wild*. The book would not have been possible without the guidance, in its first stages, of Josephine Hendin at New York University. Her intelligence and wit in reading the dynamics of American literary history and culture, not to mention her fine rhetorical sensibility, were crucial to the development of my arguments. Kenneth Silverman and Harold Bloom at NYU with generosity read the manuscript and offered sound advice on the arguments and the initial scope of the project.

In later stages, my colleagues in the English department at Muhlenberg College—Jim Bloom, Tom Cartelli, Alec Marsh, David Rosenwasser, Grant Scott, and Jill Stephen—have been helpful in reading the manuscript and offering suggestions for the shape of the book. Joe Elliot was extraordinarily generous with his time and talents in taking the pictures of the Curtis photogravures and in talking with me about his visual sense of the American West. I am grateful to Dean Curtis Dretsch for permission to reproduce the Curtis images in the collection of the Martin Art Gallery at Muhlenberg and for a grant to help with the cover art; to Kelly Cannon for reading and giving me advice on the later versions of my first two chapters; to Karl Henson for providing technical assistance when I was formating the final version of the manuscript; and to Linda Bowers and Tom Gaughan at Trexler Library for helping me locate a Curtis image from *The North American Indian* in the library's basement.

Jim Livingston read the manuscript and offered especially helpful comments, particularly about the role of naturalism in Western films. Conversations with Marc Manganaro, a fellow aficionado of the American West, were influential in my thinking about Edward S. Curtis as an ethnographer and about certain perspectives of twentieth-century Western historiography. Bruce Robbins, ever a source of innovative thought on narratives of nationalism, gave the manuscript much valued support. Patricia Rossi helped me process many ideas and shared her wisdom as a geographer and editor. Lisa Salem influenced my thoughts in surprising and important ways with her deep concern for and extensive knowledge of national mythology and literature in the context of Lebanon. Jim, Marc, Bruce, Tisha, and Lisa, together with John McClure, all provided inspiration of which they were probably unaware on several occasions late at night in the wilderness of New Jersey.

I am especially grateful to Perry Meisel for a crucial, final reading of the manuscript and for ideas inspired by his *The Cowboy and the Dandy*. I also want to thank Fred Pfeil for reading the manuscript and commenting with great precision and care on its pitfalls as well as its merits. Virginia Wiles, Anna Adams, and Jill Stephen kindly listened to ideas and helped see me through the fears and pains of illness last year. My parents, John and Frances Lawlor, and my sisters Nancy Pennington and Sarah Pearce, were also of invaluable aid to me during this time; they as well as my late sister, Lizzie Davis, gave me valuable encouragement in the early stages of the writing process.

Some years ago, my old friend Ken Shapiro was good enough to lend me his apartment in San Francisco so I could do research on the Bay Area of the late nineteenth century and visit the Bancroft Library to study the early years of Berkeley. Leslie Mitchner and Brigitte Goldstein at Rutgers University Press provided much needed guidance with the publishing process; and Jessica Hornik Evans did a superb job of editing the manuscript. Teri McLuhan graciously lent me her nega-

tive of "Mr. Herb Dunton and Model in Field," which she had converted from the original plate-glass version with difficulty and at great
expense in a lab in Paris, for the book's cover image. Last and most
especially, I thank John McClure, my husband and very best friend
through everything, an explorer-critic of the actual and rhetorical terrains of empire, whose determinism and romanticism are ever blended
in the most appealing and splendidly principled ways.

Recalling the Wild

Introduction

THE ELIMINATION OF the frontier as a category in the U.S. Census of 1890 signaled the government's official position that this public domain had come to its end. The closing of the frontier had, of course, been imagined in American literary, historical, and political commentary for several generations; but with the deletion of the Census category, it appeared to have become an actual condition. Whether or not, in view of the West's remaining unsettled space, the Census office's decision was justified, the frontier's status as a romantic geography gained new dimensions as its location in space came to be substituted by location in the imagination. Writers and artists across the social spectrum found in the topic of the vanished "wilderness" an opportunity to memorialize the open-endedness, the sense of possibility of what was now regarded as a storied zone of adventure. More than just the setting for heroic acts of exploration and settlement, the topography of the American West gained the status of an agent in a conglomerate epic of national origins.

Parallel to these artistic visions, and often contained in them, a rival motif of closure emerged as a means to represent the historical shift and its consequences for regional culture. These accounts and images portrayed the frontier as giving way to what was construed as the irresistible engine of progress and saw the wilderness as productive of unadapted, and necessarily vanishing, forms. *Recalling the Wild* attempts to track the relationships between these two modes of thinking about the West in imaginative and documentary works of the late nineteenth and early twentieth century. The generic designations I have chosen to frame the discussion are naturalism and romanticism, two notoriously playful tags that, nevertheless, seem to serve as the most useful headings for the competing modes that developed at the turn of the century for depicting and thinking about the frontier and the West.

WESTERN ICONOGRAPHY had never adhered to a single format or a single ideology, although the dominant mode for representing the American West by Europeans and Euro-Americans since at least the middle of the eighteenth century had largely been, to put it simply, romantic.[1] The frontier was typically construed as a border zone that harbored mystery and danger, but that ultimately opened onto a plentiful, inviting space where the desires of common citizens, if they were diligent and brave, might be richly fulfilled. The wide, figuratively horizontal plane featured in such prospects gave material form to the ideals of democratic possibility central to U.S. national culture from its beginnings.

Rather than discouraging these long-held notions, the image and idea of the closed frontier at the end of the nineteenth century fueled a widespread retrospection in writing, photography, and painting. Romantic paintings like Albert Bierstadt's *Yosemite Valley* and *The Last Buffalo*, Thomas Moran's *The Chasm of the Colorado* and *The Grand Canyon of the Yellowstone*, and the sculptures of Cyrus Dallin and Frederic Remington projected a revered geography and a mystical sense of frontier character. Among writers, Remington, Owen Wister, Bret Harte, and even the Mark Twain of *Roughing It* recreated a rough world of heroic characters competing with landscapes and each other for survival.

At the same time, the discourse of evolutionism and the styles of French naturalism began to challenge this traditional, romantic idiom in the United States, prompting accounts of the West in the rival terms of a colder, less resonant determinism. The overt project of those adhering to the naturalist mode was to construct a critical reevaluation of the West as a strictly material place and a historically determined culture. Thus, in the naturalist mode the West was pictured as a limited and often limiting geographical space that lacked the psychological and ideological colorings of a truly open frontier and cast regional identity as the product of material "forces" rather than of individualistic enterprise.

Emile Zola's naturalism, which started drawing attention in the

United States as translations of his novels and essays appeared in the 1880s, openly contested the romantic ideology of open space and individual will that was exemplified by traditional representations of the American West. His fiction set patterns for U.S. writers, who, consciously and unconsciously, drew on his methods as they tried to frame a post-frontier West. The determining pressures of social and historical forces in Zola's theoretical scheme rendered as illusory and misleading the romantic constructions of self and nation characteristic of what I refer to throughout this book as *westernism*.[2] I use this term to suggest any form of European-American desire for the West, even those that claim affinity for its roughness and primitiveness. My assumption is that such affinities, too, are versions of a will to cultivate non-European space in Euro-American terms.

As Zola's models found their way into U.S. fiction at the end of the century, what resulted was an emphasis on the confinement of the West within the iron cage of modernity. In this fictive world the Western environment entrapped human characters within a narrow range of possible actions, roles, even thoughts; the strong implication was that life in the West shared the social constraints and banal domesticity of life in the East.

Yet, although naturalism cast doubt on the informing principles of westernism and notably complicated the imaginative geography of the West, it certainly did not displace westernism as a national narrative. Naturalist Western fiction invoked romantic models of character, plot, and landscape in order to challenge them with determinism's rival methodologies, but in the end only partially succeeded in disciplining the older mode. Naturalism did, indeed, intensify the role of social, economic, and biological facticity in traditional plots and characterizations, and it redressed some of the problematic features of frontier ideology. But its critique of westernism was often frustrated by the fact that the two modes had things in common after all. Moreover, as often as not the limitations and confinements of the naturalist paradigm sponsored a desire in its characters for an Old West, a desire that fueled nostalgic recollections, even as naturalist theories were aimed at overriding notions of an open-ended or indeterminate wilderness.[3]

So the story I tell here is not simply one of literary conquest or colonizing, in which naturalism invades the West of the imagination and expels or exterminates an older mode. Although it did have some enduring, revisionary influence on "serious" Western representation, naturalism was too flawed as a literary and philosophical paradigm, and the attractions of westernism—for writers as well as readers—were too great for it to substantially overcome the older mode. Writers ready to challenge westernism's sense of free agency finally balked at affirming naturalism's reductions of human character and of social development to the terms of a strict environmental determinism.

This book focuses in particular on the works of Frank Norris, Jack London, Stephen Crane, and Willa Cather, each of whom took up naturalist literary methods to write about the West. Cather's work is not commonly associated with naturalism, but I argue that, even as it lacks overt references to a naturalist literary code, the models of development that Cather stages, for individual characters as for Western regional communities and national culture, often invoke the language of determinism as a medium for representing the fin-de-siècle West.

The writings of Norris, London, Crane, and Cather in a sense promise a contribution to the history of anti-expansionism in American letters by critiquing the heroic account of exploration and settlement that romantic westernism sponsored. But their biographical as well as literary ambivalences about Western regional culture, which drew on such epic material for much of its identity and inspiration, dramatically compromise the critical gesture. Although relations between the two modes were often antagonistic, at other times they were mutually influential. Thus, romanticism was at times sharpened in tone and imbued with an allegorical quality that tended to diminish the consummate value of individualism in much earlier Western writing. And naturalism, in turn, was expanded to allow for more complication of character and landscape, as landscape, precisely in its indifference, became the setting of a kind of preexistential crisis and intense meditation on the limitations of human desire. At times their overlapping effects resulted in a virtual merger, a complex generic and ideological hybrid. The chapters that follow thus describe a range of relations between naturalism and westernism, in addition to their central antagonism.

BESIDES NATURALISM, OTHER, contemporary literary and philosophical schemes contributed to a countertraditional form of Western writing in the late nineteenth century. There was the literature of decadence, which writers like Gelette Burgess and the San Francisco "Jeunes," an early Bohemian collective, identified with in personal as well as literary styles.[4] Their high-toned aesthetics and relentless irony made use of certain traditions of Western life and culture as "free" and nurturing of fine sensibilities, but these references to regional backgrounds and styles were only occasional. The posture of decadence was more pronouncedly an international mode associated with the effects of aesthetics and imagination on subjectivity rather than with any particular location.[5]

And there was local-color fiction. Bret Harte, Mark Twain, Hamlin Garland, and Ambrose Bierce, for example, often located their narratives in Western settings and made use of regional speech and manners. Like the decadents, these writers kept something of a critical distance from the idea of the West as icon of freedom. But none of their works was designed to inspire serious meditation on the impact of the historical end of the West for regional or for literary culture.[6]

At a more distant reach, the countertranscendental fiction of Hawthorne and Melville had, at mid-century, elaborately complicated the celebratory, national romanticism associated with nature and the natural landscape of Emerson, Thoreau, and Whitman. As a response to the optimistic aesthetics of an idealized democratic culture of individualism, Melville's and Hawthorne's fiction, and to some degree Poe's, cast American character, landscape, and national culture as problematic, to the extent that they were informed by notions of a mythic separateness from historical and social contexts. The notion of geographical limitation, which intensified at the end of the nineteenth century with the discourse of the closed frontier, contributed to a rhetoric of social determinism that had not existed so palpably for the "renaissance" generation.

The scientific and ostensibly antiromantic tendencies of literary naturalism emerged simultaneously in public discourse with a series of questions about U.S. life and culture that were circulating throughout the 1890s. The economic and social concerns on which many discussions of the end of the frontier turned expressed what critics and historians have since pointed to as indicators of a crisis in national identity. The best-known expression of this idea is Frederick Jackson

Turner's 1893 essay, "The Significance of the Frontier in American History." During the celebration of the quadricentennial of Columbus's voyages, Turner's thesis was presented to the American public as a response to the deletion of the frontier from the 1890 Census. His arguments gave memorable form to older questions about national identity and national culture, and in rearticulating them at that particular moment, Turner allowed these questions to fuel an enormously influential discourse about the "old West" as the central theme of a narrative about the national past.

The questions asked, for example, what concept or image could replace the frontier as an emblem of the material plenitude, freedom, and progress so central to the rhetoric of regeneration in New World ideology. What zone of opportunity would or could substitute for the space that once existed beyond the frontier? Without such space, would Americans inevitably be remade by history into beings on the naturalist model? For Westerners there was the further question of how regional identity was to be established, given the lack of a border separating East from West.

The questions and confusions at issue were sponsored not only by the rhetoric of the closed frontier but also by the free silver-gold standard debates; the financial crises of 1873 and 1893; the drift of military activities beyond continental borders into Cuba, the Philippines, and Guam as a result of the Spanish-American War; and in other developments that compromised many of the dominant terms and images of U.S. national identity that had been pinned for generations to frontier romanticism.[7]

Naturalism's intellectual coldness and its harsh schemes of human development, as well as its technological bent—its attachment to apparatuses like the camera, the telegraph, and mining equipment—suggest a tough-minded, disciplined methodology that might seem an appropriate antidote for a culture whose economic patterns, social mores, and even national identity were undergoing what would later look like paradigm shifts. But rather than provide a lasting framework for explaining the conditions of Euro-American life after 1890, naturalism sponsored a reductive account of culture and character, the appeal of which was not sufficient to substantially alter the romantic tendencies of the national imagination. Nevertheless, naturalism's way of complicating westernist plots, characters, and landscapes have had lasting effects on the tones and textures of romantic Western narratives in the generations that have continued to produce such stories long after the 1890s.

WESTERN NARRATIVE PATTERNS may seem so familiar to readers in the United States that I have been strongly tempted to assume we all recognize their central features and to proceed with analysis of the encounter with naturalism. But, of course, there is a danger in this: even such a widely known genre will be approached and understood differently depending on one's particular experiences and ways of knowing. Before taking up the complicated relationships between naturalism and westernism in the fiction of Norris, London, Crane, and Cather, the book describes in its early chapters the representational traditions and features that I associate with the terms *westernism* and *naturalism*. Chapter 1 presents a discussion of romantic westernism as a narrative genre and an ideological formula. To make my working assumptions about this genre clear, I offer models of what might be called the classic forms of westernism in John Filson's and Timothy Flint's biographies of Daniel Boone. Chapter 2 offers further analysis of classical Western narrative formations as they appear in Elliot Coues's 1893 edition of the texts of the Lewis and Clark expedition and in James Fenimore Cooper's Leatherstocking novels.

Writing in and about the West, even in a historical mode, is inevitably so entangled in U.S. national mythology that any attempt to trace its forms and meanings, particularly on the part of an American writer, is bound to miss some of its larger cultural implications. I do, however, try to keep in view the long-term effects of westernist discourse and ideology on indigenous cultural integrity. Thus, chapters 1 and 2 introduce another theme at issue, implicitly if not overtly, in all writing about the American West: the appropriation of native homelands and the reduction of native styles of being to so much inchoate wildness and test cases of adaptation, however noble Indian character and culture might occasionally appear.

Chapter 3 offers a discussion of Turner's "The Significance of the Frontier in American History" and of Edward S. Curtis's photogravures for *The North American Indian*. Both are treated as works of fin-de-siècle

westernism that overlap with the ideologies of naturalism in perpetuat-
ing the idea of the end of the romantic frontier paradigm. Turner's essay
and Curtis's images are indeed among the most influential vehicles for
"remembering" the West in the postfrontier United States. In the
fall of 1996, the Public Broadcasting System aired Ken Burns's much-
anticipated documentary series, *The West*, and even here, at this late
date, the filmmaker deployed the framing nostalgia for a disappearing
world made famous by Turner and Curtis alongside interviews with
sophisticated, contemporary critics of those ideas like Patricia Nelson
Limerick, Richard White, and N. Scott Momaday.

Chapter 4 turns to the specific, generic expectations and epistemologies of literary naturalism as they were set out by the French novelist Emile Zola, and to its importation for the representation of the
American West by Norris, London, and Crane. Here I contrast naturalist philosophical and compositional principles with those of westernism
and outline as well naturalism's affinities with the discourse of the
closed frontier.

Chapter 5 begins with a description of a particularly rich and vexed
Western landscape, that of the University of California at Berkeley,
where Frank Norris and Jack London were students in the 1890s. From
its intellectual discourses to its landscape details, the Berkeley scene
embodied the tensions of Western U.S. culture at the end of the century that would be voiced in the Westerns of Norris, London, Crane,
and Cather. As a statement of Euro-American cultural progress in the
West, the university represented an outpost of European avant-garde
thought at the far edge of the old West. In its classrooms, professors preoccupied with European ideas addressed students whose families knew
pioneer experience at first hand. The fact of the university indicated in
the clearest of material and intellectual terms that frontier culture was
now compromised by sophistication.

The remainder of Chapter 5 focuses on Norris's critical writing, his
cowboy tales, and *McTeague*. Raised partly in San Francisco and educated in Paris and at Berkeley, Norris was very consciously interested in
both the traditional stories and images of the Western region and the
more widely circulating intellectual and aesthetic trends of his time.
Norris stands as a prismatic figure whose personal as well as fictional
styles model in a highly public way the cluster of nostalgic, decadent,

and scientific modes of fin-de-siècle Western literary culture. Norris's well-known identification with naturalism and his affection for the West provide a peculiarly cosmopolitan view of a regional culture whose identity he interprets as compromised, unstable, and in many ways imitative of its own imagined authenticity. But his own fiction and critical writing are not immune to these symptoms. In many cases, he seems to be not only aware of them but openly interested in dwelling on the ironies they generate.

Chapter 6 focuses on the intellectual formation and Western fiction of Jack London. In contrast to Norris's San Francisco, London's working-class Oakland presents a rough, relatively unpolished environment. London's treatment of the encounter between naturalism and westernism is quite different from Norris's and signals the social and intellectual distances between the two writers. Raised across the bay and a fellow student at Berkeley, London shared some of Norris's cultural milieu, but he came from a very different social world. London exploits this environment in the production of his own public character and the complex ideological fabric of his fictions. This chapter traces the conflicts and compromises between naturalism and westernism in three of his works, "The Wisdom of the Trail," *The Call of the Wild*, and *Martin Eden*.

Of course not all of the writers who brought naturalism west were Westerners themselves. Chapter 7 turns to the Western stories of Stephen Crane, written after his travels to Nebraska, Texas, and Mexico in 1895 as a reporter for the Bachellor syndicate. In contrast to Norris and London, Crane positions himself, as author and narrator of the late Western scene, as something of a tourist. Crane lived in New Jersey and New York for much of his life, and he was, literally, on tour in the West. His naturalist Westerns thus lack some of the more tortuous issues of regional identity evident in those of Norris and London. But Crane's sensitivity to the West as an icon of U.S. national mythology allows him to produce a peculiarly ironic romanticization of regional society in all of its postfrontier awkwardness.

Chapter 8 looks at Willa Cather's *The Professor's House* and *Death Comes for the Archbishop*. Although Cather was much more willing to embrace her inheritance of romantic westernism than were her male colleagues, and far less attracted to the toughness of certain naturalist

gestures, her novels nevertheless engage this generic debate in comprehensive and deeply thoughtful ways. Her work focused extensively on
Western landscape as a living, virtually spiritual presence and as a finite
resource. At times almost sentimental, and at times productive of
uncanny cultural and geographical ironies, the two novels take up the
encounter of determinism and romanticism in a series of retrospections
on earlier periods of Western life. Cather's backward glance at indigenous and colonial histories explores the layers of empire in the New
World with ambiguities that are reinforced by the generic double-
mindedness.

Chapter 9 offers a brief consideration of the issue of closure for
turn-of-the-century U.S. culture. I argue here that the naturalist Westerns of Norris, London, Crane, and Cather construct images that have
the ironic effect of preserving Western wildness, by romantically recalling it and by memorializing it in analysis. Donna Haraway's readings of
turn-of-the-century preservationist work by English and American scientific naturalists in "Teddy Bear Patriarchy" provides a framework for
my closing arguments about Western literary naturalists. Haraway's
analysis of taxidermy and photography as forms in which art and science merge offers useful comparisons to my discussion of the rhetoric of
naturalist Westerns, particularly because of the problematic solutions
they extend to crises in national identity and authority. Finally, discussions of Frank Norris's story "The Strangest Thing" and Jack London's
"The Red One" take up the more theoretical matters discussed earlier
in the chapter. Focused elaborately on material as well as spiritual questions concerning death, these stories neatly encode the issues of closure
that the chapter engages.

The book concludes with observations on the connection between
American naturalist Westerns and the culture of empire at the turn of
the century. My position here is that the simultaneous preoccupations
with the wild and the primitive in human as well as nonhuman Western environments and with mapping them in terms of scientific
schemes have two central, contradictory effects. They preserve Western romanticism as a favored ideological and literary mode, and they
project it as irrevocably distanced from the enclosed and measured
spaces that make it at once an anachronism and a continuing object of
national desire.

THE CODE OF THE West, as the twentieth century has absorbed it, is perhaps most distinctly expressed in Turner's essay, clearly the best-known articulation in American historiography of the idea of the closed frontier. Some of the earliest texts to emerge from the discipline of American studies responded to Turner's analysis by introducing into the study of the frontier some of the more mythical aspects of that symbol. Specifically, Henry Nash Smith's *Virgin Land: The American West as Myth and Symbol* of 1950 and Leo Marx's *The Machine in the Garden: Technology and the Pastoral Ideal in America* of 1964 argued that both the concept and image of frontier were ideals as they had been understood in American cultural history, particularly in the later part of the nineteenth century.[8]

In the 1970s, Turner's Euro-centered conceptualization of frontier as well as the impacts of Euro-American frontier violence were taken to task by Annette Kolodny and Richard Slotkin, both of whose works offered extensive critiques of the notion of frontier in North American history and have become essential tools for the study of Euro-American expansion in the West.[9] In the 1980s and 1990s, several works of historiography and American studies attempted to describe the idea of the frontier in North America as a complex and unstable zone at the intersection of several ethnic and professional cultures rather than an isolated realm on the margins of a predominantly Anglo-American civil society.[10] These works have complicated and provoked U.S. Western studies to an unprecedented extent, particularly in their charge to cultural critics and historians to take Native American interpretations into consideration more substantially than they have in the past.

Recalling the Wild does not aspire to the breadth or comprehensiveness of these works. My ambition in writing it has been to get at the shifting meanings of the West as an imaginative geography and as a national concept at the moment when official recognition of the frontier was "deleted," so to speak, from the national register. As the vehicle for a socially oriented account of character and history in the post-Civil War United States, naturalism had the potential for introducing a substantially alternative model to the dominant construction of the West in terms of romantic individualism, especially as that construction was expressed in traditional westernist writing. But clearly the naturalist paradigm was flawed in its overly schematic reductions of human behavior and cultural development. It eliminated choice and the notion of individual responsibility as outmoded elements of character composition. The violence of its intellectual schema and demystifications were bound to provoke resistance, even in writers who thought they found its mechanisms useful and appropriate. In the wake of the confrontation between the two genres, perhaps it can be said that naturalism survives to "shadow" the continuously prominent discourse of Western romanticism in American public culture.

If the myth of the frontier is still as powerful a source of "historical" and nostalgic tropes as Neil Smith suggests in claiming geographical as well as temporal transportability for it,[11] and if the myth still sponsors the extension of U.S. ideological and cultural authority in imperialist adventures, it is not entirely free of the effects of its encounters with naturalism. Although the uses of frontier language in the representation of military activities in Vietnam and the Gulf war attest to the continuing vitality of romantic westernist discourse and imagery in popular culture, some of the more recent Hollywood Western films—*The Unforgiven, Tombstone,* and *Wyatt Earp*—are inflected with a sense of geographical and personal limitation, and with a cynicism that bears the traces of the naturalist influence. The ostensibly revisionist Westerns *Dances with Wolves, Thunderheart,* and *Black Robe* in many ways retain a classic mode of western romanticism; yet their scopes too are limited in accordance with a strong sense of historical closure, however mitigated that sense may be by the powerful presence of nostalgia for an earlier, less problematic mode of Western life and—inseparable from that imagined life—representation.

Thus, if naturalism ultimately did not overcome westernism by proposing a different, more circumscribed view of American character and geography, it did have some durable effects on the telling of certain kinds of Western stories. Even the earliest Western narrative film produced in the United States, *The Great Train Robbery* of 1903, bears the traces of a determinist perspective, as does the first Western sound movie, *The Virginian,* made in 1929. Both films project a view of the romantic landscape as something that is always, gradually, being overtaken and tamed by law, family, and economic necessity. In the process of being so appropriated, it becomes an elusive object of desire, a source of nostalgic characterization, dialogue, and certainly setting. The earliest works of Western cinema continue the dynamic of the literary narratives that had appeared just a few years earlier. The films, like the stories that preceded them, restage recollections of unframed space and open-ended character identity set against the recognition of limits and closures that make what is disappearing seem anachronistic, yet therefore all the more worth memorializing. The desire for the elusive, vanishing emblems of open-ended time and space fuels what continues in our time as a seemingly never-ending cycle of stories of the end of the American West.

Chapter 1

Romantic Westernism and the Example of Daniel Boone

Where wretched wigwams stood . . . we behold the
foundations of cities laid.
—JAMES K. FILSON, *The Discovery,*
Settlement and Present State of Kentucke (1784)

IN "THE LITERATURE OF THE WEST," an essay he wrote in 1902, Frank Norris claims that although the frontier is gone, Western character still exhibits much of the toughness associated with figures like Meriwether Lewis and William Clark. The "Epic of the West" that Norris imagines will represent the people of the West as indeed the inheritors of the explorers' models. He dismisses the currently popular dime novels as cheap imitations of older Western writing and calls for the epic to maintain a closer relationship to the romance and drama of the Lewis and Clark narratives.[1]

At about the same time, however, in "The Frontier Gone At Last," Norris wrote:

> Lament it though we may, the Frontier is gone, an idiosyncrasy that has been with us for thousands of years, the one peculiar picturesqueness of our life is no more. We may keep alive for many years yet the idea of a Wild West, but the hired cowboys and paid rough riders of Mr. William Cody are more like 'the real thing' than can be found today in Arizona, New Mexico or Idaho. Only the imitation cowboys, the college-bred fellows who 'go out on a ranch' carry the revolver or wear the concho.

The Frontier has become conscious of itself, acts the part for
the Eastern visitor; and this self-consciousness is a sign, surer
than all others, of . . . the passing of an epoch. (1185)

Whereas in "The Literature of the West" Norris campaigns for an
effective literary representation of the region's history and its heroes
"Boone and Bowie," his analysis of current cultural developments in
"The Frontier Gone At Last" plainly argues that to invoke the modes of
traditional westernism in the contemporary scene is to produce simu-
lacra—phony imitations of an impossibly lost original. However powerful Norris's affection may be for the figures and stories of Boone, Lewis,
and Clark, his more overt attitude is that they cannot serve as effective
metaphors in a regional culture that has come to understand itself as
bounded by ineluctable geographical and historical limits.

The obvious contradictions between these two positions give evidence of Norris's anxieties as well as his nostalgia for the older, romantic formulations represented by the explorers. His own Western fiction,
like London's, Crane's, and Cather's, in effect repeats the contradictions between "The Literature of the West" and "The Frontier Gone At
Last": it criticizes belated frontier romanticism but in the process
manufactures remodeled versions of the same thing.

To make sense of the changes in Western characterization, plot,
and landscape that Norris and the other writers attempted, I want to be
clear about just what constituted the earlier forms they were trying,
unsuccessfully, to avoid. At the risk of stating the obvious about these
story components, particularly for readers raised in the United States,
the following discussion attempts to map certain features of classic
Western narrative inherited by late-nineteenth-century writers
through the models of the Daniel Boone biographies, the texts of the
Lewis and Clark expedition, and the Leatherstocking novels of James
Fenimore Cooper.[2] The chapter then offers examples from the Boone
biographies. Chapter 2 turns to the Lewis and Clark texts and finally to
Cooper's novels.

A DISCUSSION OF THE common features of classic Western narrative
must give some attention to a literary category not always accorded a
central place in contemporary criticism: the construction of character.

The weight of character in the balance of Western narrative designs is simply too overt to be overlooked in a description of the genre. Two of the most common qualities of the classic Western protagonist are solitude and self-reliance, features that tend to foreground "character" as a discreet, autonomous entity that functions apart from society, history, and landscape. Isolation is a sign of individual power and a matter of choice rather than of social pressure or necessity. Alone in nature, the Western character can extend his being as far as his desire reaches, and the wilderness becomes a field of metaphors for his rich and ever-regenerative self.

Because he relates so profitably, and yet at the same time quite economically, to nature, his interactions with the nonhuman world are represented as balanced and fair. But in his encounters with the human inhabitants of the wilderness, he is often ready to resort to violence. Violence is a key factor in his life, a necessary guard for the maintenance of his own ever central, ever dominant, needs and interests.[3]

These talents for self-sufficiency and violence demand a certain physical strength and agility, which the Western hero has in abundance. Spending his energy efficiently, he generally has enough to see him through from situation to situation. He may lose his strength temporarily, or the conditions of his existence may diminish it over time; but his extraordinary facilities for reading the landscape and for living alone in the natural environment serve him well during these times. His perceptions deepen while his bodily and psychical energies are regenerated by nature's beneficial influences.

In terms of his ethical and moral fabric, the westernist hero acts on his own, natural principles, rather than on those of the society in which he was raised. His own ethical codes may appear anarchistic, but more important they are represented as simply necessary, given the facts of his situation. At times, as in the Leatherstocking stories, he runs into trouble with white society because his manners or his hunting habits are not in accordance with those established by the community. In such cases, he generally leaves rather than compromises his behavior; but the conflict is usually settled in his favor, since his individualism is at stake, and that is the key element of his being.

These features of westernist characterization are fairly simple and uncomplicated, but they often have rather complex implications when put to work in the context of a particular narrative, as the discussions of Boone, Lewis, and Leatherstocking that follow illustrate. One of the most vexing of these difficulties is the westernist character's desire to find and live in his true self. This mystical goal is only momentarily achieved and continuously deferred because of the exigencies of travel and the practical needs of survival. In addition, the perceptions and experiences that go into the making of the expeditionary self take shape in writing, mapping, and other forms of representation primarily intended to serve the needs of the sponsors of the journey. Their interests are more often than not political, commercial, and scientific. Not only do these tasks interrupt the romantic, presumably indescribable processes of the explorer's efforts to know and be his true self, but to the extent that they reveal elements of character, such tasks invade his hallmark privacy—his isolation from the gauging and demanding presence of civil society. In the case of Boone and Lewis, this issue is particularly complex, since it always threatens the purity of the hero's most "aboriginal self," to borrow Emerson's term.

This jealously guarded privacy of the westernist hero is the means by which he manages to slip from the public obligations that would otherwise bind him, to become someone else in the immense, uncharted zones of the wilderness. But civil responsibility after all determines and accounts for the very project of exploration. The hero's effort to distance himself from that responsibility produces one of the central conflicts of westernist narrative, since his status as representative of nation and national culture continuously obstructs the attempt to retain his essential, irregular character.

It should be evident from these comments on westernist characterization that it can be adequately comprehended only in relation to what often appears as the immigrant subject's most demanding antagonist, Western geography. At the outset of the Boone, Lewis and Clark, and Leatherstocking texts, as in many others like them, narrative attention is divided between explorer-pioneer characters and the landscapes that lure and challenge them, such that two separate and antithetical fields of being are projected. Western space gets represented as *wild*—as either too inchoate or too empty to be regarded as a viable geopolitical entity. Yet at the same time, this zone of otherness is regarded as open to, and potentially supportive of, the explorer's interests, as it is to the narrative of Euro-American history. It offers an invitation as well as a threat; going West thus entails an ordeal of exposure to loneliness that must be survived in order to achieve that more naturalized relation in which the European is "at home" in the great spaces of the West.

This perceived availability of the wild but richly endowed Western landscape has inspired a cluster of influential romantic ideas having to do with regeneration—economic, psychical, social, even spiritual—in classical American frontier writing. Hence the West gets constructed less as a geographically stable zone than as a shifting, liminal space between wilderness and East, a space in which it is possible for map makers to live beyond maps, farmers beyond fences, in a zone simultaneously open to exploitation and free of the confinements of industry, property, and law.

The transience of the "West" and its susceptibility to easternization are recognized in westernist texts, but as long as there is more wilderness ahead, the full implication of these processes can be deferred and evaded. Thus, Western explorer-heroes often see for themselves that the regenerative effects of the frontier world are or will soon be compromised by the very processes of Euro-American settlement. The actions that result from this attitude constitute a singularly important dynamic of Western narrative. The Western adventurers addressed in this chapter, for example, negotiate relationships between the wilderness and civilization that make the settlements possible, but they are themselves compelled to evade those settlements and to continuously "light out for the territory." The territory in this sense was, as Twain's Huck Finn imagined it to be, a country that had not yet been domesticated in any way at all.

The plot of continuous escape and settlement is intricately tied to notions in these stories of an ideal, authentic West that tends to exist not in the present but in the past. The hero's nostalgia for a wilderness uncontaminated by European hands or eyes might even be activated at the moment of his first encounter with a particular place. In imagining the future he heralds, he can only experience the West present to him as something already fondly remembered.

This kind of recollection memorializes a disappearing wilderness devoid of the codes and structures of European America—a true West imagined in retrospect as the origin of more modernized scenes. In the biographies of Daniel Boone, the Leatherstocking novels, and the expeditional writings of Meriwether Lewis, John Fremont, Kit Carson, and others, this ideal West influences the standards by which the hero evaluates the more settled frontier scenes that evolve from his work. As temporally distanced source of the present, it also continues to exist in an imagined geography beyond the Western horizon that promises a return to the uncompromised conditions of the past. More than a material zone whose borders periodically shift, the West becomes a series of narratives whose meanings accumulate at the same time that they insist on their reference to a pure, primary essence that transcends history.

Thus, these texts sustain, in their way, a more complex view of Western character, landscape, and narrative than they might appear to at the outset. The modernizing impulse and the conservative, nostalgic one regularly and abruptly interrupt each other once some degree of success has been achieved in the settlement of the West. Simultaneously wishing to preserve the enchantments of a place unvisited by agents of European culture and to take possession of them in that culture's name, the hero inhabits an ambiguous temporal zone between past and future. This liminal position illustrates his critique of civilization, but in most cases his nostalgia for the wilderness is simply a complicating yet integral piece of the same narrative of modernization. The critique justifies the hero's escape and allows for further exploration of "undiscovered territories," which are always followed by settlement.[4]

BIOGRAPHIES OF DANIEL BOONE, which began to emerge in his own lifetime and continue to appear on bookstore shelves at the turn of the twentieth century, crystallize elements of frontier character, geography and plot.[5] The iconic forms set by the Boone biographies appear in subsequent fictional as well as historical U.S. expeditionary writing, somewhat at the expense of the often claimed originality of the central figures at issue in these texts.

Early biographies of Daniel Boone present him as a quasi-literate woodsman who explores and maps the Kentucky wilderness with the toughness and violent intelligence he has adopted in his relations with the Shawnee. As a promotional figure in pamphlets adzvertising Kentucky land sales, he was well known in the Atlantic states and much

admired in his own time. In *Regeneration Through Violence*, Richard
Slotkin writes that "it was the figure of Daniel Boone, the solitary,
Indian-like hunter of the deep woods, that became the most significant,
most emotionally compelling myth-hero of the early republic" (21).
Slotkin continues, "This figure caught and held the national attention
for half a century despite varying sectional evaluations of the moral and
social character of the frontier" (23).

Slotkin portrays Boone as the servant of an aggressive colonial
state, the informing myths of which are expressed in his confident yet
awkward, rough yet gentle, and wild yet naive character. In the emergence of official American ideology after the Revolution, Slotkin
argues, Boone's figure had these mythical values and functioned in a
series of stories that could be repeated and varied—a folkloric cycle, as
it were, wherein ideology could reproduce itself.

John Filson's 1784 *Discovery, Settlement and Present State of Kentucke, with the Life of Colonel Daniel Boone*, and Timothy Flint's 1833
Biographical Memoire of Daniel Boone, as well as several other accounts
of Boone written in his own time and later, construct the explorer's
career in slightly different ways. But each of them projects him as a
designer of his own character and history and as a self-conscious actor
in a series of events, the potentially epic proportions of which he is
somehow aware.

Filson had been a Pennsylvania schoolmaster before the Revolution, when he migrated to Kentucky. There he met and accompanied
Boone on several expeditions into the forests, during the process of
which, as he explains, Boone dictated to Filson his own and Kentucky's
history, which were inextricably bound up in each other. The account
of Kentucky that Filson subsequently published provided a material and
historical record and also served as an enticement to potential settlers.
In this sense it was, precisely, a real-estate pamphlet. The text introduced Kentucky into the emergent geography of the United States and
attached it as well to the dynamics of the national marketplace.

But more than an alienated commodity, the landscape projected in
The Discovery, Settlement and Present State of Kentucke appeared as a
romantic field, portions of which might be appended to the identities
and fortunes of individual citizens. These could be adapted from the
model that Filson offered of the whole of Kentucky, which was histori-

cally and figuratively bound up with the life of Boone. The explorer's life was thus shaped by the images of the territory that he mutually constructed. Generating the wilderness that generated him, Boone became the quintessential figure of the West, imaging the whole field of its possibilities in his presence or in the simple sound of his name.

In the close association of Boone's character with that of the land he represents, he becomes something of a hybrid creature, designed in part out of the elements of the wilderness to which he is so strongly attracted. His hybridization is also the product of willful self-fashioning, in which Boone designs himself as an Indian. His minimal acquisition of the Shawnee language is bolstered by a style of dress, gesture, and simple English speech that mimic what his biographers imagine as "Indian." But at the same time, he is agent of the ordering systems that follow. Filson's encomium to white accomplishments in Kentucky initiated by Boone, repeats this dichotomy of his character in relation to the territory itself: "Where wretched wigwams stood . . . we behold the foundation of cities laid."[6]

The dynamics of this appropriation mean that Boone must always retreat, since cities and foundations are antithetical to his expeditionary nature. This is a key feature of what John Mack Faragher refers to as the "romantic myth" (5) that Filson made of Boone's life; but it is precisely his access to this wildness and its infinite possibilities that makes him the rich source and vital seed of U.S. civilization in the West.[7]

The Boone biography that follows the description of Kentucky in Filson's book constructs an idealized, heroic being whose interests are readable in the rich, natural phenomena he "discovers." Kentucky gives shape to Boone's character and complicates his subjectivity by standing as the exoticized other that bears the marks of, in fact is, his desire. His overcoming of the difference between himself and the pretextual Kentucky is a process of violent satisfaction of that desire and of absorbing the landscape into his own history. As representative agent of the commercial interests and national ideals of an emergent U.S. culture, Boone understands Kentucky as a stage for the enactment of those interests and ideals and as a romantic image of the new society's most evident future.

This absorption of the Kentucky wilderness is the central action of

Boone's story and the central, shaping dynamic of his character. But it depends on a pseudoantithesis in which the landscape is first positioned as a nearly unconquerable antagonist and Boone is the disadvantaged newcomer. Rather than affirming a genuine difference between protagonist and geography, however, this dichotomy uses the Kentucky landscape to image and complicate Boone's figure in romantic mechanisms more often associated with Filson's English contemporaries William Wordsworth and Samuel Taylor Coleridge. The shapely contours of its hills trace the outlines of his horizon and serve as boundaries for him to cross, to extend his experience and his visionary power. The dark woods cultivate the danger he foresees, which is met by his own danger in advance.

Beyond his bravery and physical agility, Boone's greatest talents lie in his uncanny ability to read and make sense of the landscape, a practice that casts the territory itself as a text for him to interpret and simultaneously as a personality for him to comprehend. His innocence is progressively compromised as he penetrates the forest and learns its wily ways, a fearsome initiate of its special, often unholy mysteries. In the process, the woods accumulate the characteristics of a willful agent, matching Boone's own canniness by prompting, tricking, pleasing, and thwarting him. As he describes his passage, he thus describes a conscious Other, the sensible contents of which express a message and a mood, directed toward him.

And yet one of the more complicated and powerful of Boone's attractions in Filson's biography, as in those that follow, is the peculiarly resilient quality of his innocence: however much the hero learns, and however adept he becomes at using his knowledge, he continues to appear unrehearsed, unequipped—a recipient of endless surprises. The natural gifts that sustain him do not emerge from any source but his own, self-contained being. For Filson in particular, this combination of fierceness and innocence seems to have the effect of justifying his every violent act against the Shawnee people and their land, for he is presented as having no design or motive other than the maintenance of his own freedom.

The relentless innocence of Filson's Boone is also closely connected with his presumed originality. Like other adventurer figures in his image, he might be said to repeat the late Renaissance project of

Northern Euro-American origins: the will to be new, to start things over again. His continuous encounters with zones he has never seen before provide him with a continuous engine of regeneration. Ever a new man, he is not placed by any of his surroundings, but rather places them in his wake, as newly created elements of the national body he helps to shape.

Claiming his own originality and detachment from causative factors, Filson's Boone projects this form of innocence in a variety of ways. One of the most effective is his putative lack of sophistication in the techniques of representation, verbal or visual. Rather than generating his own life story, Boone simply dictates it to Filson. On the first page of his book, Filson explains the history of its production and points to its source in "Boone's language," the explorer's own rough and simple speech. In introducing himself, the biographer explains that he greatly valued Boone's spoken words, "which I esteemed curious and interesting, and therefore have published them from his own mouth."

Neither he as writer nor Boone as speaker, Filson implies, engage in complex literary models or rhetorical devices; the events and phenomena described simply speak for themselves. But, presumably because Boone's utterances are so raw, Filson edits his words and rhythms so they will suit the conventions to which his readers are accustomed.[8] Thus, while Boone is described as dictating the story of his life to Filson, the gap that remains between the words that appear on the page and those that originate in Boone's voice position the explorer as simultaneously close to and distant from the text.

This peculiar relationship to his own biography, which is virtually composed in his presence, seems to set a pattern for subsequent lives of Daniel Boone. However distanced in time, these works typically sanction their authority by claiming a certain proximity to the body and speech of their subject by, for instance, establishing an affinity that the writer has with Boone's history, or by presenting previously undisclosed stories about him. But at the same time, the thematized mediations of the biographer's research and writing underscore their distance from the original Boone, whose protean, ever-regenerate being and Odyssean survival skills make him an impossible biographical subject to "capture" on the page.[9]

The magisterial elusiveness that Boone acquires through the course of his many adventures is the object of Filson's literary desire. But to account for it in any substantial degree also means compromising his mystery; and Filson's transcriptions of Boone's rough, natural language, in attempting to better describe him, ultimately avoid the compromise by the gap they ensure.

THE MANY STORIES of Boone that followed Filson's, some fictional and others more attentive to historical documentation, kept to the outlines that Filson set in casting Boone as a mystically simple, rough character; and they maintained the tradition of his never-ending innocence. Perhaps the most interesting revisions occur in the shaping of the character in relation to Western geography. The narrative process in Timothy Flint's 1833 *Biographical Memoire of Daniel Boone*[10] still centered on the problem and resolution of a preconquest tension between the explorer and the wild zones he encountered. But unlike Filson's methods of imaging the Kentucky landscape, Flint's representation of the wilderness as a woman expanded its romantic reflexivity and promised the ultimate erasure of difference in a familial form of settlement.

Flint had read and written about Filson's account of the adventures of Daniel Boone and conducted his own research on the explorer's life, which included interviews with surviving relatives.[11] Like Filson, he heard from Boone himself the stories of his life and of the Kentucky past, which became the material of Flint's *Biographical Memoire*.[12] The *Memoire* shares patterns of characterization, plot, and certainly ideology with the models established by Filson.

In Flint's biography of Boone, the Western landscape emerges as a feminine figure, and the metaphor is extended in the story of Boone's wife, Rebecca Bryan. Rebecca makes her appearance as an explicit image of wild femininity and its dangerous lure. Although Boone, like other wilderness heroes that follow him, resists the very notion of marriage in his lust for the forest, Rebecca nonetheless becomes his wife, and together they reproduce the most powerful icon of the civilization of the wilderness, the settlement family.

Boone's first sighting of Rebecca is a seminal moment. Hunting deer at night with a friend, Boone "shines the eyes" of a creature at the edge of the forest. It immediately turns to flee. Enchanted by something in the quality of the eyes, Boone pursues what he still thinks is a deer all the way to his neighbor's property. Once he encounters Rebecca, now safely in the house, he recognizes the eyes and immediately falls in love. In mistaking her for a deer, Flint's Boone associates his future wife with the nonhuman, natural world. Her appearance within the depths of the wilderness suggests a certain animal nature that justifies Boone's choice of her as a mate; she is as wild and as natural a creature as he is. Like the wilderness itself, she appears virginal and, at the same time, mysterious.[13]

But this enigmatic presence is fleeting, for almost as soon as Boone encounters her, he begins reshaping her life to his. Rather than a speaking subject or even a real, sexual body, she stands for the pure naiveté of a Rousseauian wilderness, which may be overtaken by the explorer or inspire him to greater visions of himself, but will rarely get recognized on its own terms.[14]

Boone's overtaking of Rebecca Bryan results in his being "captured" as well. Concluding at her parents' house, the story of their first meeting moves in a steady pace toward Boone's settling into domesticity. Rebecca, no longer a figure of nature, becomes arch-emblem of the family. Her presence, along with their daughter's, on ensuing expeditions compounds the dangers Boone must expect and complicates his physical prowess and agility, even though the narrative proudly claims Rebecca and the daughter to be "the first white women that ever stood on the banks of Kentucke river."

Eventually, Rebecca more or less disappears from the story and occupies only a periodic, marginal place in it as the means of Boone's reproduction and part of his social identity. But even with such a limited presence, she serves the important function of relating him to a family structure and a civil society that demand his attention. Embedded in these relationships, Boone finds himself limited and compromised, no longer living by the impulses of his aboriginal self.

In his movement to the next frontier, whether Rebecca accompanies him or not, Boone, as Flint's account and many others suggest, presumes to extricate himself from social relationships and from the histories they conduct. These escapes, so to speak, constitute Boone's critique of the Euro-American civilization he has made possible; but, of course, far from disconnecting himself from domesticity and colonization, he only extends these systems in making his expeditionary moves, which in turn simply clear the way for more settlement to follow.

THE BOONE FIGURE'S reading of the landscape and interpretation of physical data as if they functioned like a code seem to cast the territory itself in many ways as a text for him to negotiate, a tendency that becomes emphatic in nineteenth-century accounts. His innocence is progressively compromised as he penetrates the forest and absorbs its wily ways, a fearsome initiate of its unholy mysteries. Thus his ego is constituted by virtue of this wilderness, as a claimed innocent working against it. His violence and highly sophisticated machinations, however, demonstrate the very civilized, codified wilderness that he himself is. Finding his interests in the landscape and absorbing what he takes to be its own desire—the language of the natives, the tempers of nature— he inscribes the forest with paths that lead progressively to the rivers that run westward for the subsequent traveler to follow quite naturally.

The issues of character and subjectivity implicit in this occupation of tracing one's presence, or rather imaging presence for one's traces, raises this question: What space does the Boone figure, as representative Western subject, occupy? Like the figure in a photographic negative, he is formulated as the interstice between material objects that therefore become his margins, and he theirs. Movement is his condition, and the protean figure takes his limit, his shape, from the matter of forest, as he, mutually, limits it. The oxymoron of this constant negotiation allows the figure to elude figuration, to escape representation; but in so spending himself he leaves behind a streak that articulates the wilderness, maps it with his paths, and draws him in drawing the direction of his desire.

More than anything else, after all, Boone seeks to represent himself by virtue of charting his passage. The marks that make him also make the woods, in the interest of reproducing themselves, and it is at this juncture between the initial—and, as it were, accidental—laying down of a mark and the wish generated in this act to remember itself that the character of Daniel Boone functions.

To the extent that Boone and other frontier heroes styled after him recognize this dynamic, they maintain a sense that primary wilderness conditions are ever threatened by time and by the civilizing processes that heroes themselves make possible. In this, they anticipate the pre-occupations of naturalist Western characters of the late nineteenth century, who in one way or another seem to continuously express anxieties about geographical enclosure and about the loss of wilderness as a crucial emblem of nineteenth-century concepts of new world freedom.

The stories of Boone and of Boone-like characters produced by Filson, Flint, Cooper, and others participated in important ways in the development of literary models for figuring national experience. The signature adaptability of character and geography featured in their stories made it possible for the narratives themselves to have the same quality.[15] Replayed with endless variations through the generations of U.S. cultural history, the narrative of Western adventure retains a recognizable set of features that justify referring to "it" as a genre. A revisable text, the Western narrative offers itself as a national myth; and the classical forms of westernist subjectivity and geography operate along with narrative as the necessary means by which the myth is reproduced.

Boone's figure is particularly useful, and in this sense mythical, because the most constant feature of his character in the many stories produced about him is precisely his adaptability. As Leslie Fiedler, Richard Slotkin, John Cawelti, and others have suggested, his type is a transferable figure, appearing as cowboy, soldier, spy, businessman, spaceman, and politician in subsequent generations of Euro-American cultural history. The imaginative geography of Boone's Western space retains a mythical vitality as well, despite the erasure of its historical and territorial bases.

The vehicles of character and geography invite the retelling of a story about the regeneration of individual and national being as goal and justification for the overtaking of successive indigenous territories. American personal and cultural power "ceases in the instant of repose," writes Emerson in "Self Reliance"; "it resides in the moment of transition from a past to a new state, in the shooting of a gulf, in the darting to an aim."[16] In this sense, then, westernist character and geography as modeled in the Boone stories sustain the continuous revitalization of Western narrative. They exist not only in specific narrative time, but in mythic all-time, as a form that can be invoked in the different social and aesthetic contexts of subsequent generations.

Scenes of Visionary Enchantment: The Lewis and Clark Narratives and the Leatherstocking Novels

*The hills which we passed today exhibit a
most romantic appearance. . . . With the help
of a little imagination and an oblique view,
at a distance [they] are made to represent
elegant ranges of lofty, freestone buildings. . . .
As we passed on it seemed as if those scenes
of visionary enchantment would never have
an end.*

      —MERIWETHER LEWIS, *History of the
Expedition . . . To the Sources of the
Missouri River (1814)*

FILSON'S LIFE OF Boone was widely read by the end of the eighteenth century, and it presented a model of Western character, plot, and landscape for subsequent frontier narratives, fictional as well as historical. Filson's Boone "caught and held the national attention for half a century."[1] If Meriwether Lewis and William Clark reproduced features of Boone's story and colonizing fervor in actual, historical events that shaped the future course of empire, James Fenimore Cooper adapted them to fictional forms that had lasting influence in their own right. Several critics and biographers nave noted that the forerunner of Cooper's Leatherstocking was Boone, with the implication that the novelist had read Filson's and later Flint's biographies.[2] Whether Lewis and Clark actually read Filson or consciously modeled their own characters in the expedition notebooks after Boone is impossible to determine, but their self-portraits, their descriptions of the trans-Mississippi West, and certainly the ideological romance of their narrative bear close resemblances to those of Boone's story.[3]

In 1893, at about the time that Turner's essay appeared, a surgeon and former secretary of the U.S. Geological Survey named Elliott Coues brought out a new edition of the *History of the Expedition Under the Command of Lewis and Clark to the Sources of the Missouri River*, the first to appear since the *History*'s initial publication in 1814.[4] Appearing in the thick of the discourse of the closed frontier, Coues's edition participated vicariously in the adventures that constituted the government's nominal opening of the West; he joins, as it were, the "Corps of Discovery," as the expedition personnel were officially known, by rewriting and adding to its inventory of the contents of the American West. His heavily annotated edition of the *History* supplements the original material not only with updated ethnographical, botanical, and zoological data, but with exhaustive etymologies and astonishingly intricate stylistic analyses of the explorers' writing. Read as a nostalgic repetition or as a scientific revision of Lewis and Clark, Coues's edition is representative of a widespread interest in frontier history in the U.S. during the 1890s and of a trend toward reinterpreting the Western past in openly romantic as well as specifically evolutionary terms.

Coues refers to the expedition text as "our national epic of exploration" and "the *Robinson Crusoe* of fact." The analogy with Defoe is possible, Coues argues, because of the explorers' "acute powers of observation," which match the English author's "startling verisimilitude" (vi). In so openly celebrating what might be called the literary realism of the *History*, Coues calls attention to its adherence to stylistic trends that had become dominant in his own time. But his appreciation also begs the question as to whether Lewis and Clark romanticized the country in the process of describing it. Indeed, if the scientific clarity of their account is all the more noteworthy because, unlike Filson's biography of Boone, it is cast in fluent literary language, then it might also be said that the explorers' often poetic narratizing of their data maintains its authority through the scientific rhetoric that frames it.

In offering so complex a response to the language of the expedition texts, Coues exhibits some of the key aspects of the anxious and porous opposition between scientific and imaginative forms of representation as these modes were understood in his own cultural milieu. The American naturalist writers who were Coues's contemporaries shared in his and Turner's efforts to account for the evolution of the present by reference to strictly materialist, presumably factual evaluations of the historical past. But these efforts were often thwarted by a nostalgic lyricism that would surface in reflections on that past, its characters and landscapes.

In Jefferson's "Memoire of Meriwether Lewis," which heads the text proper in Coues's edition, the president justifies his choice of Lewis, his twenty-eight-year-old secretary, as head of the expedition by describing traits he shared with Boone—his "courage," "firmness," and "perseverance of purpose." But, unlike Boone, Lewis was educated, and his knowledge of botany was crucial to the expedition's mission to inventory the physical make-up of the territory.[5] Although he requires some technical training, this preparation will guard him "against losing time in the description of objects already possessed . . ." (xxii). Invoking in his language the ancient formula that to name is to possess, Jefferson points to the profound importance of Lewis's Linnaean eye as a means to legitimate the originality of the expedition's scientific work. For if Lewis cannot catalogue exotic species, the contents of his notebooks will be, in effect, familiar and domestic—hardly deserving of the caption "discoveries."

The figure of the wilderness hero as American Adam, naming and possessing what he sees in an originating act, is a conventional one in New World expedition narratives from Columbus to Boone. For the duration of the expedition, from May 1804 through September 1806, Lewis and Clark made daily notes of what they saw, of the actions of their party, and of encounters with Indians and other *voyageurs*. These were regularly revised, copied, and returned to Washington whenever means were available. In his edition of the expedition correspondence, Donald Jackson comments that Lewis and Clark "were to become the writingest explorers of their time. They wrote constantly and abundantly, afloat and ashore, legibly and illegibly, and always with an urgent sense of purpose."[6]

Jefferson instructed Lewis to copy "at Leisure times" all of his descriptions, measurements, and impressions. In this way Jefferson even accounted for the travelers' inactive moments, as if they were characters in a narrative conducted under his own management.[7] And indeed, the copious details and collections of static images in the journals serve as counterpoints to the flow of narrative time along the river. This alternation between picture and movement in the journals places the explorers as figures in their own literary production of the expedition.

But the literary, political, and commercial intentions are glossed by Jefferson and Lewis in the expedition's key tropological systems of innocence and natural necessity. At the same time that Lewis is well prepared intellectually for what he is asked to do, he, like Boone, is cast as an innocent whose agenda only emerges from nature. In his "Memoire of Lewis," Jefferson describes him as particularly suited to the work of naming because he is "honest, disinterested, liberal, of sound understanding, and a fidelity to truth so scrupulous that whatever he should report would be as certain as if seen by ourselves—with all these qualifications, [he is] as if selected and implanted by nature in one body for this express purpose . . ." (xxii).

Here the namer functions like a humble window on the true West, as if the land were simply being presented in such a way as to speak for itself; thus its images and dimensions appear to impress themselves on the writer's mind without subjective interpolation. The unmediated relation between subject and object in such a concept of "natural" writing suggests Lewis's possession by and of the Western landscape. This perfect exchange will be passed along by Lewis to Jefferson, so that the same pure and unmediated communication might be repeated between the West and Washington. In this way, the expedition appears to have no "design" of its own, but merely effects a natural and necessary transference through Lewis's innocent accounting.

By submitting his projects and his compositions to the register of nature, Lewis, like Boone, attempts, however consciously or unconsciously, to minimize the appearance of ideological and private interest. In a similar way, Coues, Turner, and the literary naturalists contemporary with them, defer to evolutionary "force" as the real author of their own rhetorical designs and interests. In both eras, the writing is understood to record only what is somehow understood as necessary.

"Necessity," a key term in Jeffersonian rhetoric, suggests of course a major trope for post-Darwinian discourse—the field from which Coues speaks in his retrospective glance at Jefferson's Western projects. The plainness of style that Jefferson advocated, combined with the vehemence of his interests, effected a radical efficiency in his political and social texts. The apparent effort was to make Lewis's prose operate as if discursively self-reliant, the product of careful observation that required minimal argumentation.

This emphasis on linguistic self-sufficiency and on the visual clarity of simple literary language are crucial compositional ideals for late-nineteenth-century naturalism. In his manifesto for that movement, Emile Zola claimed to take the stylistics of the eighteenth-century physiocrats, a school of political economists of the generation to which Jefferson belonged, as his models. In this earlier theoretical discourse, Zola wrote, he "found the word" for naturalism.[8] Thus, rather than reacting against this particular Jeffersonian ideal, American naturalists often aspired to it, and in this sense had something very much in common with classical Western representation, where truth and accuracy are assumed to be achievable through undesigning observation. Whether or not naturalist writing was any more successful in this effort than romantic Western writing had been, it shared with romantic westernism the assumption that little interpretive energy need be spent in the presentation of what is deemed purely natural phenomena.

But necessity in the Lewis and Clark journals works in complementary ways with the equally important expeditionary category of wildness. And indeed, the chorographies and ethnographic portraits that Lewis and Clark provide make full rhetorical use of that category. Rocks and flowers are seen as "wild" not only in the sense that they do not appear arranged or cultivated by human hands but because they have not yet been categorized or named within the grids of European science. Thus, the expedition's descriptions do the necessary work of codifying these objects.

For Lewis and Clark themselves, the wilderness and its people presented a scene of instability and promiscuity—in the landscape itself, as well as in the language and promises of the people they encountered. The most common example of this instability is the very vehicle of their excursion, the Missouri River. As the explorers neared the headwaters of the river in the summer of 1805, they were troubled by the multiple channels into which the main course divided. Lewis noted, "I found it impossible to lay [the courses] down correctly."[9] His frustration continued when they approached the Three Forks:

> I walked down to the middle fork and examined and compared it with the S.W. fork but could not satisfy myself which was the largest stream of the two, in fact they appeared as if they had been cast in the same mold, there being no difference in character or size, therefo e to call either of these streams the Missouri River would be ;iving it a preference. (DeVoto, 168)

During the first phase or the voyage, when the explorers were still unaccustomed to the river's tendencies, Clark noted on several occasions the tendencies of banks and sandbars to shift during the night as the expedition crew slept. On September 21, 1804, he wrote:

> At half past one o'clock this morning the sandbar on which we camped began to undermine and give way which alarmed the sergeant on guard. The motion of the boat awakened me; I got up and by the light of the moon observed that the sand had given away both above and below our camp and was falling in fast. . . . We had pushed off but a few minutes before the bank under which the boat and pirogues lay gave way, which would certainly have sunk both pirogues. (DeVoto, 30)

Such surprises and misreadings of the river have their social counterparts in transactions between the explorers and the people they encounter along the river. From their earliest encounters with the Yankton Sioux to their later meetings with the Clatsop at the mouth of the Columbia, misunderstandings and confusion characterize verbal exchange. On many occasions, communication required virtual translation chains.[10] The lack of clarity as to the significance of words, gestures, and facial expressions maintains a steady level of nervousness among the expedition personnel, particularly the leaders. Lewis's anxious efforts to communicate with the chief of the Shoshone in preparation for the Rocky Mountain portage ended in a cloud of distrust. Lewis confided in his journal:

> My mind was in reality quite as gloomy all this evening as the most afrighted Indian but I affected cheerfulness to keep the

Indians so who were about me. . . . I slept but little as might be
well expected, my mind dwelling on the state of the expedition
which I ever held in equal estimation with my own existence,
and the fate of which appeared at this moment to depend in a
great measure upon the caprices of a few savages who are ever
as fickle as the wind. (DeVoto, 201)

Unrecognizable and unrecognizing, the territory and its people
eluded Lewis and Clark's attempts at representation; they were too
unstable to be accounted for on their own terms. This unrepresentabil-
ity had its political as well as scientific implications, for it justified the
explorers' project to give the wilderness an order and a set of meanings
that would make it operate within the emerging national culture of the
United States.[11] The very rational schemes by which they finally organized Western nature produced a map in which the various entities
could take what were deemed their inevitable places.

In contrast to this codifying process, Lewis's and Clark's writing at
many points renders everything, including the seeing subject, as elements of one great, harmonious vision. Shortly after entering the upper
Missouri River, for example, Lewis, having spent several days confined
to the boat, decided to "amuse [him]self on shore . . . and view the interior of the country." Ascending a hill, he notes:

The country breaks off . . . into a fine level plain extending as
far as the eye can reach. From this plain I had an extensive
view of the river below. . . . Young grass had now sprung to a
height of 4 inches presenting the live green of the spring. . . .
This scenery already rich pleasing and beautiful was still farther
heightened by immense herds of buffalo which could be
comprehended at one view . . . (DeVoto, 28)

What Lewis observes is a scene of abundant riches, witnessed not from
the marginal perspective of the river, but from the depths of the country's
"interior." The young grass and the general liveliness of the prairie
spring (even though the entry is made in September of 1804) bespeak
the fertility of the area, which in turn bears the familiar poetic meanings of rebirth and bounty, as well as the reproductive power of the
West to image Jeffersonian ideology. The buffalo inflect the gentle pastoral of the scene with a fierce energy that again attests to the vitality

and plenty of the plains. The view extends "as far as the eye can reach," as if encircling Lewis in its breadth. At moments like this, Lewis represents himself as someone who, like Mary Louise Pratt's figure of the "seeing man" (7), looks passively on the landscape to admire rather than conquer it; but his gaze ultimately takes possession of all he sees. His "extensive view" encompasses everything in the horizon, as if it were inviting him to claim it. The promise of the landscape in this and many similar passages lies not only in its richness but more significantly in the offering it makes of itself to Lewis's enlightened eye.

In the spring of the following year, nearing the Marias River, a series of peculiar sandstone cliffs caught Lewis's attention:

> The hills which we passed today exhibit a most romantic appearance. . . . The water in the course of time in descending from those hills . . . has trickled down the soft sand cliffs and worn [them] into a thousand grotesque figures, which with the help of a little imagination and an oblique view, at a distance are made to represent elegant ranges of lofty, freestone buildings. . . . In other places on a much nearer approach and with the help of less imagination we see the remains or ruins of elegant buildings. . . . As we passed on it seemed as if those scenes of visionary enchantment would never have an end . . . so perfect indeed are those walls that I should have thought that nature had attempted here to rival the human art of masonry had I not recollected that she had first began her work. (DeVoto, 123–124)

As if seeing Filson's prophecy in the cliffs, that "where wretched wigwams stood we behold the foundations of cities laid," Lewis converts them in the act of seeing to figures for the civilization to come, drawn in the lines and contours of urban architecture. Here Lewis's poetic vision is brought into full view, as he thematizes his romantic interpretations of the landscape.

This romantic way of seeing had become the topic of an entry just one month earlier, when Lewis remarked, upon setting out from Fort Mandan after their first winter camp, that "the state of mind in which we are generally gives the coloring to events when the imagination is suffered to wander off into futurity." The landscapes through which he travels get shaped by his representations, as, according to his more romantic reveries, the landscapes shape his ever-moving subjectivity. Thus, Lewis constructs himself as a protean, ever-regenerative figure whose mutually influential relationship with nature is representative of the national culture he heralds.

In this sense, then, Lewis's character joins Boone's in taking on the mythic proportions of an adaptable and reproducible figure. And the landscapes he produces have the mythical value, again to cite Neil Smith, of being "transportable over space" beyond their "constitutive geography." Capable of representing anything for which it might be substituted, Lewis's West becomes an exchangeable object for the mythology of the United States, signifying immensely the dream of regeneration—from anything to anything.

But implicit in the literary, commercial, scientific, and political purposes of Jefferson's project in the Lewis and Clark expedition is a wish characteristic of westernism to recuperate an earlier, primary condition that has been lost in the developments of history and culture. This progress for the sake of conserving—the most respected oxymoron of Western narrative—implies the contradictory but entwined elements of simple, wild primitivism in a "natural" scene and energetic, ordered progressivism in a consciously motivated one. Together these elements work to repeat their imagined origins, as in the Daniel Boone stories and the Western narratives that follow them beyond the historical closure of the West.

The generic criteria of romantic frontier narrative are exemplified in James Fenimore Cooper's Leatherstocking novels.[12] The heroic figure of the man who is half-civilized and half-wild, whose life is spent in the liminal space between the settlement and the forest, is Leatherstocking himself. The landscape of endless, uncharted wilderness is there in Cooper's forests of upstate New York; and the story of continuous evasion of civil society for the wildness of still Western frontiers is in place from the first Leatherstocking novel, *The Pioneers* of 1823.

The central character of the Leatherstocking series has the dress, speech, manners, and talents of Filson's and, in later novels, Flint's Boone. Cooper also found models for his characters, incidents, and settings in the Lewis and Clark expedition narratives.[13] Leatherstocking, also known as Natty Bumppo, is renamed Hawkeye, Trapper, Path Finder, and Deerslayer over the course of the series that concluded in

1841 with *The Deerslayer*. In each of the novels, the hero negotiates the gap between settled and wild territories, just as Lewis and Clark and the Boone of Filson's and Flint's narratives do. In each case, the explorer-hero repeats the dialectic of expansion and settlement with each phase of his own life and that of the white culture he represents.

The early Leatherstocking novels are preoccupied in general with an opposition between written law and proprietorship on the one hand and oral tradition and unarticulated land claims associated with Indian culture on the other, an opposition that they cannot successfully maintain. However, the later novels shift the opposition to one between written and visual ways of knowing. It is as if the later works relinquish the exhausting attempt evident in the earlier ones, as in Flint's *Memoire*, to represent a frontier character who functions beyond culture. Instead they emphasize seeing as a power different not only from that of books and the mediated kind of knowledge with which they are associated but from verbal epistemologies in general. Vision in this sense takes on the properties of revelation and of truth as unmediated presence in a highly romantic articulation of the wilderness.

Invoking nature as a power that precedes humankind and as a physical unity much larger than the specific location of his story, Cooper introduces his last Leatherstocking novel, *The Deerslayer*, in humble and self-effacing tones. The painterly descriptions of landscape attempt to recuperate a wilderness whose integrity exists in being untouched and in having a looming, unquestionable consciousness. Unlike the indifferent nature of later nineteenth-century writing, Cooper's woodland scenes absorb the desires of his characters—as in the exemplary mirroring of Glimmerglass—and effect a readable transference, understood as intelligence for military, commercial, or survival purposes, or more grandly as "the book of nature."

Such regard for nature as either the province of an absolute, masculine deity, or as the privileged signifier of the most transcendent signifier of the same, is countered by a second tropological system that operates perhaps closer to the ground and cathects the wilderness with a feminine, sexual design. Natty's orientation is with the less specific, more disseminated manifestations of nature's power as father; Judith Hutter, a virtual frontier Venus, most demonstratively stands for the variations of bodily, reproductive nature that women represent in the novel. In this opposition, the representation of gender in *The Last of the Mohicans* is turned around; Hawkeye, whose physical and sensory energies are so crucial for knowledge, acquires as the Deerslayer a nearly spiritual integration with nature wherein his differentiation exists largely in his eye. Serving like a window, Natty's eye presupposes a subject-object relation between him and the environment. Like the relation between Filson's Boone and the Kentucky landscape, in this one the subject and object determine each other; but in Filson's text, the figure of the hunter is almost mystically dissolved in the texture of the landscape. Glimmerglass attracts Leatherstocking not because it is picturesque but because it possesses an "air of deep repose—the solitudes that spoke of scenes and forests untouched by the hands of man."[14] The repeated admiration of Glimmerglass and of Judith's face, as well as the use of the "glass" to focus on long distances, draw attention to the act of looking—not looking for trails, but a more overtly romantic and reflexive kind of looking, or contemplation, that makes use of the pun Emerson elaborated several years earlier, in "Nature," of the "eye" and the "I."

Judith, in subsuming the other women of the novel as well as feminine sexuality in general, is represented as picturesqueness itself, her good looks always arresting those who look at her. But the other side of this power is Judith's notorious vanity, which leaves her open to sexual exploitation by the British officers and really marks the difference between her kind of knowledge and Deerslayer's. The adventure's general ethic is to denounce the kind of physicality that Judith represents; tedious biblical lessons are woven through the utterances of Hetty and Leatherstocking and through the narrator's insistent moralizing. Deerslayer rejects Judith's affections and proposal of marriage for the sake of his continued existence as an individual par excellence, but his Moravian sensitivities inflect this decision with a priestly mission: to serve the masculine god of nature by refusing to submit his body to the terms of Judith's desire and by sustaining his celibate character. But nature becomes distinctly androgynous in his response to Judith's insinuating question, "Where, then, is your sweetheart, Deerslayer?" He replies: "She's in the forest, Judith—hanging from the boughs of the trees, in a soft rain—in the dew on the open grass—the clouds that float out in the blue heavens—the birds that sing in the woods—the wet springs where I slake my thirst—and in all the other glorious gifts that come from God's providence!" (616–617).

This long-winded answer, which Mark Twain ridiculed with such delight in "Fenimore Cooper's Literary Offenses," confirms Natty's priestly service to a list of traces that constitute nature, his true bride. Unlike the version of nature understood as an abstract consciousness, this version seems to exist in the aesthetics of the visible prospect. His repeatedly mentioned devotion to truth telling is necessary because, in both understandings, nature is everywhere, and anything he might say is registered by its implicit witness. As a lover, nature regards Leatherstocking from its own distinct perspective. Nature as witness to truth telling suggests that the record of his behavior will be tallied at his death. It might be argued that the metaphor lends a note of self-consciousness in the storytelling process, a note that recalls Cooper's earlier anxieties in the elaboration of Natty's character—anxieties also present in Filson's and Flint's representations of Boone—as an entity beyond culture. But the pressure of truth telling is also indicative of Deerslayer's great self-consciousness in the form of a narcissism that assumes his every utterance has meaning and effect; and in this sense, nature is a presence simultaneous with his own, that extends beyond him but in his own line of vision. Contrary to Deerslayer's denials of vanity in relation to his physical appearance, this close attention to his own utterances amounts to an equivalent fetish of himself as voice rather than body. In both cases, consciousness is simultaneous with self-representation; listening to and looking at oneself are recording acts that imply a departure from the immediacy of being and cancel Leatherstocking's as well as Judith's innocence.

In a curious reversal of reproductive powers, *The Deerslayer* ends with Natty's return to Glimmerglass fifteen years after the incidents that precede it, only to find that Judith's name is no longer remembered and no account of her whereabouts can be secured beyond a vague rumor that she is living on the estate of a British officer who has not married her. The sexuality that exists for its own sake in her portrait is posed against that of Hist, who marries Chingachgook and gives birth to Uncas, the Apollonian hero of *The Last of the Mohicans*. Hist, however, dies by the time Natty and Chingachgook return to Glimmerglass. In spite of the implication that Hist and Judith are different kinds of women, they are both instances of the same kind of nature—specific, embodied, sexual, and feminine. The limitations of the particular, material nature they represent result in literal and figurative death. On the other hand, Leatherstocking, like Uncas and Chingachgook, continues into time, reproducing himself in new names and adventures through a kind of disembodied vision, never allowing domesticity to touch or to limit him and never representing himself through the inheritance of a family lineage. Thus, his figure, as aware of itself as Narcissus was, represents and reproduces ideology in sterility, while Judith, who bears all the marks of a fertile sexuality, is frustrated in her desire to marry Natty and reproduce in the form of children. The family lineage that she wishes to initiate is, of course, one of the dominant means by which the European order is able to secure its articulations of the wilderness and to ejaculate its ideals of property and representation onto the tabula rasa of the forest. But families must always be alien to Natty Bumppo's wilderness, even though the narrative of generation derives from the same phallic episteme as Natty's celibate progressions.

IN ARGUING THAT "the existence of an area of free land, its continuous recession, and the advance of American settlement westward explain American development," Frederick Jackson Turner also called attention to what he thought was a crisis in the fact that "the frontier has gone."[15] But he also worried about the fate of individualism as a national character trait and about the cultivation of the kind of images and stories that the nation would need to sustain itself. In Turner's analysis of the situation in 1893, the three dimensions of time, character, and space were central; and his manifesto to reconceive the national purpose, in effect to reconceive national identity, was also a call to rewrite the national narrative so that it both respected the Western past and went beyond it.

Turner's call to revise this narrative still assumed the centrality of individualism as the core feature of national life and as a principle that new narratives of national purpose and identity, without the aid of a frontier setting, would need to sponsor. The many Boones, Lewis's, and Leatherstockings that Turner used as his hypothetical frontier Americans were, as he stressed again and again, images of this individualism; but the rhetorical services they performed had more lasting social effects than did the material conditions that initially sponsored their mythical individualism.

Frederick Jackson Turner, Edward S. Curtis, and the Romance of Disappearing

Chapter 3

It is true that advancement demands the extermination of these wild, care-free picturesque Indians, and, in the language of our President, we cannot keep them or their lands for bric-à-brac.
—EDWARD S. CURTIS, *Scribner's Magazine* (1903)

W HAT FREDERICK JACKSON Turner called the "closing of the frontier" in 1893 fostered an extensive sense of loss in U.S. public discourse. This mood centered around the deactivation of a vital cultural symbol and the ostensive disappearance of an actual space in which key promises of a democratic national narrative could be acted out. Turner represented the deletion of the frontier category from the 1890 Census as a crisis, since it marked the end of "the existence of an area of free land" upon which the country's "vital forces" formerly exercised themselves; thus "its going has closed the first period of American history."[1]

Although Turner's argument would be refuted by subsequent generations of historians, it was tremendously influential in his time and has to the present day maintained the status of a major statement in American historical writing.[2] Before the congress of the American Historical Society at the 1893 Chicago World's Fair, he offered a lyrical interpretation of the depletion of the public domain.[3] His analysis was not only thorough and rhetorically sound; it also effected a highly romantic review of Western history. The essay looks back on the chronicle of Euro-American movement across the continent and argues that the frontier has played a crucial role as safety valve in the history of the United States: social, financial, and personal troubles that surfaced in the finished, or civilized, parts of the country could be eliminated by a dramatic change of venue and by constructive effort in the open spaces of the West. The essay does not so much insist that demographic and economic statistics have in fact attested to these salvaging functions of the West, but that the very possibility of starting over had been a key figure in American thinking.[4] With the deletion of the category of the frontier, American national culture would have to situate its aspirations elsewhere.

In Turner's mind, this condition called attention to the lack of serious study of the West and its patterns of experience, now that it was about to disappear from history. The fervent elegance of his prose celebrates the origins of Euro-American expansion in the Columbian expeditions and urges those who would grasp his point to appreciate his question and to begin seriously considering its implications for the future of a model American will-to-progress:

> Since the days when the fleet of Columbus sailed into the waters of the New World, America has been another name for opportunity, and the people of the United States have taken their tone from the incessant expansion which has not only been open but has even been forced upon them. He would be a rash prophet who should assert that the expansive character of American life has now entirely ceased. Movement has been its dominant fact, and, unless this training has no effect upon a people, the American energy will continually demand a wider field for its exercise. (57)

As a highly influential voice among the many that were working to define the modernity of U.S. national culture at the end of the century, Turner helped sponsor an intellectual and artistic tendency to look backward and forward at the same time. His attention to the past evoked a distinct sense of loss in the images of the frontiers he so eloquently recalled, but his concerns about the national future projected an implicit optimism based precisely on the drive and ingenuity that he appreciated in the past. The contradictions were seemingly resolved in his stance that this particular history was an inevitable story, determined by natural courses that led to an unavoidable conclusion. Nevertheless, this evolutionary determinism, however intellectually avant-garde its analytic framework, had the important effect of sustaining a rich nostalgia for what was left behind in the sweep of history.

Something like worshipful reverence for a formerly unconverted wilderness zone is common in accounts and images produced by Europeans in North America since long before Turner. But the finality of Turner's essay meant that such retrospection could become all the more articulate and romantic in its imagining of a wild, natural zone that would never be recuperated or replaced with a new frontier.

Turner's organizing metaphor for the country is the palimpsest. History and location are thus conflated on a continent laid out like a scroll, on the surface of which the periods of discovery, settlement, and development are inscribed, one on top of the other. The earliest layers are still readable through the skin of the later ones; and this pile of history is imaged as repeating itself in an overlapping movement westward. Since the continent has been thus accounted for to its very edge, Turner argues, free space can no longer function as the informing principle of regeneration.

In drawing the metaphor of the layered writing surface, Turner resorts to the vocabulary of geology—one of the most fashionable disciplines of the late nineteenth century—to make an analogy between his own historiography and the scientific analysis of the earth's surface. In distinguishing the layers of physical development, the geologist reads the history behind a contemporary titled and mapped landscape, just as Turner reads the layers of development in the composition of his contemporary American West. The strain of evolutionism in his vocabulary strongly implies a note of inevitability in his interpretation of Euro-American history, an inevitability that seems to naturalize the writer's argument and the history he constructs of his culture.

The idea of the closed frontier that Turner's essay articulated gained currency amid the accumulating influence of literary naturalism, and that genre furnished many of Turner's organizing tropes as well. Naturalist space generally closes in on human figures rather than liberating them; and nature itself is ostensibly conceived as an indifferent field of objects and processes rather than a series of signifiers that romantically formulate the subject's desires. The claustrophobic limits of space stand in what appears to be direct opposition to the open horizons and inspiring vistas of the Western frontier that Turner's essay had proclaimed to be closed. In fact, his own naturalist vocabulary and metaphors of evolution partake of the modernity that the essay argues has overtaken the continent.

One of Turner's central claims is that the environment of the frontier—its natural, economic, and social facts—has determined North American character and culture. But his argument treated these elements of the environment in terms of the dominant ideas of character and culture in his time, thus allowing environment to be shaped in clearly discursive, culturally sanctioned, ideological modes. In other words, although Turner claims to argue that environment determines culture, his essay persuades the reader that the obverse has an equal, if not greater, degree of truth. Indeed, the waves of immigrants whose purposive movements constitute the essay's central narrative are presented as exerting a distinctly shaping force on the environments they encounter. When Turner represents them as being shaped by material factors, he does so by invoking very familiar conventions of westernist characterization, particularly those found in stories of explorer-pioneers for whom the tests of frontier life served to strengthen and regenerate heroic being.

Rather than demonstrating that pioneers responded to radically new realities in the West by substantially altering their interests and epistemologies, Turner cites these inherited models of heroic individualism that the pioneers acted out. The concerns that they brought to the wilderness are projected onto the empty or chaotic space of the West rather than stopped and renegotiated at a frontier of cultural difference. Immigrant actions are thus described as material interpretations and appropriations of the West, not as necessary responses to its demands.

As many late-twentieth-century histories of the West have argued, Turner's account of the concept of frontier does little to address the dynamics of exchange and influence among different groups whose interests and activities coincided at the various border locations he cites.[5] Nor is it concerned with drawing distinctions between a physical and a conceptual meaning of the wilderness: the frontier is as much a state of mind for Turner as it is anything else. His intentions aside, the "significance of the frontier" develops the rather literal meaning of absorbing whatever value is projected onto it by the searching pioneer. In its adaptability to immigrant intentions, the frontier's significance is thus literal, in the sense that it provides a continuous source of signifying material for the shaping of individual and national narratives.

Turner's dualism was shared by contemporary writers of naturalist Westerns, whose stories sought to preserve Euro-American Western traditions and to recognize their passing at the same time. The vehicle of literary naturalism was in many ways the perfect medium for Frank Norris, Jack London, Stephen Crane, and Willa Cather to express their willed modernity, but it served their latent romanticism perhaps even better. Like Turner, they found in determinist models a way to articulate their ambivalence about Western culture and cultural identity. The nostalgia in the work of these writers, as well as its critique of Western romanticism, has been repeated many times over in frontier narratives of the twentieth century. It seems plausible to say that, more than simply accounting for the closure of the frontier, Turner's essay regenerated a constitutive nostalgia in Western representation for a once unarticulated landscape, a nostalgia that might fuel endless reproductions of a mythical last West, a final frontier.

After Turner, representations of the West would perpetuate its value as a receding phenomenon and thereby sustain its image. At the same time, Turner's eloquent projection of the social and psychical implications of geographical closure for U.S. national culture, like the claustrophobia of naturalism, inflected Western representation with the more grim tones of determinism. The closure that came with the completion of the imperial project left everything accounted for; and the work of naturalism was not only to make use of this situation in order to show that the classical American narrative of free individuals in free space was a faulty paradigm; but also to complain that the energy of empire had made precisely this paradigm impossible. Frank Norris's 1902 essay "The Frontier Gone at Last" works in this way, as did several of the earliest narrative films produced in the United States. In these works the strains of romanticism and determinism often compete with each other for the control of narrative meanings. But in many ways they fuel each other in alternating series of plot movements and images—as in *The Searchers* and other films by John Ford, Howard

Hawks, and Sergio Leone—that now promise possibility, now constrict that openness to an ineluctable set of limits.

Turner's way of orchestrating this alternation was to memorialize the open landscape and infinite possibilities of the frontier, and, in the process of doing so, to frame it as a completed history. His questions about the future directions of U.S. national culture and identity assume the importance of recalling the frontier as a historical engine of development rather than as a romantic Euro-American concept. But clearly the concept was given powerful articulation in the detailed account of its disappearance.

In Turner's estimation the frontier is for Euro-American culture what Michel Foucault would have called an *episteme*. Its enormous seductive power lay largely in its capacity to absorb any number of projected meanings or desires, and in its mechanism of recession—of sliding ever out of reach in the pioneering subject's accumulation of horizons. Turner's focus on the disappearing public domain dramatized the loss of a wilderness understood as primary and invigorating to a system of highly organized social exchanges. In doing so he contributed to the palimpsest that he designed in his essay and offered it as a record for modern Western nostalgia to maintain. In this sense, Turner invented the West for the twentieth century by closing it, and he invented the "Western" by opening the possibility for repeating the loss of the West in fiction.

IDENTIFYING HIMSELF WITH Lewis and Clark, the photographer Edward S. Curtis took on the role of explorer and student of the West with wide open, romantic eyes. "Through the Lewis and Clark Journals I had followed in my mind that great exploration on the Columbia River," Curtis wrote. "I wanted to see and study the region . . . as had the Lewis and Clark party. I wanted to camp where they camped and approach the Pacific through the eyes of those intrepid explorers."[6] At the same time, he saw the region as a finite space and its populations as fated to be consumed by the programs of natural selection.

Among Curtis's photogravures for his series *The North American Indian*, perhaps the most familiar are the portraits of individual men and women, very present to the camera, whose faces, postures, and costumes shape them as instructive representatives of Native tradition and nobility. But the series, produced from 1898 to 1930, offers other equally affecting and yet more complex sets of images. One theme that recurs throughout the thirty-two-year period of publication might be termed Curtis's liminal picturing of indigenous life—in these images, individual Indians are just barely visible, sitting, as it were, on the edge of perception. As if straddling a border between presence and absence, the subjects of these pictures seem to be disappearing before our eyes.

The compositions of these "vanishing Indians" attest not only to Curtis's own peculiar aesthetic and technical styles but speak as well to events and issues in the public culture of his time. A close understanding of the liminal photogravures depends on an appreciation of the social contexts in which they were produced—in particular, the diminishment of Native American cultural vitality that made possible what Turner referred to as the closing of the Western frontier.

Curtis's liminal images of Indian subjects were produced at a time when it was commonly thought that Native American traditional life was on the brink of disappearing. Most indigenous people in the United States were, in fact, assigned to reservations administered by the Bureau of Indian Affairs, some of them quite distant from traditional homelands. Since 1887, with the passage of the Dawes Act, these reservations had been "allotted" into separate parcels set aside for each Indian, such that the traditional notion of a tribal land base—a cornerstone of native cultural and personal identity—had been severely compromised. The intention of the bill, in the minds of its sponsors, was to help Indians assimilate to the dominant culture through the potent effects of owning private property; but since the Dawes Act also allowed for the sale of this property, it not only diminished tribal identity but opened the door to white settlement on reservation lands as well.

Besides these changes in land usage, important shifts had occurred in Indian society as a result of the government-sponsored education system that had been in place since 1877. Under this system, native children were taught the language, religion, and culture of the dominant society, in many cases at boarding schools where tribal languages and traditions were systematically and severely repressed. The idea of the program was not only to reshape cultural identity in the children, but, through them, to diminish tribal lifestyles on their return to the reservations. But often, when graduates went back to their reservations, the training only served to alienate them from home and to provoke a host of psychological and social problems.

These incursions on Native traditionalism and daily life came, of course, in the wake of more openly genocidal actions conducted by the United States military throughout the nineteenth century. In 1890 they came to a dramatic conclusion with the massacre at Wounded Knee, South Dakota. Occurring just eight years before Curtis began his project for *The North American Indian*, this incident involved the slaughter of more than three hundred men, women, and children by the soldiers of what had once been George Armstrong Custer's regiment. Wounded Knee effectively broke the back of Indian resistance to the extension of U.S. authority in the West; for contemporary American Indian society, it is probably the most densely remembered incident in what many consider the centuries-long holocaust directed against indigenous people in North America.

But as Turner's thesis makes very plain, the West was more prominently considered lost to whites, not to Indians, by the time Curtis began his work on *The North American Indian*. Curtis's project interprets Indian subjects as quintessential elements of this passing West. Like the culture of the frontier, tribal cultures throughout the trans-Mississippi zone are portrayed in his images as disappearing. Emblems of a primal, original West, Curtis's Indian figures prompt the viewer to imagine the sources of "America" in such natural nobility and at the same time to see, with Curtis, that Native American tribal communities are in many ways simply unable to adapt to the practices, beliefs, and ideologies of the now dominant culture of European America. His writing—in *The North American Indian* and elsewhere—as well as his visual images clearly demonstrate Curtis's sense that the Native Americans are simultaneously romantic, heroic figures and nonparticipants in the irresistible march of progress. In 1903 Curtis wrote in an essay for *Scribner's Magazine*: "It is true that advancement demands the extermination of these wild, care-free picturesque Indians, and, in the language of our President [Teddy Roosevelt], we cannot keep them or their lands for bric-a-brac."[7] Yet he complains bitterly, nevertheless, about the execution of Indian policy by government officials and politicians. Curtis's complex reaction mixes sympathy with "science" as he resigns himself to the idea that, left out of the long run of natural history, the Indians must either revise themselves to meet the culture of the dominant society or be marginalized to the point of extinction.

For Curtis, these "facts" of nature are as true as they are sad. His work for the *North American Indian* involved not only making photogravures in native locations but extensive studies of Indian cultures. His knowledge of the tribal communities he visited was extensive, if not comprehensive. He spent long periods of time with the communities he studied; and his writing exhibits a great deal of affection, respect, and sympathy for the people who became his artistic subjects. So familiar was Curtis with the residents and ritual life of the Hopi at Walpi village in Arizona that he was initiated into the tribe and became a priest. The photographs speak eloquently about his perceptions of the beauty and wisdom of Native America.

"The Vanishing Race," taken at Navajo nation in 1904, was the first photogravure in the portfolio accompanying volume 1 of the series. In this picture, we barely distinguish a line of riders who are heading away from the camera toward a dark horizon in the distant background. The light on their path contrasts sharply with their shadows and with the murkiness of the distant destination, such that the image seems divided into two halves. Curtis's caption reads:

> The thought which this picture is meant to convey is that the Indians, as a race, already shorn of their tribal strength and stripped of their primitive dress, are passing into the darkness of an unknown future. Feeling that the picture expresses so much of the thought that inspired the entire work, the author chose it as the first of the original series.[8]

In many ways the picture can be said to serve as a coda to Curtis's vision of Native America, and thus its position at the beginning of the series' portfolios is apposite. For the Navajo figures are not interesting in themselves—we can barely even see them—but function more as elements in an allegory, which the caption stipulates. That allegory is clearly of an ominous nature: rather than riding toward a new phase of life, the figures seem to be moving in the direction of something that looks more like death. The riders at the head of the line are in fact so dark and difficult to see that they are indistinguishable from the dark,

Figure 1. "The Vanishing Race" by Edward S. Curtis. Photo reproduction by Joseph Elliott, courtesy Martin Art Gallery, Muhlenberg College.

upper portion of the picture, where representation ends. Engulfed in the darkness, the leading figures have, in effect, already disappeared into the depths of the hillside.

The invisibility of the characters in this picture invests them with mystic appeal. Curtis composes the image in elegant symmetries; the barest suggestion of light just touches the backs, heads, and shoulders of the riders in the foreground. The silhouettes, and the aesthetically pleasing but barely discernible shimmer of the aura that surrounds them, elicit the viewer's desire to see more. Thus, Curtis's vanishing figures appear coated in mystery, assuming an exotic moment of being, a kind of destined movement into death, as the Navajo direct themselves out of the picture plane, out of this world.

At the same time, alongside the suggestion of movement into a mythical, epical death, the image shapes an immense, silent sadness in which the Indians appear resigned to a less heroic, slow removal toward a more banal destination. The sadness of the picture suggests the grim resignation to marginalization, neglect, and the boredom of reservation poverty that accompanies the diminishment of traditional Navajo culture. In this reading the glitter of light on the shoulders and the symmetry of the composition point not so much to the glamour or exoticism of mythical death but starkly to the minimal continued existence of each figure, as of the group. Curtis's uncanny ability to capture this condition attests to a great empathy on his part, far beyond aesthetic appreciation of a more romantic kind of vanishing.

It is important to note that "The Vanishing Race" was extensively "worked on" in the darkroom. Photographic historian Christopher Lyman writes that the photograph

> is as much the result of retouching as it is a product of the
> original negative. The sticks in the lower right-hand corner
> were apparently enhanced by strokes of the stylus, and the
> shapes of the Indian riders were defined by highlights which
> were enhanced with a negative retouching pencil. Even the
> hopeful aura of light running along the horizon was retouched
> into the image. (80)

In many more instances in *The North American Indian*, Curtis manipulated his images, at times quite dramatically. Given this practice, along with the romantic anxieties about the closing of the West in Curtis's imagination, one is compelled to question just what is being expressed in "The Vanishing Race." Is the picture about Indians and the problems they face; or is it about issues of cultural politics and identity that beset Euro-Americans, particularly those calling themselves Westerners?

For all of Curtis's great sympathy with and interest in Indian life and culture, does the picture even attempt to record the experiences of Indian people? James Clifford and others have suggested that Curtis's work in general perpetuated white notions of "Indianness"; but to what extent might we also say that his images—and "The Vanishing Race" is representative—record the somewhat displaced self-pity of a vanishing white culture (that of the frontier) which depended on the presence of Indians for its own romance? Mick Gidley proposes that, rather than asking whether "white culture(s) depicted indigenous cultures with verisimilitude, in the manner of the repeated claims that tribal people depicted in Curtis's images were 'wrongly' dressed, it would seem that the appropriate question to ask today of one of the dominant (white) culture's products would be, What aspect of itself has it represented?"[9]

Figure 2. "Crying to the Spirits" by Edward S. Curtis. Photo reproduction by Joseph Elliott, courtesy Martin Art Gallery, Muhlenberg College.

Gidley traces the dichotomy in Curtis criticism between, on the one hand, those who find him a producer of "authentic incarnations of essential Indian nobility and spirituality," and on the other, those who foreground "the powerful element of staging in the photographs" and who treat the work "almost as if it had been produced by a charlatan." Avoiding either of these positions, I, like Gidley, take Curtis to be typical of artists and writers of his time and his work to be "paradigmatic" (11–13).

The designedness of these pictures and the sense one gets that they are, after all, enlisting Native American subjects in the production of a narrative about white Western culture increases when one looks at a few more of Curtis's liminal images. In 1908 Curtis made the photogravure known as "Crying to the Spirits," depicting a statuesque figure, which he included in volume 4. Describing the Hidatsa tribe, of which the picture's subject was a member, the caption to the image reads: "Their habitat for many generations has been along the Missouri from Heart River to the Little Missouri, in North Dakota. According to legend, their emergence was a mythical one from the underworld." The choice of this comment, of all the information that might have been offered about the tribe, suggests that the gravure was designed to illustrate something about emergence or the spiritual consciousness of emergence on the part of the unnamed subject. Although the figure is certainly more visible than are the Navajo riders of "The Vanishing Race," the perpendicular line of his body vanishes into the darkness at the top of the picture plane. His feet are equally planted in darkness, such that the figure does, in a sense, appear to be emerging from the earth and at the same time merging with the sky.

The subtle but focused light on the forehead seems to invest the man with a form of mystic wisdom. In this as well as the distribution of light about his body and in the act of "crying to the spirits," he bears a transcendent aspect that would be hard to miss. The figure, shot from below so that he looms over the viewer, appears stationed between a material, earthly life in the present plane of existence and another, more distant, zone inhabited by spirits. In addressing himself to the spirit world while still inhabiting the present, his figure exemplifies the tradition of the noble Native in the literature of the United States from Cooper's Chingachgook to Jack London's Sitka Charley. He is also representative of Indian populations throughout the continent that Curtis understands to be on the brink of extinction, and thus in closer communication with the spirit world than with the everyday one of modern, material reality.

To enhance the visual articulation of these ideas, Curtis touched up "Crying to the Spirits" in the darkroom, as he had "The Vanishing Race." Lyman explains that "Curtis had the sky burned-in in the darkroom. Instead of appearing white, as it does in the unmanipulated image, the sky displays a gradual darkening of tones" (74). The "unmanipulated image" that Lyman reproduces in his book is much brighter and less shaped for dramatic effect. In any case, if it does tell a story it is a different one from that of the more openly processed image. In contrast to the white background, the figure actually appears darker; but his presence on an earthly plain is more evident.

Again, questions arise about the topic of "Crying to the Spirits." Does it record a native reality; or is it another expression of white concerns and interests? Without presuming to know just what Curtis knew about this particular, unnamed Hidatsa or his experience, it is tempting to read the Indian figure as the sign of an elusive and at the same time earth-bound spirituality that had come to be part of many white Americans' myth of the self and its identification with the land. Read in this way, the picture suggests that citizens of the United States, inheriting the strength and endurance of the Western settlers, had also inherited the Indians' natural connection to the landscape. Although the indigenous Americans could not survive the course of history, they could and did bequeath their spiritual affinity with Western nature to those who overcame them. Thus, the process of adaptation and natural selection worked to permit the victors to absorb what had been a key factor in the Indians' losing the contest for survival.

Considering himself a privileged inheritor of these spiritual traditions (and not just because he had been initiated into the Hopi priesthood), Edward Curtis not only appreciated but cherished the passing Native cultures. In his general introduction to *The North American Indian*, he wrote:

> The great changes in practically every phase of the Indian's life
> that have taken place, especially within recent years, have

been such that had the time for collecting much of the
material, both descriptive and illustrative, herein recorded,
been delayed, it would have been lost forever. The passing of
every old man or woman means the passing of some tradition,
some knowledge of sacred rites possessed by no other;
consequently the information that is to be gathered, for the
benefit of future generations, respecting the mode of life of one
of the great races of mankind, must be collected at once or the
opportunity will be lost for all time. It is this need that has
inspired the present task.[10]

"The present task" positions Curtis as mediator between the spiritual
life of the Indians and the more modern one of his largely Euro-American viewers. Teddy Roosevelt affirmed Curtis's presumed inheritance of
some of this Native spirituality in his foreword to the series. Curtis, he
wrote, "has not only seen their vigorous outward existence, but has
caught glimpses, such as few white men ever catch, into that strange
spiritual and mental life of theirs; from whose innermost recesses all
white men are forever barred."[11]

If "Crying to the Spirits" offers a glimpse of Hidatsa spirituality, in
"Before the White Man Came," made on the Agua Caliente Reservation in southern California, Curtis pictures an imaginary Native world
completely unknowable to Euro-Americans from a time before "history" began. The female model in the foreground looks out on a dry,
rocky little canyon filled with palm trees. She, like many of Curtis's
images of women, is pictured in a moment of daily domestic life. With
a basket on her head, she appears to be working; although she has
stopped for a moment to look at the scene before her in the location we
now know as Palm Springs. This image is not so liminal as the others I
have addressed, and yet the model's posture, her back turned to the
viewer, suggests a way of being that we cannot see, a way of seeing that
we cannot emulate. Even though it was produced in 1924, much later
than the others, the picture's retrospection takes it back in time to what
Curtis fantasizes as an ancient homeland untouched by white influence. A certain irony develops if one notices that the image can be
seen as harking back to the Old Testament, the quintessential text of
Judeo-Christian civilization, picturing "the white myth of Eden: the as-
yet-unashamed Eve [awaiting] her fate."[12]

Figure 3. "Before the White Man Came" by Edward S. Curtis. Photo reproduction by Joseph Elliott, courtesy Martin Art Gallery, Muhlenberg College.

Curtis's romanticism is more evident than his evolutionism in this picture; the location has a pastoral resonance, even though we are presumably being asked to view the woman as stopping by the springs on a sunny day while working. The potential rest and recreation associated with Palm Springs by 1924 seems to distract the woman from her "traditional" duties. The natural landscape is reflected in the water, and she seems perfectly a part of it. But the explicitly imaginative composition ignores any present-tense Indian existence in California and in doing so assumes, at a certain level, their total disappearance. The picture is perhaps more of an advertisement for Palm Springs and for romantic American notions of the self alone in nature than an illustration of anything Native—even as it makes use of the romance still associated with the figure of the vanishing Indian in the fashionable culture of southern California in the 1920s.

NEITHER WOUNDED KNEE, the Dawes Act, nor the boarding school system, in fact, entirely erased Indian culture, even if to a great extent they did accomplish what they set out to. Many, if not most, of the Indians whom Curtis went to study were only barely holding on to traditional economies, ritual practices, ways of dress, and so forth; but Indian populations themselves were not, in fact, dying out, and have not in our own time. In many cases contemporary tribal cultures have maintained important traditional practices, beliefs, and even lifestyles. Just as in Curtis's and Turner's moment, the means of "being Indian" remain in many cases difficult to negotiate. One can appreciate the aesthetic qualities of Curtis's work and the usefulness of its preservation of late-nineteenth-century images of Indianness—whether their provenance lies sheerly in Euro-American expectations or to some extent in Native self-images; but its real power for us, I would argue, has a great deal to do with his writing them into Euro-American stories of conquest and loss.

Chapter 4

Importing Naturalism to the American West

We live in a world of wanton and importunate fable.
—HENRY JAMES, *"Emile Zola"* (1903)

THE MODEL OF geographical closure that the American naturalists took from Frederick Jackson Turner projected an overpoweringly material world. If Turner's West of "The Significance of the Frontier" is on one level a disappearing landscape where imagination met geography in a conquering sweep, on another it is a dated and gridlike part of the continental body whose essence is limited to its physical and economic proportions. In the naturalist Westerns that share this vision, even the most wild-seeming element of Western landscape or character is accounted for in advance by the legal, commercial, and scientific codes that had comprehensively mapped the continent. The disenchantment of these landscapes presumably lay in the idea that the population of the West had increased to such a point that its entire surface was effectively titled and, if not precisely settled, then certainly accounted for. But, of course, disenchantment also came as an effect of evolutionist thinking that saw history as a set of fiercely material processes, the conclusions of which were inevitable. Thus romantic geography was converted to naturalist environment, and the largeness of the West was reconstituted as a potentially claustrophobic, totally socialized zone.

For Norris, London, Crane, and Cather, literary naturalism emerged as a highly appropriate medium for representing the shifting prospects and ethics, indeed the confusions themselves, of contemporary regional culture. Naturalism had been circulating in U.S. literary markets since the 1880s, when Emile Zola's Rougon-Macquart novels began appearing in English.

Of particular use was the convention of the distanced narrator, which had been central to Zola's naturalist program from the start. The naturalist narrator's position was to be like that of an experimental scientist, distanced from the material rather than enmeshed within it. From such a perspective the narrator of a novel, no less than the author, could presumably study the dynamics of environment, character, and event without muddying their clarity, since his own psychical propensities would not be part of the picture. By directing readerly attention to the story and deflecting it from textuality—from the processes of story-telling—the naturalist narrator could avoid romanticizing his own point of view.

The advantages Zola hoped to gain by pursuing this problematic goal centered on the resistance that the observer's stance might pose to romantic articulations of character and story. Among the many problems Zola found in romantic writing, perhaps the most objectionable was the loosening of the observer's or speaker's will onto the dimensions of the material addressed and the working assumption that the psyche of the subject might be original and self-generating. In 1906 he wrote, "I hate romanticism for the false education it gave me; I am caught in it and it makes me wild."[1]

The observer-narrator Zola described in "The Experimental Novel" would interpret the psychical processes of character as effects of the social environment as well as of family and cultural history rather than as the products of idiosyncratic, autonomous sources in the self. Geographical settings were not intended to function as images of character psychology or as vehicles of inspiration. Instead the reverse would be more true: human figures would bear the traces of historical and social processes as embodied in such settings. Such determinations, then, would have integral roles in the narrative economy as characters and communities recognized, encountered, and negotiated them.

The Western naturalists had other models for this privileged, rational viewer as well. In the traditions of romantic Western writing, which their work in many ways sought to revise, a precedent for the authoritative observer lay in the figure of the expeditionary narrator whose naturalness and innocence rhetorically ensured the integrity of his text. Daniel Boone's dictation of his story to John Filson, for instance, and Filson's transcriptions of the oral source, are presented in *The Discovery, Settlement and Present State of Kentucke* as pure media that give the most unprocessed vision possible of Kentucky's history and of Boone's life. In Jefferson's "Memoire of Meriwether Lewis," the honesty and intelligence of the explorer's scientifically trained mind ensure that his pen will serve as a transparent window on the Western territories. In these ways, the gaze of the expeditionary narrator is offered as a pure medium of communication, whose affinities with wild nature ensure his clarity, his unique and even exotic self.

By contrast, the naturalist narrator's innocence is clinical, sanctioned by scientific integrity and the distance he has from the material he studies. But the effect is similar, and in both cases the narrator acquires authoritative clarity by virtue of a presumably special capacity to see what is simply there in all of its actual dimensions. Naturalist Westerns typically begin by upholding the authoritative stance for the narrator evident in both orthodox naturalism and classical westernism. In the case of Frank Norris and Jack London, and in a less overt sense Stephen Crane and Willa Cather, the construction of the narrator in relation to the world to be represented has powerful affinities with the westernist construction of the American explorer-pioneer in relation to the wilderness to be charted and domesticated: the social field and individual human psychology are both treated as wild zones to be mapped and thus brought under the intellectual control of "science" or the logical categories of empirical thought.

But this kind of authority is commonly subverted in the course of the narrative. As the thematic and structural motif of limitation develops, the observer's privileged distance and clarity often get compromised. Telling stories about Western life and culture at the height of the discourse of the closed frontier put special pressure on the narratists to present their credentials and purposes. For while the postfrontier West was legally as well as scientifically mapped, regional identity was not, insofar as its traditional bases in wilderness romance were viewed as dramatically compromised. Thus, the narrator's own authority and identity, particularly as they pertained to regional knowledge, were sub-ject to question.

To be a capable interpreter of contemporary life, a writer needed to have first-hand knowledge of Western language, manners, and customs. This residual tradition of Western romanticism too remained in natu-ralist Westerns. But to the degree to which the features of Western life were considered to be destabilized, the speaker of a given text could have this knowledge of the local only if he was unaware of the cultural shifts that made them things of the past. In such a position, a speaker could not be relied on to give an efficient portrait of the contemporary scene. But to include this awareness in the representation would, in effect, mean that one was memorializing rather than offering a living, first-hand account of frontier experience.

Given these complexities and compromises, it was openly prob-lematic to assume that an observer who understood the region well enough to represent it with sensitivity and accuracy could maintain a transcendent position toward it—a position outside its blurred ethics and epistemologies. In attempting to establish their authority, the nar-rating voices of these texts produce a variety of reflexive references to their own voices and to their aesthetics, somewhat at the expense of the confident portrayal of the material and social dimensions of West-ern life. Thus their narrators share not only the integrities of their westernist predecessors, but the ethical confusions they saw in contem-porary regional culture as well.

The naturalist Westerns addressed in the following chapters recog-nize this problem in varying degrees, and some of them openly attempt to manage it. Frank Norris deals with the problem in several of his short stories by splitting the work of narrative presentation between an intel-lectual outsider, or host of the story, and a rougher insider whose expe-rience of the true West is both vouched for and interpreted by the outer speaker. In this way narrative authority is secured and regional knowl-edge vouched for; but the arrangement is rather elaborate and calls a good deal of attention to the process of storytelling itself.

Norris's *Vandover and the Brute* offers one of the more obvious examples of the muddying of the authority of the narrating voice. The "speaker" of that novel at times hovers over Vandover's and his parents'

figures, describing, interpreting, and moving them through given situations, particularly in the first two or three chapters. But as Vandover's
integrity as a character and a personality begins to disintegrate, so does
the presence of a distinct narratist's sensibility. The book's perspective
is still directed largely from Vandover's point of view, but not by free
indirect discourse nor by adherence to his perceptions. Rather, the narrating voice seems to take a position separate from that of Vandover
and yet at the same time to share in his murky and incoherent way of
seeing the world.

A similar confusion of authority occurs in the later sections of Norris's *McTeague*. As the central character flees progressively further from
the structures of the city that previously gave him shape, he also seems
to slip from the controlling definitions of the narrator. The perceptions
that come with his "sixth sense" are certainly not those of the manag-
ing voice, and yet that voice virtually merges itself with McTeague's
sensibility.

Crane's narrators in "The Blue Hotel," "The Bride Comes to Yellow Sky," and "Moonlight on the Snow" are often as awkwardly situated as his central characters. Familiar with the peculiarities of the
moment of cultural history in which they are located, these narrators
seem at times as lost as their characters are about what to think and
how to act in the postfrontier West. The authority figures in the three
stories share a perspective on the ambiguities at issue in their situations;
but they, like their narrators, are finally lost in the strange shuffle of
things, and no one offers an authoritative analysis.

London's Klondike tales, on the other hand, tend to reimagine the
plausibility of a narrator's ideal comprehension of character, event, and
landscape. But this is only achieved by exceeding the limits of naturalist rationalism. The speaker's focus on the evolutionary materiality of
the frozen north is so intense that the physical begins to dissolve into a
peculiar form of mysticism. Just as the most fit Arctic travelers acquire
an uncanny ability to interpret the data of the forests and the motives
of their companions, so their narrators speak as if they could read the
thought processes and hidden desires of these figures from the evidence
of their biological and genetic constitutions.

The most palpable instance of this virtually supernatural knowledge comes in *The Call of the Wild*, when the narrator's authority is

demonstrated by his ability to share in Buck's primeval, unmediated perception of the mystic heart of the wilderness. Such ecstatic comprehension is achieved at great expense to the materialist principles that London poses as cause and effect of all phenomena in the first several chapters of the novel. In relinquishing this logic to the story's accumulating mysticism, the rationalism and certainly the authoritative distance of London's narrator are openly challenged.

In these and other ways, then, the narrators of naturalist Westerns appear nearly as vulnerable to epistemological and ethical confusion as the characters they describe. Initially, they seem to share the presumptive authority of Zola's narrators. But the problems that implicitly arise in the repressed contradictions of scientist observation in French naturalism are more evident, and in many cases more openly thematized, in naturalist Westerns. For all these reasons, the observers in Western fiction seem to be considerably affected by the environmental dynamics that they attempt to represent, whereas Zola's are less likely to admit their susceptibility. The Western narrators lack the power to sustain environment's distanced, indifferent witness and, unlike Zola's observers, are more likely to position themselves among the human figures of their stories, at least in terms of cultural knowledge and rationalizing capacities. Rather than taking on the weighty task of narrating the actions of the many different kinds of forces that operate under the general rubric of "environment," these narrators tend to focus on geography as environment's privileged representative. The craggy, frozen, and dehydrated landscapes of their fictional postfrontier West often figure as emblems of not only territorial closure but of economic, social, and natural limitation as well.

The particular force of environment that serves as the dominant, causative drive of events in a given story may be any of a number of material powers. It might consist of an evolutionary momentum that demands adaptation by human and other species to the conditions of a specific natural zone. Or it might be a sheerly social matter of population growth and the development of community in a given location that necessitates interpersonal exchange and other forms of relationship. The determining force of environment may also be a set of commercial forces—for example, real estate schemes, involving the literal marking out and titling of ground lots, by large-scale mining, ranching, and farming interests. Above all, geography is the dimension that most commonly and most powerfully is made to stand for all of the others in naturalist Westerns. The often inviting geographical landscapes of naturalist Westerns thus reveal themselves, in one way or another, as the visible manifestations of the many forces that systematically thwart human ambitions, and thus take on the qualities of pointed allegory.

The old romantic field of imaginative geography thus has the new task in naturalist Westerns of demonstrating not the power of individual subjects but the material forces that stand in their way. Landscapes from this point of view are not the romantically nurturing or challenging horizons that they are in traditional westernist narratives but rather brute entities whose most evident attribute is indifference. If Western geography is cast in a broad panorama, the narratives of Norris, London, and Crane toy with the expectations of promise or regeneration that such images might imply. While the horizons may elicit the Westerner's desires for the satisfaction of these expectations, they are not intended to respond to them; and they lack the leading edge of a frontier open to a number of possible futures.

In addition to projecting this mute, inconvertible surface, the fictional West of Norris, London, Crane, and Cather was located closer to the modernized settlements of European America than it had ever been in previous U.S. literature. They acknowledged the increasing urbanity and gridlike lines of the West in their fiction with differing stresses and differing degrees of recognition. Norris quite openly assumes that the West is lost, and yet he also plays with the possibilities of its continuing to exist in the heart of the city. Crane ironizes the West of the past just as he does the confusions of contemporary Western regional culture. London, on the other hand, celebrates what might be called the remnants of the old West in the Klondike and in the substitute frontiers he found in the Pacific. In *The Professor's House* and *Death Comes for the Archbishop*, novels addressed in chapter 8, Cather locates her West in Santa Fe and Hamilton, small but rapidly developing cities where she finds traces and memories of older traditions of character and action.

The romantic, open West is often replaced in their stories by what William Cronon has called "second nature." This processed natural zone is schematized for the purposes of real estate or agricultural, pastoral, and extraction industries connected to some metropolis but positioned at a distance from it.[2] In this space, the visionary and gothic images of Western romanticism are mixed with the exhausted and disenchanted scenes of naturalism. *The Call of the Wild, White Fang,* and much of London's Klondike fiction; Norris's *McTeague;* Crane's "The Bride Comes to Yellow Sky" and "The Blue Hotel"; and Cather's *The Professor's House* frame these belated wildernesses with the urban and suburban environments whence the characters emerge. Voicing something between the Whitmanian "barbaric yawp" of "man in the open air" and the self-consciousness of urbanized moderns, their frontier he-men, like their landscapes, demonstrate the ideas adhering in the competing literary codes of naturalism and westernism. The discursive field produced in these texts constitutes a borderland of a different sort, in which the two generic modes collide.

The sharp focus on geography in these stories and the special role it plays in representing the general category of environment is, perhaps, a central factor in the failure of naturalist Westerns to produce a more optimistic interpretation of the social dimensions of regional culture at the end of the nineteenth century. Rather than proposing models that recognize potentially productive forms of social and economic exchange, the articulation of the historical shift focused instead on the revised meaning of landscape. This shift was registered in a teasing action of Western landscape—in a beckoning toward beauty, which finally was indifferent, or perhaps fatal, given its fierce powers. But this teasing action required recalling a romantic landscape that was humanistically meaningful in its promise of individual regeneration. This shadow image, while pushed to the background for the sake of the naturalist ideology, was nevertheless entirely readable. The national iconography of the recalled frontier was not to be read as a collective promise but as an image and elicitor of individual desire for each immigrant who witnessed it. The foregrounded scene, rather than substituting this vision with another one based on the perceived newer conditions, dwelled on the dimension of loss of the romantic promise and the implications for individual imaginations.

This preoccupation with loss distracted textual attention from the immanent issues of social and economic constraints, the growing role of community in the West, and the appropriation of the region by corporate powers. The social relations and institutional powers that Zola attempted to thematize as features of modern life demanding close attention are seen in naturalist Westerns only as the grim limits, the unwelcome developments that come with geographical and cultural change. However much Zola's socialist ethics were overtly espoused by Norris and London, they were not persuasively developed in the contexts of their naturalist Westerns. The ideas of social limitation and exchange served more dominantly as ideological backgrounds against which the challenges of modernity for individual American subjects were dramatized.

But if environment is subsumed as geography and deviates from Zola's program in these ways, the characters of naturalist Westerns are drawn more precisely along the lines suggested in "The Experimental Novel." In their characterizations, Norris, London, Crane, and Cather each attend to the particular historical logic of the discourse of the closed frontier: they dramatize the reordering of imaginative geography in their characters' suddenly anachronistic beliefs, behaviors, and perceptions. Ethics are reshuffled but not quite codified. Western characters stumble over the need to alter their moral imaginations in order to accommodate a Western world constructed as in many cases surprisingly amoral, but amoral in a different sense from that in the legendary past. For the evolutionary attitude that sees nature and natural processes as indifferent constructs social and geographical adaptations as ethically blind. But rather than inviting ethical anarchy, this combination of indifferent nature and amorality more often produces in naturalist Western characters a cautionary attitude and a perception, however cloudy, of the need to compromise on wishes and impulses dictated by instincts.

The motif of cultural confusion serves in many instances as both cause and product of the standard emptiness of naturalist character. The personnel of naturalist Westerns commonly figure as the playthings of environment; they also exemplify the slippery and problematic venture of representing the Euro-American character generally in the 1890s. What, for instance, is the psychological and cultural status of a person who continues to see a wilderness and to look for enchantment in a belated, well-mapped world? What are the parameters of speech and manners in the new West? What does a wide horizon signal in terms of adventure or liberation if it no longer signals a frontier?

Although such questions imply a naturalist limitation to individual character, they also suggest answers rich in dramatic possibilities.

In general, the quality and intensity of character emotions in re-action to the ineluctable momentum of forces that shape them are ini-tially drawn in simple, unsubtle terms. This simplicity is suggestive of the limited and uninspired perceptions accorded to naturalist char-acters in Zola's theoretical agenda. But in the process of trying to com-prehend their situations and to negotiate the spaces and communities of the postfrontier West, they wrestle with their own expectations and with the limits now placed on older ethics and epistemologies. Thus invested with a jarring self-consciousness, they acquire extra dimen-sion, and their simple emotions turn in upon themselves. While these figures still appear as the ciphers of environment and history, a form of self-analysis, however dim or shallow, doubles their thoughts and move-ments, and at the same time inflates them with something akin to romantic literary subjectivity.[3]

These intracharacter struggles between resistance and adaptation are often further complicated, in the work of Norris and London in par-ticular, by what Donald Pizer has called "evolutionary ethical dual-ism."[4] This dualism, which found more comprehensive theoretical articulation in the writings of contemporary scientific philosophers like Joseph LeConte at the University of California and the widely known English sociologist Herbert Spencer, accounted for human psychical dynamics as the effects of a tension, or contest, between primitive and more developed inclinations in human character.[5] The division destablized subjectivity and made it vulnerable to catalysts in the envi-ronment that could activate either set of inclinations. Like other con-temporary theories of human agency, most notably those of Sigmund Freud and Josef Breuer, LeConte's and Spencer's tended to convey the human psyche as always in process, a complex and slippery entity that eluded dependable representation.[6]

The articulation of character as a tension between base drives and properly socialized consciousness was also a key piece of Zola's original formula for naturalism. The baser mode of being had no conscious agency and was largely expressed in accidents and transgressions of common social codes, as well as in the all-knowing descriptions pro-vided by Zola's ideal narrators. But whereas in his work primitive drives

function as controlling energies that compete with and often overwhelm other factors constituting "character," in the work of the American naturalists they tease the character in question with a momentary
wildness that bears the traces of more traditional westernist subjectivity.

The immutably primitive mechanisms of human character often
become associated in naturalist Westerns with sensory "instinct," a
material way of knowing encoded in biology but which at the same
time can allow for unmediated contact with geographical environment,
actually a capacity for *being with* that environment's most affecting features without sharing in its powerful determinations. This transcendent
apperception, added to the proper emptiness of character, allowed for a
kind of protean shifting of subject positions. Given the absence of an
account of character content in its own right, these figures had the
potential of slipping from any particular psychical or social position and
acting on any other catalyst that might conceivably drive them.

This elusive aspect of naturalist Western character recalls a similarly slippery quality in romantic Western characters, whose idiosyncratic, mysterious powers were expressed most effectively by it. The
appearance of these "instinctual" powers in the belated frontier subjects
carries a weight of nostalgia and loss not evident in the French formula
for naturalism. One of the more effective means by which the naturalist Western narrators resisted identifying these traits with romanticism
was to characterize them as the manifestations of brute, material drives
that constitute unanalyzed selfhood as an effect of environment and
heredity rather than as inspiring sources of autonomous subjectivity.
The preservation of this wild, nearly unrepresentable condition in naturalist Western character justified the observer's analyses in the same
way that the projection of a promiscuous wilderness justified the rationalizing of romantic Western narratives. In both cases, Enlightenment
reasoning imposed its sanctions against otherness while maintaining
otherness in order to situate and secure itself. Naturalism's avant-garde
experimentalism thus retained one of the most central features of westernist ideology in presuming to map what it construed as wildness in
"modern" terms.

Given these affinities between the naturalists' sense of self and
project and the sense of self and project inscribed in Western romanticism, we can expect the naturalist text to be infused with some respect,

however unacknowledged, for its deluded protagonists. And indeed, for all of the differences between naturalism and romantic Western representation in terms of ideology and the distribution of space, both genres position the subject in an encounter with a social or natural presence that elicits an effort, however plausible or doomed, to overcome the limits to personal power. A key feature of Western romanticism, the drive to regenerate and extend the American self, does not necessarily disappear in naturalist Western writing. The closing of the West no more closes such desires, as Turner predicted it would, than does naturalism's dismissal construct a curbed American subject. The enclosing effects of naturalist environments—both natural and urban—position this subject differently, but the differences in spatial imagery, where the extension of the self occurs, can often be understood as a shift in which the horizontal line of frontier is simply turned on its side in the more vertical designs of naturalism.

THE SERIES OF BOOKS normally assigned to the category of literary naturalism share a sense of belatedness, of being situated in a moment of literary history when nineteenth-century epistemologies appeared exhausted. This exhaustion is accompanied by a sense that choices and opportunities for human action within a limited set of possibilities have been depleted. The determining agents of these possibilities, set in motion at some privileged point designated as original, act on the receiver at the end of a hereditary, or narrative, line. The causal factor—in a sense, the will of naturalism—is presumed to exist in the present as the accumulated momentum of something initiated long ago. Perhaps the geological tropes that the American naturalists were so fond of using spoke to this residue of age in what they imagined as the forces of natural and environmental power.

But the logic of evolutionary thinking did not sponsor the naming of specific originary phenomena. Authority, something understood as responsible, is absent. One of the central ironies of even the orthodox naturalist theories lies in this lack: for if human subjectivity is only a construct of forces of the environment and inheritance, and if the authority of natural reality does not materialize in any palpable representation—the thing itself of evolutionary agency—then wherein lies responsibility? Who is accountable for social, cultural, and historical phenomena? If the project of naturalism was initially to give adequate representation to social relations, institutions, and processes for the sake of sponsoring a socialist literary imagination, how could this be achieved without a more comprehensive account of agency and individual responsibility?[7]

Rather than answering these questions, American naturalist fiction tended to dwell on the effects of determining forces on particular subjectivities and on the romance of environment's ancient origins. Naturalist Westerns did not configure natural or social forces as respondents so much as antagonists to the individual will. These forces could loom over the puny human figure because of their sheer material power and the accumulative momentum that came with their long histories. This relationship, rather than providing a paradigm for socially inflected romantic agency, traced out the lines of an individual existential angst that competed with more traditional forms of Western romanticism, and at the same time refurbished that mode with a new set of parameters. These revisions allowed for the darker, more pessimistic projections of settler and explorer history in twentieth-century Western cinema—for example, the films of John Ford and Howard Hawks. They had significant effects on the telling of frontier stories and complicated the meanings of Western imaginative geography by adding limitation and frustration of individual desire to its stock of more promising referents. But despite naturalism's challenges and alterations, westernism continues to this day to thrive as an important myth of national culture.

Chapter 5
Frank Norris and the Fiction of the Lost West

He had so lively a sense of the value of accurate observation and so eager a desire to produce that in the very face of death he could set down a description of his surroundings, actually laying down the rifle to pick up the pen.

—FRANK NORRIS, "A Memorandum of Sudden Death" (1902)

BECAUSE GEOGRAPHY HAS such a privileged role in the representational systems of naturalist Westerns, it is worthwhile to take into consideration the geographical contexts and the specific landscape conditions of the West in which these stories were produced. This is not to assume that literary settings simply reproduce historical ones, but that the shapes and contents of physical places have some transformational bearing on the very landscape-centered narratives of the regional culture that naturalist Westerns dramatize. Beyond the importance of geographical settings for the representation of late Western cultural identity, the dimensions and the textures of the places these writers knew seem to leave their impressions on narrative structure.

Taking a look at the Berkeley and San Francisco landscapes in the 1890s helps to give a geographical context to the tensions in the fiction of Frank Norris and Jack London in particular. Not all of their stories feature San Francisco as an iconic Western setting, but the myths and ideals of frontier romance that their work typically engaged—whether to celebrate or critique or both—are in many ways emblematized in San Francisco's geography and public culture.

In Norris's critical writing about Western life and literature, he in effect calls for the retention of what might be termed an unself-conscious regional style. In doing so, he asserts the continuous existence of an ideal, pure Western mode of being, unmediated by the structures and methods of civil society. Without self-consciousness, without the secondary level of performance that he thought characterized more contemporary Western subjectivity, this primary state could be achieved simply by being in and speaking from one's most unrehearsed, unscripted Western self. The spontaneous "nature" of such unself-conscious being would serve as the proper source of representation of the Western landscape and its people, even in the postfrontier era. The mystical access to the true meanings of the West, and the simple language style of its speakers, would preserve and at the same time revitalize romantic westernism as it had functioned in the narratives of Daniel Boone and Meriwether Lewis.

Norris attempted to put his ideas into practice in three short stories and the novel *McTeague*. The contest between what gets construed as spontaneous Western vitality and belated, or self-conscious, observation and action in these tales complicates both categories. Norris tries to recuperate the asserted distinctions, but his stories are, in the end, more successful at demonstrating the implausibility of modeling "true Western" character or speech in the age of Turner. Norris's naturalist interpretations of the historical moment help him to frame these incongruities with some integrity. But a residual fondness for older westernist types and stories featured here remains in view, even as Norris distances himself in various ways from identifying with them.

THE CALIFORNIA STATE CONSTITUTION of 1849 had provided for the establishment of a university, and plans for its realization had begun to take shape in the same year. But it was not until well after the Gold Rush, with the state legislature allocating funds in 1862, that construction actually began. The Gold Rush had brought inflation; and inflation had made the rather wild city of San Francisco conscious of itself as an urban complex with economic and fiscal responsibilities. The city in a sense, and perhaps somewhat reluctantly, settled down to law and order—and to family life. Many of the forty-niners who had stayed on the west coast had brought out their families from the East or married the children of new pioneers who came to the West with no apparent lust for gold or even particularly for adventure.[1] These post-rush settlers were more often than not simply taking part in a migration that by 1868, with the completion of the Union Pacific Railroad, had become quite plausible, and that by the late nineteenth century was virtually conventional.

By 1890, when Frank Norris began studying there, the campus of the University of California at Berkeley was spread across more than 160 acres of irregularly graded terrain, wooded largely by oak trees. Its water supply, a reservoir and a creek that forked through the campus, was poorly distributed for the needs of the roughly seven hundred people who worked and studied there. But the system was being redesigned to include new wells and wider pipes that would replace the old lines installed when the University was founded in 1868. The grounds were pock-marked and pitted from the digging; they hardly matched the design authored for the University in the late 1850s by Frederick Law Olmsted, the landscape artist of New York City's Central Park. Later in the same year a project was initiated to level and shape the grounds to suit the Olmsted plan more closely, but this work, which extended over several years, contributed to the tattered look of the school as it approached the end of the century.[2]

In spite of its unfinished state, by the late nineteenth century Berkeley was a mark of Western society's cultural sophistication. And indeed, given the accumulation of stable civic institutions among American residents after the middle of the century, the construction of a university on San Francisco Bay seems in retrospect like a reasonably predictable event. The civility that it stood for meant the diminishment of Western regional culture's most distinguishing features: its roughness and its free-form social as well as geographical contents. Nevertheless, Westerners continued at least through the 1890s to include in expressions of their regional identity some reference to an invigorating wilderness—material and conceptual—that marked their difference from the Eastern culture that they were coming to resemble increasingly with each decade. The culture that the University at Berkeley was intended to mirror and uphold was still claiming a difference for itself from the terms of Eastern refinement. Thus, the University's appearance was symptomatic of the liminal quality of civil society in the Bay Area at the end of the century.

The strain of this Janus-faced identity, leaning eastward for its future but relying on a tenuous Westernness for its core of distinction, nurtured an already habitual nostalgia in the rhetoric of the American frontier. That nostalgia, envisioning what it construed as a once pure wilderness compromised in the present, is evident in European-American frontier narratives—historical, fictional, and scientific—since the eighteenth century. Yet the blurring of different cultural conditions in the highly unstable zone of the frontier seemed repeatedly to elicit a drive on the part of explorers and pioneers to grid and chart the West for an Eastern culture to follow. In romantic narratives of the regional past, these processes were seen as having compromised what was retrospectively imagined as the original, true West.

The planning of the West and its continuous representation as a mysterious, wild zone resulted in a complicated cultural situation that riddled Western regional identity with anxieties and contradictions. Norris and Jack London were both trained as writers in this milieu, at the university as well as in San Francisco and Oakland. Their fiction projected a mixture of exuberant, romantic regionalism and a more circumscribed cultural modernity. These contestant modes were evident in the academic discourses to which Norris and London were exposed at Berkeley; and, as instanced by the reception of Turner's essay, they were current in the country at large as well.

The University of California exemplified in various ways the complications at issue for regional identity, particularly in the efforts of its founders to mark the existence of "high culture" in their West. Previous to the legislature's allocation of funds, the question of the location of the college had become a surprisingly difficult one. Problems concerning water supply, terrain, and proximity to populated areas eliminated one available site after another until in 1856 Henry Durant, who became the university's first president, saw the current grounds. At that moment, a companion reports, he stood in his carriage and shouted "Eureka! . . . Eureka! I have found it. I have found it."[3] Whether the conventions of the mining experience had actually found their way into the language of this eminent educator is probably an unanswerable question. But the story itself—told during a memorial address for Durant in 1875—attests to the steady currency of the memory of a wilder West in the fin-de-siècle frontier's image of itself. The association in the Durant exclamation of higher education with the popular culture of the Gold Rush is symptomatic of the self-conscious atmosphere of rough gentility in Berkeley's early history, as in other sectors of Bay Area society in the late nineteenth century.

For members of the University community, such roughness had to be contained as a regional style; the presence of substantially cruder character was not easily accommodated. In the spring of 1889, John H. C. Bonté, secretary to the Board of Regents of the University since 1883 and professor of legal ethics, had expressed relief in his *Annual Report* over the disappearance of certain "notorious visitors" to the campus during the past several years. Instead, he was happy to report, the visiting public consisted mostly of "numerous well-behaved families with their children." The previous visitors, whom Bonté also called "the worst possible people," had approached the grounds "in great numbers," "disgraced" the scene with their drunken behavior and destroyed property.[4]

The university officially maintained an open relation to the community where it was located; it was, after all, a state-funded institution that existed by public support. Bonté's reports suggest that ever since the school had moved from Oakland to the Berkeley Hills, the people that he complained of had been a regular nuisance to the civil institution that the Regents and scholars represented.[5] Those who made up the "evil element"—another of Bonté's terms—are a difficult group to identify. They may have been migrant ranch workers or drifters from other parts of the state, looking for work in a depressed economy. They are barely sketched in Bonté's reports, enough only to appear as inappropriate figures in the scene he wanted to describe and as trespassers who treated the landscaped lawns of the university as a comedy. His complaints came in an effort to dissociate Berkeley from such society; this was necessary not only because the two worlds existed side by side but because San Francisco newspapers and Berkeley pulpits were complaining about the drunkenness and debauchery of the university's own students in much the same tones as Bonté used to disparage the "evil element."[6]

If the manners of the mountain men and the college students over-
lapped in places, this was only symptomatic of the hybrid culture of the
American West since the term "frontier" had been used to mark it. The
distinctions that Bonté's annual accounts attempted to draw were tenuous; and wild Western behavior was no more natural in this scene
than were Ivy League manners. Whoever the figures were that appeared
in his report, they bore, to Bonté's eye, the marks and manners of a
rougher West, a supposedly disappearing culture, that people of his class
and generation would have recognized as anachronistic.

But those of Bonté's milieu would also likely have viewed such
characters from another perspective: as much as embarrassing morons,
they were also romantic remnants of a singular, true West. For educated, middle-class observers to recognize these crude individuals as
nostalgic reminders of a bygone era would have been to underscore
their own own access to, but difference from, the culture of the old
West. This doubleness was a key component of the anxiety in regional
identity: life in the new West was not life in the East, yet the audience
for Bonté's *Reports* kept a distinguishing distance from the characters
who hewed too closely to old West ways. If these middle-class observers
never took advantage of the anarchic freedoms that Bonté's "evil element" ostensibly symbolized, the presence of that element kept a note
of risk in the air, a sense of openness and possibility that the lateness of
the frontier at the same time seemed to deny.

Much of the writing of Norris, London, Crane, and Cather thematizes this contradiction in contemporary Western character. Their literary designs for this peculiar moment had much in common, although
each of them makes different use of the elements of wildness in frontier
character. Taken together, they suggest that once the wild has to be
recalled, its belatedness is simultaneously the material of romantic loss
and awkward anachronism.

The conflict here is symptomatic of a condition that the American
West has always had to negotiate: because its physical boundaries have
been so protean, "West" has a stronger sense of relativity in American
culture than does "the East," "the South," or "the North." This relativity makes Western regional identity more dependent on the meanings
and identities of the other regions, particularly the East, than are the
identities of those regions on the West or each other. Bonté's position

is, in a sense, that of an Eastern colonialist; his effort to identify Berkeley with a particular kind of West, a place where elegant manners and traditional academic knowledge were sustainable, was plausible only insofar as Eastern codes did not altogether cancel the viability of Western difference. Like others of his region and experience, his references to Eastern culture often situate it as distinctly different from that of the West, but this means that some model of the East has to be evident in order to be rejected or revised. In light of the West's relativity and its standing vis-à-vis the East, Bonté's cultural identity, and hence that of the educated, moneyed sector of the California population he spoke for, might be understood as anxious: identification with the metropolitan East as an affirmation of civility and class position stood side by side with the desire to claim an affinity with Western character and regional culture. This problematic subject position was dramatized in naturalist Western literature, particularly Norris's, not only at the level of character but of narrative authority.

Norris and London, coming of age as writers in this atmosphere, were demonstratively designers of themselves as much as they were of literary texts. At various times in his brief career, Norris adopted the postures of Parisian aesthete, practical Western journalist, and urban *élégant*. London's self-fashionings, by contrast, ranged across a spectrum of Western he-man roles, but he also positioned himself as a worldly and sensitive theorist of class difference, urban poverty, and evolutionary development.

The intellectual and personal styles that Norris cultivated at Berkeley supplemented the urbane and worldly manners that he had acquired at the Académie Julian in Paris, where he studied painting from 1887 to 1889. After Berkeley, he spent a year at Harvard studying French language and literature and creative writing, an experience that further situated him in an academic milieu that fostered fin-de-siècle European ideas. But however worldly Norris's public persona became, he, like London, sustained a counterpoint identity, a more local and unpolished style of being that contested his own cosmopolitanism.

These contradictory styles of selfhood at once distanced and secured Norris's relationship to Western life and culture. Their simultaneity is evident in the peculiar ways that he claims narrative and critical authority, as a bearer of local knowledge and as a more broadly learned interpreter of the postfrontier West. The self-consciousness that emerges with the conflicting subject positions by which he situates himself as speaker both memorializes and obviates his claim to Western authenticity.

IN CONTRAST TO THE SETTING of Berkeley, San Francisco, where both Norris and London worked at different times in their careers, was less likely to cultivate a homogeneous public culture. Its rambling, often dramatic dimensions suggested a far more haphazard past and unpredictable future than did Berkeley's. The strains of romantic westernism in San Francisco circled about an ever-unachieved presence, imagined retrospectively to have been the proper, original substance of the anxious contemporary West.

The material of the San Francisco environment to which Norris and London both so attached themselves—its dramatic physical dimensions, its pioneer social vitality, its giddy culture of profit—functioned as a kind of rhetoric. This rhetoric cast Western life, in its ideal form, as a field of open-ended possibility and a unique experience in European and Euro-American cultural history, even as the idea of the closed frontier was circulating. Geology, architecture, language, and finance projected a horizon of optimism and a sense of spontaneous energy in the course of daily public life.

Now that the course of Manifest Destiny appeared to have been fulfilled and exhausted on the North American continent, San Francisco in the 1890s, positioned as it was at the end of the closed frontier, became an emblem for Euro-American Western desire, carrying the double burden of its own and national questions of cultural identity. . . . As the site of a pioneer culture, San Francisco at the turn of the century was being planned and revised in ways that aimed not only to construct the city as a physically and economically workable metropolis but also to assert a regional identity. San Francisco had a highly international character by the 1860s, but rather than a multiethnic community it was more a series of separate neighborhoods. The city's heterogeneous architectural outline, which included European and Asian national influences in addition to evolving Greek, Roman, and Gothic fashions in civic building, did little to lend any specifically Western aspect to San Francisco façades.[7]

The continuousness of city planning, like the countless efforts to rebuild individual structures and redesign neighborhoods after fires, floods, and earthquakes from the 1850s through the turn of the century, undermined even the stability of these polyglot neighborhoods and muddied any potentially developing architectural contribution to a peculiarly San Francisco identity. Since each new plan and design displaced previous ones, the result was a virtual palimpsest of images and a history of image production as much as it was a history of functional community development.

Aside from its jumbled contemporary appearance and its compromised position in relation to the rhetoric of the closed frontier, San Francisco in the 1890s had accumulated a record of extreme rises and falls through its rocky nineteenth-century career. The city's history, full of great booms and losses, rehearses the dialectic of expansion and nostalgia evident in the history of Euro-American conquest in the West generally. A brief selection of the many dramatic events of the latter half of the century points to the nearly continuous shifts in social relations and even physical proportions of the metropolitan area. The Mexican War; the Gold Rush, together with its inflation of the local economy and the panic that followed in 1855; the periodic resurgence of vigilante violence in the early 1850s; the Nevada silver strikes and the wild fluctuations they caused in San Francisco stock gambling; the many significant fires from the late forties through the sixties and the two major earthquakes of 1865 and 1868 that razed substantial portions of the city; the debates over the authority of the Southern Pacific Railroad that began in the 1860s and extended through the last decade of the century—all of these events revised the city's culture in myriad ways. But the string of calamities and successes in the nineteenth century both fed and enacted San Francisco's revisionary propensities, fostering a regional culture in which the vertiginous and the liminal were aspects of everyday life.

While its history and material composition provided a palpable image of European activity in North America, San Francisco, like the rest of the nation, had reached a conglomerate of limits by the 1890s.

The youthful culture of the forty-niners, now either dead or aged, continued to inform the city's spirit, but the 1893 financial crisis and the discourse of the closed frontier, like the sophistication of the West in general, made that spirit seem anachronistic. This sensibility is evident in the literature and other arts of the period, but it did nothing to halt the rituals of accumulation and conquest that were contemporaneously being described, in the language of the germ theory, as endemic to Anglo-European culture.[8]

Kevin Starr summarizes the arguments of California historians concerning the effects of the Gold Rush on "the California personality" as "a permanent internationalization of flush times, an attitude of recklessness and swagger and competitive democracy."[9] In 1898 and 1899, this outdated swagger was thinly justified by San Francisco's connection to the Klondike Gold Rush. But by now it had largely become an anxious expression of regional and national vitalism, prone to embrace a range of popular theories of culture and behavior that, like the germ theory, were distinctly racist in tone and theme. Strains of Eurocentrism and national chauvinism that thrived in the rest of the country were equally evident in San Francisco, which by the 1890s had developed a history of exclusion and discrimination on the parts of Euro-Americans toward Asians and the relatively small number of blacks who had settled in the city since the Gold Rush.[10] In 1898 it served as a point of embarkation for military ships assigned to America's first extra-continental imperialist missions in the Philippines and Hawaii during the Spanish-American War and, at the turn of the century, in Panama with the construction of the canal.

The spirit of conquistador vigor of what had been until 1870 a largely male and Euro-American population in San Francisco continued, however belatedly, to assert its voice in the wake of Turner's discovery of the closed frontier.[11] San Francisco's paradoxical image as end and launch point of the Euro-American colonial drive expressed the modernism of the 1890s and an appended melancholy about the loss of an idealized openness presumed to have existed in the past. At the same time, its iconic history and physique seemed to excite ideas of further American advance into the Pacific region—ideas that in practice would rehearse the dominant social politics of Euro-American continental expansion.

San Francisco's ups and downs, as well as its capacity to emblematize the narrative of Western conquest—the reach of desire and the contraction of settlement—advertise aspiration, risk, and nostalgia as conditions of life in the West. Its image as the end of the West recapitulates this narrative once again; and at the height of the discourse of the end of the American frontier, the old anxiety of wishing to be new was stimulated again. Now, however, citizens were exhibiting their westernism very problematically, and in many cases all the more tenaciously.[12]

LOOKING AT SAN FRANCISCO'S outline from the ferry docks, Norris's character Condy Rivers in the autobiographical novel *Blix* is fascinated by its tenuous strength, the heap of geology and architecture tilting in the direction of the Pacific as if at every moment it were leaning farther toward some apocalyptic cave-in. The risky tilt of the San Francisco landscape and the flatness of Berkeley offered to Norris's vision a pronounced display of the surface of the region. Placed on this surface is an image of a city and of a university imported from the East and from models of landscape and planning that were already available in Euro-American design. But the simultaneous assumption of uniqueness, of being in some way specifically Western, and deriving of cultural validation from Eastern forms adds a kind of shadow to the primary outline. Similarly, the physical, intellectual, and social shaping of the University that was taking place in the 1890s resulted in a college with a frame around it.

The consciousness of surface and of simulacrum in Norris's prose is of a piece with the self-consciously dramatic designs of these places. The string of art forms—of sketches, paintings, photographs, kinetoscopes, operas, songs, and poems—that collect in his fiction call attention to the work's own status as composition. Norris's habit of alluding to these works also signals the difficulty of constructing a realistic representation of Western city or rural life without calling attention to the representation itself.

Even though Norris's critical writing often called for a Western literature that could get at the heart or core of Western life, his own novels and stories imply that that essence is a highly elusive ideal. His actual Bay Area home and the fictional versions of it that appear in his

novels and stories both display the designs of late frontier culture, the
elements of which hardly stand still in the measurable dimensions of a
simply real place. The West he saw and the West he wrote were equally
the constructions of a European culture that had expeditiously established itself in northern California in the later nineteenth century.
Norris's San Francisco exhibited a self-consciousness that emerged
from this belatedness, as well as from the challenge to regional identity
in the idea of the closed frontier. His references to a precursor, less-
developed West-aimed at projecting a temporal dimension, a sense of
history and authenticity that would adhere to his time and place.

The effort to project a sense of age was continually frustrated not
only by the city's interests in appearing as developed and as modern as
its Eastern counterparts but by the massive repression of Native American cultures that had far predated European settlements in the area.
The scope of this study is too limited to address the situations of Native
American populations in California during the 1890s; but it assumes
their suppression as a condition of the European presence in the West,
both Spanish and Anglo-American, and as one of the major reasons for
the lack of depth in the history of that presence.

NORRIS'S RECOGNITION OF THE poetic value in San Francisco's landscape was underscored by his recognition of the city's inventiveness—
its tendency as a culture to promote, if not always actually to produce,
new social and financial processes, technologies, and ways of thinking,
as well as its status as a city in the process of being invented. His writings for the *Wave* and the *Chronicle* bear the marks of such inventiveness and novelty in their impressionistic manner and in the topics of
life in the city, where such inventiveness was daily enacted, that they
reported. His constructions of local culture in many ways call attention
to the designs of his own writing. Norris's self-conscious rhetoric suggests a playful and yet vexed attitude, not only about representing San
Francisco, but regarding the practice of writing the West in general. In
a dramatization of this attitude, Norris's fictional journalist Condy
Rivers of *Blix* simply makes up much of his material and is far more
interested in writing his novel than in newspaper reporting. As Kevin
Starr puts it, Condy "finds it all too easy to fake material, to achieve a
veneer of realism through the judicious use of a few details."[13]

If realism is only a matter of manipulating details to achieve a recognizable image of the Bay Area and its people, then anyone might produce it, and anyone might be fooled by it. For all his appreciation of
William Dean Howells, Norris associated the genre with what he saw as
the small scope of Howells's own fastidious portraits of problems in
average social situations. Norris objected equally to what he called the
"everlasting dramas of conscience" in the fiction of his time, which, as
he described them, focused on the interior life of the psyche and the
finer emotional dimensions of character relationships. Norris's own call
for a literature of the West demanded writers' attention to the common
people of the docks and the streets, not for their averageness but for
their colorfulness and their adventures. His great interest was to see
young Western writers take advantage of the "gusto" and "life" available as literary material among the working people of San Francisco.

In an essay of 1901, "A Plea for Romantic Fiction," Norris reduc-
tively defines realism as the nit-picking fiction of daily life and indicts it
as the drama of the "broken teacup." He points to what he sees as clear
examples of a dichotomy between what he calls "Life" and "Literature":
essentially, he argues that when adventure romance is effectively written, it gives a sense of the palpable excitement of "Life" in its most elemental forms, whereas mere realism is self-conscious and composed of
literary conventions that record very contained, predictable emotions
and manners.

In his interest in models provided by common people, and in his
asserted emphasis on social and material forces rather than on complex
psychical careers, Norris shared with Howells a disdain for romantic literature. This can be a difficult issue to understand in Norris's critical
thinking, since he also overtly championed romanticism, particularly
in "A Plea for Romantic Fiction." Defending romanticism against realism, he offers a very loose definition of romantic literature as "the kind
of fiction that takes cognizance of variations from the type of normal
life" and "an instrument with which we may go straight through clothes
and tissues and wrappings of flesh down deep into the red living heart
of things."[14] The argument relies heavily on realism and sentimentalism
to help clarify what true romanticism is not; but the examples of
romantic motifs offered are not sufficiently elaborated to make them
appear distinct from sentimentalism: "A heartache (may-be) between

the pillows of a mistress's bed, and a memory carefully secreted in the master's deed box. . . . an affair, or great heavens, an intrigue, in the scented ribbons and gloves and hairpins of the young lady's bureau" (1167).

While Norris complains about realism's limiting of attention to the surfaces of things, there is nothing in these examples to suggest "the unplumbed depths of the human heart, and the mystery of sex, and the problems of life, and the black, unsearched penetralia of the soul" (1169), nothing indeed beyond the surfaces of very conventional literary images to concoct secrecy and problems in the manner of the "conjurer's trickbox, full of flimsy quackeries" (1165) that control the mechanisms of "cut-and-thrust" stories which, he complains, have stolen the good name of romanticism.

In trying to name the deep core of throbbing life and passionate emotions that he claims are not traded openly in Howells's brand of realism, Norris only comes up with tropes and definitions that sound more like what he is objecting to. In turning toward theoretical abstractions, he gains even less clarity about what "romantic fiction" means in the context of his discussion. He worries as much in asking his reader, "Is all this too subtle, too merely speculative and intrinsic, too 'précieuse' and nice and 'literary'? Devoutly one hopes the contrary" (1165).

Norris's literary regionalism, as well as his naturalism, have much in common with Howellsian realism, including an interest in the lives of common people, their social contexts and material environments, and a resistance to distractingly decorative or highly metaphorical language that might be considered too flagrantly artistic or "literary." But important differences exist in Norris's fascination with and anxiety over narrative authority and point of view. These concerns are much more intensely and regularly thematized than anything of the sort found in Howells's writing. Thus Condy Rivers's faking of newspaper material offers Norris an opportunity to expose journalistic authority by parodying it and at the same time to critique the methods of realism that after all inform much of his own work. In this sense, Norris parodies himself simultaneously with his treatment of Rivers's narrative authority. Such self-consciousness in Norris's writing is not simply a matter of humorous entertainment but a recognition within the story of problems that he saw in any effort to give literary coinage to the life and culture of the American West.

The elusiveness of this true West for literary representation matched the elusiveness of regional identity for San Francisco and its residents. Its continuously deferred essence did little, however, to diminish its palpability for Norris; and indeed he gave it mystically real status in calling it "Life." While he celebrated this "Life" extensively in theory, it could not be embodied in his fiction, and this contradiction gets aired in the parodic tones of Norris's Western stories. As long as he assumed the presence of "Life," he associated it with the gusto, optimism, and recklessness that were so anachronistic and yet so heartily supported by the public culture of late-nineteenth-century San Francisco.

In his oddly simultaneous parodies and celebrations of Euro-American westernist vigor and aggressivity, Norris engaged naturalist literary practices that both foregrounded such drives and showed them to be finally powerless. In celebrating Western romance, he expressed a nostalgic sensibility that was common in his time. Giving emphasis to the social and the biological, he lowered the value of the individual; but charging his narratives with the appeal of frontier as crucible of "Life" and stage of character essence, he participated in the rhetoric that fostered the continuation of Euro-American expansionism in the national imagination by revising westernism so it could accommodate, and thus survive, the naturalist critique.

NORRIS WAS JUST BEGINNING his writing career in San Francisco when Turner's essay on the frontier appeared. The tenuous opposition between wilderness and civil culture that strains many representations of Western life in the 1890s can be mapped onto the unstable distinctions that he drew between the artistic modes of "Life" and "Literature." Indeed, this dichotomy became an important analytical tool in his critical works on Western writing and troubled both that criticism and his fictional accounts of the West. His call for "Life" in Western literature expresses a wish evident among many writers and artists of the West in his time, including Stephen Crane, Jack London, Willa Cather, Ambrose Bierce, and in some cases Mark Twain, to understand the region as different from other sections of the United States by virtue of

its roughness and its spontaneous energy. But by embracing these qualities, an author risked the possibility of losing whatever respect and
serious attention contemporary representations of the West might have
accumulated among Eastern audiences. The works of Cooper, Francis
Parkman, Richard Henry Dana, and others of the earlier nineteenth
century had gained secure places among the texts of classic American
literature, but their descendants in the later generation were reworking
the tradition to include comedy, parody, and a form of self-consciousness not usually evident in serious or "good" literature.

So much spontaneity at the level of literary character and regional
culture also meant so much instability, in social forms, ethical values,
and individual psychic life. Aside from anything intrinsically problematic about such instability, its rhythms tended to obviate possibilities
for understanding the particular phases of the region's or of an individual's activities, by Western as well as Eastern analysts. An effect of
emptiness or superficiality easily accumulates, leaving performance to
resemble spontaneity. The region's famous recklessness was thus often
celebrated in a compromise that drew equal attention to the inheritance of traditional Eastern and European motifs—what Norris would
categorize as "Literature"—in anxious denunciation of models that he
certainly used.

But the freedoms associated with spontaneity and instability, even
in their opacity and fleeting elusiveness, are themselves comprehensi-
ble in terms of European notions of escape from a standard social norm.
Certainly concepts like wilderness and recklessness have histories and
distinct values in European cultural history. In themselves, they carry
the weight of familiarity, even if what they refer to is ultimately some
notion of emptiness or insubstantiality. The irony in this is that the
exemplary characteristics that Western regional culture seeks to attribute
to itself have long since been registered in the categories of European,
and certainly Euro-American, thinking. This is not to argue that Western American art and culture are implausible or doomed from the start;
on the contrary, these complexities, which might be understood in
terms of what Harold Bloom identified some time ago as the anxiety of
influence, often express instructive and provocative literary and social
questions.

In Norris's fiction, this troublesome opposition is often posed by an intellectual, urbane protagonist who seeks to understand, or to render in art form, an unsophisticated and in some degree mute environment. The tension is important in several of Norris's novels, particularly *The Octopus* and *Vandover and the Brute*. But the enormous psychological, social, and political themes tackled in those novels overshadow the difficulties implicit in the tension between "Life" and "Literature." The efforts in some of his shorter fictions to realistically portray a nonliterary West, a place beyond any culture's conventions, inevitably produce an interpretation of the West as if it were a text.

While Norris's efforts are surely genuine, his playfulness with representation in puns and metaphors that express the belated processes of writing and visual arts suggests an aesthetic sensibility that has already relinquished the effort to refer to something so teeming with spontaneous energy as life itself. In this sense it seems plausible to understand him as a student of his contemporary, Walter Pater, whose aesthetic theories he most likely read or heard about in his courses with Charles Mills Gayley at Berkeley.[15] Pater's lyrical interests in the effects of art on a perceiver's sensibility, and of that sensibility on the critical evaluation of form, pointed elaborately to subjectivity as the central factor in the determination of artistic substance and value. It would seem that in his assumption of a specific material as well as metaphysical reality in Western culture, Norris, as critic of it, might have looked more to the theories of Matthew Arnold, whose work he would also have studied at Berkeley, than to Pater's rhapsodies on individual artistic perception. Arnold's notion that the function of the literary or cultural critic was to focus his attention on "the object as in itself it really is" assumed a certain stability of literary and other objects of study. But it might be argued that the privileged moment of perception in Pater is precisely what Norris wants to encode in the heightened pulse of his literary category "Life," given the quick of experience that Pater raises to nearly spiritual status, and the elusiveness that makes representation of that experience such a complicated matter.

Literary criticism was a way for Norris to directly expound what continually eluded him in his own fiction. In essays, he could forcefully state his claims that the realm of the intellectual and the realm of the natural or instinctive were easily separable, and that the instinctive is more desirable because it is more true to life. But here, as in the fiction, his senses of the natural and the synthetic overlap and tend repeatedly to bleed into each other. His efforts to articulate the differences between "Life" and "Literature" constitute an urbane, sensitive project, an intellectual formula for representing raw, unsophisticated experience. "Life" becomes a form of art in his essays, and despite the ontological distinctions he steadily tries to draw between them, this category, like "Literature," is removed from the immediacy of being and functions as a conventional mode of knowledge.

More immediately, the figures of the robust cowboy and the effete dandy that Norris modeled in his personal styles and in his writing tend to personalize the concepts of life and literature; but the two categories are inextricably bound up in each other, and analysis of them that attempts to divide experience from representation only reproduces some of Norris's most incessant literary problems.

However problematic these two terms appear to be, they are so important to his critical vocabulary and have such a bearing on the thematic oppositions of his novels that they have drawn quite a lot of attention from twentieth-century readers. The confused play of distinctions between them has been addressed as either a fault or at best an attempt at freedom from the constraints of logic found in a more mature or conventional writer. Larzer Ziff and Warren French see an awkward but likable vitality in the tenuous differences Norris draws between "Life" and "Literature." Donald Pizer accounts for the problem by referring to Norris's unstable polemics: "He believed that fictional form is an intellectual problem in selection and organization for the achievement of plausibility, effect and theme, and that there are few substitutes for a considered and painstaking intellectual solution."[16] Pizer sensitively notes that "Life" and "Literature" are Norris's "inadequate symbols for two rich and opposing clusters of ideas and values." In his argument, both function as intellectual categories; and Norris's preferred "Life" represents one of the many anti-intellectual philosophies in the history of American ideas. Yet, Pizer writes, for Norris, "without life as a foundation, no amount of technical training would benefit a writer" (xiii). The ideal novel "was primitivistic in content and then sophisticated in form" (xv). To separate form and content is a troublesome project, and Pizer's comment demonstrates that difficulty in attempting to define the autonomy that Norris grants the two cate-gories.

William Dillingham has written that the difficulty for Norris is in distinguishing between "genuine feelings—the deepest and best impulses—and those deceptive poses which are the product of the intellectual."[17] Dillingham argues that the problem is very really resolved because it stems from an early preference for academic painting to impressionism, genres he studied as a very young man at the Académie Julian in Paris. Academic art can thus be associated with Norris's "Life," since it "distrusted subjectivism and glorified competence, clar-ity, disdained inspiration and preached hard work" (23). Dillingham cites Norris's 1897 "The Green Stone of Unrest," a parody of Stephen Crane's *The Red Badge of Courage*, to show how the aesthetics of the two naturalists differed: the impressionist style, to Norris, was emo-tional, poetic, and subjective. But the intellectual tradition invokes a heavy consciousness of the past in academic painting, which brings it close to the overt degree of stylized representation in impressionism: history and traditions' priorities not only impose themselves but make the artist's competence possible. Dillingham concludes that Norris "respected and tried to practice a philosophy of art and life alien to his nature" (23).

Larzer Ziff explains Norris's shunning of the literary and the pre-cious in art by pointing to a biographical anxiety: "Norris was not asserting the claims of life . . . as a defensive measure against the learned. . . . Rather, [he] was trying to break through from his inherited position of comfort and genteel taste, which, he felt, offered him only a substitute for life."[18] Ziff finds in the zigzagging of Norris's ideas "a fidelity to life's amplitude and complexity, in contrast to the theories of unity and simplicity that he rhetorically offered as the organizing prin-ciples" (251).

All of these arguments assume a respectable difference between life and literature. But the dichotomy itself is a profound problem for Norris, a serious dilemma that he was constantly trying to settle. His struggle concerns nothing less than the nature of language, and his work provides a vivid illustration of the problem of how to reconcile representation and source in any artistic enterprise.

In a May 1897 article for the *Wave*, he addressed young regional writers, urging them to satisfy a lack in San Francisco fiction: "Give us stories now, give us men, strong, brutal men, with red-hot blood in 'em, with unleashed passions rampant in 'em, blood and bones and viscera. . . . Think of the short stories that are happening every hour of the time. . . . It's the Life that we want, the vigorous, real thing, not the curious weaving of words and the polish of literary finish . . ."[19] The implications are clear, and we have a vivid idea of what he means by "Life." But the passage sustains a note of the struggle for authenticity in all of his criticism. The "blood and bones" he begs for are those of the real-life San Francisco waterfront. But "blood and bones" is itself a conventional trope and a metaphor as much as a metonymy for a recognizable, indeed generic, sort of dockside violence that would have been available to Norris not from any experience of his own but from Kipling and Scott.

Several years later, in "Why Women Should Write the Best Novels: And Why They Don't,"[20] first printed in the *Boston Evening Transcript*, Norris claimed "of all the masculine occupations that of writing is the first to be adopted by women." The reasons for this are that women have more leisure time and, most often, are better versed in the subject—that is, they have read more. He concluded: "Would not the inference be strong, that—given an equal start—women would write more readily than men, would do so because they could do so; that writing is a feminine . . . gift" (34).

This privileging of the feminine in the world of letters is surprising, considering Norris's preference for what he understands as a more masculine literary style on several other occasions. But his purpose is to show that what is essential to quality fiction is experience, in the life of the writer and in the writer's work. Women simply do not have the worldly experience necessary. The paradox here is in the cancellation of the initially privileged position Norris gives to learning, reading, and private time in one's study—the stuff that should make women better writers—and its substitution by the absolute necessity of experience. To which does Norris actually grant first place? Given the title of the piece, one wonders how Norris can say that a refined life of letters is what should best prepare one for writing, only to topple this claim several paragraphs later. He clearly emphasizes the importance of experience, but nonetheless allows his essay to go into print with its confusing "should" in the title and at various points in the text.

The experiential quality that Norris seeks to represent is, by his own admission, a troublesome one to grasp: "Of all the difficult things that enter into the learning of a most difficult profession, the most difficult of all for the intended novelist to acquire is the fact that life is better than literature" (35). Young writers are vulnerable to the influence of older, more accomplished ones, according to Norris, and must learn at some point that what they take from a master in terms of structure and style must be eventually bolstered with experience. The problem for women is in the difficulty that they cannot hope to surmount but which men can: "she lacks the knowledge to use knowledge . . . gained [from a mentor]" (36). This knowledge to which men do have access is brought to experience as a tool for articulating and framing experience—an entirely cerebral process. Whether the writer be male or female, the point is, in Norris's words, a matter of knowledge: one must know how to write. Experience thus falls within the category of literary knowledge.

In "The Nature Revival in Literature,"[21] an article published posthumously in 1903, Norris welcomes a new trend for the 1890s, the resurgence of outdoor life in fiction. He cites the works of Ernest Thompson Seton, Alfred Ollivant, J. P. Mowbray, and other popular writers as examples of a nature-oriented fiction that is replacing the "literature" that had filled bookstore shelves before the nineties. The latter, full of "humans with their everlasting consciences, their heated and artificial activities, filled all the horizon, admitting the larks and the robins only as accessories" (42). But now, writes Norris, with the influence of Seton and Mowbray, "The sun has come in and the great winds, and the smell of the baking alkali on the Arizona deserts and the reek of the tar-weed on the Colorado slopes" (42). The distinctions he draws between the two modes is clear enough; but it remains the case that what Norris is championing here is another form of literature, as carefully sculpted, shaped, and crafted as the arabesque romances of conscience he so happily dismisses.

Concerning the necessity for shaping and controlling artistic material, he has some curious things to say in the 1901 "A Problem in Fiction: Truth Versus Accuracy."[22] Here we encounter the comment, "Life itself is not always true; strange as it may seem, you may be able to say that life is not always true to life—from the point of view of the artist" (56). This peculiar statement makes a bit more sense if we compare it to Henry James's declaration at the outset of his 1903 "Emile Zola" that "we live in a world of wanton . . . fable." James complains of the lack of experiential knowledge and the excess of research in Zola's writing. In "Truth Versus Accuracy," Norris is speaking of actual events that provide poor material for fiction because of their theatrical—their artistic—appearance. As an example of incidents that are not true to life, Norris tells of informing a man that his brother has just died. The man throws up his arms and staggers backward "precisely as they do in melodrama." At this point it is tempting to ask: if arabesque literature is not "Life," and if life is not "Life," what is this elusive "Life"?

But Norris's argument is after all an understandable one: he likes literature that is simple and at the same time powerful. And he likes unaffected, un-self-conscious behavior as a source for representation. The term he applies to these phenomena is nevertheless clearly problematic though, for "Life," even as he employs it in quotation marks, implies a kind of photographic authenticity, which is not at all a part of Norris's oeuvre or of his theory.

He admits as much in "Truth Versus Accuracy":

> Of course, no good novelist, no good artist, can represent life as it actually is. Nobody can, for nobody knows. Who is to say what life actually is? . . . Not even science will help you; no two photographs . . . will convey just the same impression of the same actuality. . . . Even the same artist will not see the same thing twice exactly alike. His personality is one thing . . . before dinner and another thing after it. (57)

He strikes out farther from an autonomous concept of "Life" by explaining how a painter will use a smear of blue in a study of a brown horse. "This is inaccurate. The horse is not blue, nor has he any blue spots." But the effect, when a viewer stands back from the painting, is "true." Thus, he permits a highly stylized and manipulated version of reality to pass as "truth."

ON THE OCCASION OF the closing of the frontier Norris wrote about the difficulty that Western culture would have in absorbing the concept of a finite landscape. In "The Frontier Gone at Last,"[23] he writes: "We liked the Frontier; it was romance, the place of the poetry of the Great March, the firing-line where there was action and fighting, and where men held each other's lives in the crook of the forefinger" (1183). He eulogizes the once real cowboy figure, replaced now by stylized versions who, nonetheless, are "more like 'the real thing' than can be found today in Arizona, New Mexico or Idaho" (1185). These imitations, obnoxiously successful, look the part but do not satisfy Norris's desire for a lively depiction of "truth"; they might fall in with the category of dime novels, which he complains have come to be the major vehicles for representing Western life.

In several of Norris's Western stories, the implications of a struggle to articulate a difference between vigorous experience and belated observation are manifest. "The Passing of Cock-eye Blacklock," "A Bargain with Peg-leg," and "A Memorandum of Sudden Death," all written in 1901, are set in the Southwest, with cowboys, gamblers, marshals, and gunslingers as characters. Published posthumously in *A Deal in Wheat and Other Stories*, each of these tales establishes a situation in which two tellers deliver the story, and narrative authority is ostensibly shared between their literary and experiential orientations. The arrangement—the figure of the writer, a sophisticated man of letters, posed against the "strong, brutal men" who embody Norris's troublesome ideal of "life"—aims for readability and authenticity.

In each story, the original teller is portrayed as a rough-and-ready man of the wilderness whose material is passed along to the reader by the more sophisticated narrator; the encounter with the first teller and the hearing of the tale then become part of the sophisticate's own story. Kenneth Lynn provides a useful account of this sort of narrative distancing in the literature of the American Southwest in his *Mark Twain and Southwestern Humor*.[24] From William Byrd to Twain, Lynn traces the conceit of the gentlemanly narrator, who, like a journalist, recounts a story delivered by a rough provincial. The narrator gets credit for recognizing the entertainment value of the story but does not have to take responsibility for its composition. In comparison with the provincial tale-teller, the urbane host appears thoughtful, identifiable with his audience, and different from the wilderness represented in the story.

But it is precisely in this latter effect, as Lynn describes it, that the technique differs in Norris's work. While his narrator's formal English diction grants the story more plausibility than the primary teller would be capable of, his difference and his role as mediator underscore the enviable spontaneity of the man of the ranges, the quick of "Life" which the sophisticate cannot express in his own voice.

The first two tales are told by Bunt McBride, who is introduced by the narrator of "The Passing of Cock-eye Blacklock" as "one of a fast disappearing type. . . . He had fifteen separate and different times driven the herds from Texas to Dodge City, in the good old, rare old, wild old days when Dodge was the headquarters for the cattle trade and as near to heaven as the cowboy cared to get" (80).[25] After a fawning and elegantly worded description of Bunt and the landscape as remnants of a dying culture, the narrator seems to remove himself from the story and to leave the tale-telling almost entirely in the hands of Bunt; but the control of Bunt's material never slips from the narrator's hands. He is the one who recognizes the story's value in what might be called the literary "economy" of an authentic West, only so many of whose elements remain as material for realist representation. In the manner of an anthropologist, he works along the lines of what James Clifford has called a "salvage paradigm," effectively a mechanism for taking possession of another's culture, which would, without the account provided, disappear without record.[26]

The writer's function appears to be to simply transcribe what Bunt relates. Norris relies on the topos of journalism in order to cast his illusion: Bunt is raw, barely literate experience, the author urbane intelligence; neither would be capable of the other's contribution to the story. But as journalist, the narrator relishes the impressions that his observations allow and offers his own recapitulation of the material. The exquisite perceptions of his Paterian sensibility are devoted here to the aestheticizing of a Western twang and to nostalgia for a passing type. What we read is a heavily stylized, almost caricatured version of the rough frontiersman. Bunt's dialect, as well as his yarns, remind us of the "red shirt" literature, or synthetic portraits of the cowboy tradition, which Norris deplores in his 1902 "The Literature of the West."[27] His attempt to depict "Life" and "Literature" in harmony results in a highly orchestrated literary exercise.

In the opening of "A Bargain with Peg-leg" we hear little from Bunt—only his monosyllabic announcement to the narrator that it is time for his "chaw," dinner in the supposed argot of the frontier. The introduction is for the most part handled by the voice of the narrator. Later, Bunt begins to speak, and the two voices alternate for a while before the narrator's fades and all but disappears, except for an occasional narrative link, and effectively reemerges only at the end.

The differences between the two voices unmistakably distinguish the men in terms of interest, values, perception, and class. Here is the narrator, early in the introduction: " . . . we emerged from the cool, cave-like dampness of the mine and ran out into the wonderful night air of the Sierra foothills, warm, dry, redolent of witch-hazel" (61). While the language of this description bespeaks the narrator's education and elegance, the landscape it projects has the naturalness and unmediated life of Bunt and his story. The pungent air bears the metaphorical weight of ideal Western purity, at the same time that the exquisite prose betrays the outer narrator's processed imagination and belated, modern affection for his inner narrator's primacy.

Bunt himself speaks a dialect completely unlike that of the adjective-trained voice of the city and the university. He begins his story by describing his protagonist, "a cow-rustlin', hair-liftin', only-one-born-in-captivity, man-eatin' brute of a one-legged Greaser which he was named Peg-leg Smith" (62). To more fully characterize Peg-leg, Bunt continues: "He was shy a leg because of a shotgun that the other man thought wasn't loaded. And this here happens, lemme tell you, 'way down in the Panamint country, where they wasn't no doctor within twenty miles, and Peg-leg outs with his bowie and amputates that leg hisself" (61). The passage invokes Western speech and tale-telling to the point of caricature; if this is the fulfillment of Norris's own critical injunction to give respectful representation to the real life of the West, it misses its mark by resorting to parody. The peculiar tone not only airs the difficulty of the injunction, but it suggests the lack of positive narrative values in his imaginary West. Like the absence of substantial content to the rhetoric of optimism and possibility in the city of San Francisco, the lack of a balanced and serious representation of Western regional life in Norris's story suggests the problematic terms of a culture whose most pronounced interest is the elimination of limits.

Any content, any substance that might stand as the referent of regeneration, or of the far side of the frontier would cancel the energy of possibility. The lack of substantial narrative values in Norris's story, and in his Western fiction generally, produces the plethora of marks and signs that punctuate his fictions as if to mimic the narrative itself in its attempt to represent anything. The curious pattern of amputations in his works often seems to be associated with this lack and with the question of a human being's ability to signify, even in its physical person, a meaning, a power or a purpose.

But the passage quoted above has generic qualities beyond Norris's own habits. It is an instance of the Western tall tale, which late-century written versions depict, somewhat nostalgically, as originally a purely oral form. The tall tale is every bit as stylish as the "red shirt" literature of the contemporary scene, but its oral mode is made to appear free of canny literary design and to preserve a sense of unmediated communication in the bodily presence of the speaker's voice and the listener's ears. Norris's story is full of slapstick cowboy comedy; antics of the dime-novel Western are everywhere evident. As such, this aspect of the story appears to work like satire, and we can assume from his argument in "The Literature of the West," which calls upon writers to honor traditions exemplified by the Lewis and Clark expedition, that the satire implicitly calls for a more authentic and thoughtful depiction of Western life. But the story frustrates this expectation and offers no model alternative.

"The Passing of Cock-eye Blacklock" has a similar structure: Bunt tells the narrator a story of his past that centers around the antics of a dangerous troublemaker. Like Peg-leg's, Cock-eye's behavior is explained as the psychological result of a physical shock. Years before he and Bunt had spent a night in a blizzard and nearly frozen to death; Bunt survived intact by rubbing tobacco juice in his eyes to keep himself awake, thus avoiding hypothermia. But Cock-eye somehow did not come through the night in good order, "for he went bad afterward."

In the frame of this story, Bunt provides a brief opening monologue while the narrator muses to himself on his companion's history, on the beauty of the night and the landscape, on the silence of the herd. As if two voices were speaking at once, Bunt's tale is in progress in the background while we read the narrator's private thoughts in the foreground. And indeed the latter seems kept to an appropriate whisper, since the narrator's artistic language would embarrass a character of Bunt's type: "There was not a cloud. Toward the middle watches one could expect a moon. But the stars, the stars! In Idaho, on those lonely reaches of desert and range, where the shadow of the sun by day and the courses of the constellations by night are the only things that move" (81).

The landscape rhapsody serves to set Bunt's own clarity and natural simplicity; but again the language of the prose advertises the outer narrator's own sophistication. This speaker lyrically describes the few sounds and sights he witnesses, and his meditation seems aimed at bringing the natural elements to life in writing. But the story after all betrays the narrator's ambivalent wish to, on the one hand, identify with the inarticulate being of Bunt and the pastoral Western landscape and, on the other, to exercise his own writerly worth in the face of the deadly silence of nature.

Eventually Bunt and the narrator begin to talk. The stuff of their conversation is highly intellectual, but the narrator excuses this: "It is astonishing to note what strange things men will talk about at night and in a solitude." Thus he feels free to describe their talk: "That night we covered religion . . . astronomy, love affairs . . . history, poker, photography . . . and the Darwinian theory. But . . . we came back to cattle and the pleasures and dangers of riding the herd" (83–84). Here Norris connects the two dialects that he has been trying both to separate and reconcile to one another. Two men, one a litterateur, the other a cowhand, pass the evening in conversation that bridges their respective worlds in a reconciliation that one imagines Norris himself would have liked to achieve. But the actual content of this dialogue is not given; we do not read the details, the phrases, the turns or innuendoes of speech. This conversation, like Bunt, the stars, and the cattle, is used as an image of a harmonious merging of Western life and literature. Its status is purely formal, purely artistic; the work of a writer who sees himself operating within a foreclosed, determined, social and geographical environment. But Norris's sense of his situation produces, simultaneously, a mood of resignation and a rival, romantic celebration of the innocence and primality of Bunt's wilderness.

One is tempted to read this section of "Cock-eye" as a playing out of two aspects of Norris's imagination. The primary identity of the outer narrator is that of a litterateur, no matter how much a man of blood, guts, and passion his wish-fulfillment cowboy tales allow him momentarily to imagine being. But if the cowboy and the man of letters are kept so cleanly apart—and we have no trouble seeing the Norris persona in the figure of the narrator—a question arises as to whether Norris desires their separation. Does he want somehow to clarify his posture as a sophisticate in relation to this coarse material, even as the material represents the object of his desire? Emerging in difference and distance, his desire holds the object of his affections at arm's length, or projects it onto the horizon in an operation that looks like observation, like so much journalism that wishes to let the object of its gaze speak for itself.

We get a clear sense of the control that the narrator maintains over the presentation of Bunt's story in his long introduction, his periodic interruptions of the monologue, and in his closing, which again turns to the landscape where he and Bunt are located. But at another level the narrator's manipulations of Bunt's material are so evident that they suggest the scene is worth recalling only *as* a story. As Bunt puts it, their meeting "is what a man like [the narrator] ought to make into one of your friction [sic] tales." This hole in the world of the story is patched up somewhat by a brief explanation from the narrator: "Ever since I once made a tale (of friction) out of one of Bunt's stories of real life, he has been ambitious for me to write another, and is forever suggesting motifs." (84–85).

The comment clarifies the fact that Bunt has an unsophisticated imagination, is perhaps even illiterate, and that the stories told here—"Peg-leg" is implied—are the products of his memory polished and framed by the author's craft. The narrator secures credibility for himself by demonstrating his competence and powers of discrimination in making Bunt's raw material into literature. The comment also implies that Bunt is a more interesting figure and has a richer memory than the narrator, who goes to him for material. In the same moment, Bunt's rough, un-self-conscious experience is both glorified and subtly denigrated. As the cowboy's tale ends, the sun begins to rise, and the narrator notes, "All in a minute the night seemed to have closed up like a great book." Almost destroying the fictional illusion, this phrase suggests that the whole affair has been strictly literary. In calling such attention to his story as an art form, Norris risks eliminating the difference between the two figures by demonstrating that they constitute two simultaneous and mutually determining modes of telling the true West.

A slightly different kind of narrating device frames the tale told in "A Memorandum of Sudden Death." Here the narrator acquires a manuscript belonging to an Albuquerque harness maker who has come into possession of it from a bone-gatherer named Bass. Bass has picked up the pages from the desert floor where the fight they describe has taken place. The strange mutuality of the pages on the desert and the desert on the pages provokes an imagistic rhyme, in which the flat, dry surface, marked by the fading signs of battle, recalls a dramatic moment whose time has passed. But the minimal traces of life sustainable on the visible surface of the page as well as the desert suggest that the fading liveliness is a mirage and a textual illusion. Of the two, the manuscript itself is the more dramatic evidence of the former action. The narrator describes it thus: "In two or three places there are smudges where the powder-blackened finger and thumb held the sheets momentarily" (106). More than a referent of the prose, the action is readable in the very materiality of the page. The para-text of smudges and thumb prints speaks of a vitality that writing could never hope to attain; but even these accidental marks have only a tenuous, liminal connection to the "Life" of action, insofar as their meanings are built on retrospective, imaginative interpretation.

While the New Mexican desert is an icon of westernist location, its place in "A Memorandum of Sudden Death" is rather attenuated by the story's leveling of its different narrative voices. As the manuscript travels from the hands of its author, Karslake, to Bass, the harness maker, and finally the outer narrator, the desert setting of the story's events, so integral to the act of composition, gets deferred to textual imagery as the pages are passed along. Mirrored in the pages that both describe and lie upon it, the desert originally has a close physical as well as logical relationship to the text; but as the manuscript moves, the presence of its action and its setting become more distanced from readerly experience. The process of composition, distribution, and consumption thus parallels the contours of classic frontier narrative in positing and continuously attempting to contact an ever-receding, quintessential West.

The manuscript is the work of Arthur Karslake, a well-known journalist and novelist who has studied law and ethnology, served with the government coastal survey, and traveled to the Caribbean as well as the western United States. He has recently enlisted in the U.S. Army Cavalry but has not seen active duty, "until the time when his narrative begins" (105).

The narrative frame is virtually bibliographic in its attention to the history of the manuscript. These bookish interests of the narrator are underscored by his listing of Karslake's writings and by his observation that they will be recognized by Easterners who would have read them in New York publications. The opposition between this Eastern literary sensibility and the material realism of the Western account in the manuscript is duplicated in the account's own division between reflection and action. The problem that the story undertakes is in fact to represent Karslake representing an elusive *now* in such a way as to respect entirely the authenticity of his engagement with its unique emergence in time. The narrative develops as Karslake writes it; and the story enacts a competition between action-adventure and reflective recording, as he moves back and forth between the two operations.

But the narrator attempts to downplay Karslake's contemplative, writerly character so as to foreground his status as a figure of Western "Life." He is indeed quite a "man of action" for allowing himself to be part of a dangerous expedition, for partaking in the fight, and for not succumbing to the paralysis of fear. But his involvement is that of a greenhorn: the outer narrator explains in his introduction that this is Karslake's first experience of active duty. That he has no rifle with him but only a revolver indicates not only the amateur's lack of preparation but also, possibly, a lack of awareness of the potential danger in the mission. Not until Bunt dies does Karslake gain possession of a carbine; and we can be certain of only one enemy death that he is responsible for. What he is doing most of the time is writing. He notes what the others do—shots they attempt, positions they take, the frighteningly energetic choreography of the Apache attacks. Karslake is so concerned to write the experience down that he does so in the face of his own death. The story ends in midsentence, as Karslake writes his last words, "It will—," which simultaneously kill the story and its writer.

Karslake's way of experiencing "Life" is undeniably literary. So much attention is drawn to his role as scribe that the story is every bit as concerned with the manuscript and its composition as it is with the gunfight. Early in the account, he writes, "this business of today will make a good story to tell. It's an experience—good 'material.' Very naturally I cannot see how I am going to get out of this [the word "alive" has here been erased] but of course I will" (107; bracketed phrase appears as such in text). The note of writerly self-consciousness intrudes on the illusion of the story and begs the question of how the narrator can know that the term "alive" has been erased? The only explanation that would leave the realism of the story intact would suggest that the words were faintly visible beneath the erasure. This erasure recalls Frederick Jackson Turner's model of Western culture, the palimpsest, on whose primary, bottom layers are inscribed Euro-American history—the source, one could say, of a present condition that aspires to understand and recuperate its past. For Norris's writing, "alive" is an equally remote condition and an object of desire—a condition that his literature creates in the attempt to recuperate it.

Is the situation an experience for Karslake or is it a story? He may not be sure that he will survive, but his words will. From the introductory material, we learn that he has enlisted in the army as part of a plan to write a novel of military life in the Southwest: "wishing to get in closer touch with the milieu of the story, [he] actually enlisted in order to be able to write authoritatively" (105). Karslake writes rather than shoots because the story is more important to him: it is to be understood as a potential contribution to his military novel, and thus the action is at the service of the story. He has "so lively a sense of the value of accurate observation and so eager a desire to produce that in the very face of death he could set down a description of his surroundings, actually laying down the rifle to pick up the pen" (105). Of course, without the battle there would be no story for Karslake, so that one cannot dismiss the action as simply replaceable "material."

During a break in the crossfire shortly after Karslake has killed "the Spotted One," he gazes on the twilight landscape and muses extensively on his own imagination. "No doubt the supreme exaltation of approaching death is the stimulus that one never experiences in the humdrum business of day to day existence" (120). The association of violence and writing demonstrates the issue of power at stake in Norris's sense of verbal representation. On the one hand, it seems that, in his understanding, to represent something is to kill it; and on the other, it is to preserve it. Both writing and fighting can be construed as dangerous activities, in that they require constant attention in order to avoid falling into nothingness, into abysmal indifference where conscious effort is consumed in an overwhelming storm of accident. The strain to resist this fall accounts in part for the peculiar beauty of violence and death that fuels Karslake's imagination and his obsession with writing. But the exhilaration, immediately upon being felt, is referred to literature.

Norris writes the words of his protagonist's manuscript so that they will look as if preceded by great thoughts. Karslake declares, for example, "Oh! if I had time now—time to write down the great thoughts that do throng the brain. They are there, I feel them, know them. . . . Unintelligible, but if I had time I could spell them out, and how I could write then!" (120). His romantic monologue continues, an artistic image on the same order as the intellectual conversation between Bunt and the narrator of "The Passing of Cock-eye Blacklock." We get no sense of the ideas that the language names. Karslake insists that his mind contains, at some level, certain profound and transcendent thoughts: "I feel that the whole secret of life is within my reach; I can almost grasp it." But the vision never comes: "It is not meant to be. There is a sacrilege in it" (104).

Karslake's meditation on life and the cosmos develops in form and content into a meditation on language, or more precisely, literature: the words themselves refer to nonexistent thoughts, and the anxiety produced is a literary one. Karslake's dilemma recalls the narrator's attempt in "Cock-eye" and "Peg-leg" to articulate the glories of his setting while at the same time being true to them. The narrator who introduces "A Memorandum of Sudden Death" alludes to the quick of life that Norris imagines at the core of Western experience, a throb of vitality that, in this story, is too elusive for language to name. By contrast, silence does a better job, as the narrator notes in describing certain elisions in Karslake's manuscript: "the very breaks are eloquent while the break at the end speaks with a significance that no words could attain" (121).

Norris's rhetorical mechanism in this section of the story is to make something out of nothing; to suggest a content to Karslake's meditation by presenting it as too powerful to name. The elusiveness of his realization does nothing to diminish its value. On the contrary, the difficulty of grasping and naming it only increases its desirability for Karslake.

Such elusiveness and erratic mobility are hallmarks of westernist characterization and narrative movement. Elusiveness charges figures like Karslake, Daniel Boone, Leatherstocking, and even Meriwether Lewis (as Lewis tends to construct himself) not with dense content but precisely a lack of content, and their trademark journeys become quests to fill the void. As empty subjects of barely articulated desires, they serve as ciphers to draw the narratives where they appear through the thickets of possibility and danger in the project to contact the aboriginal Euro-American self.

What Norris would have his readers experience as the unspeakable quick of being—the real, understood as simple or sublime—is created by the words that aspire to duplicate it, and thus the source of the real exists not outside but inside the necessary illusion of his language. "Life" for Norris is just this elusive vitality that is always some steps ahead of language but created as an object of desire in the very substance that misses it. By dying in midsentence, the writer escapes the limits of language, conflated here with the limits of consciousness. Death becomes the most eloquent break in text, apparently bearing with it the "significance that no words could attain" and "the whole secret of life."

THE GOLD FETISH AMONG the characters in *McTeague* is an expression of profound respect for an object that operates in the text as the very image of signification. As Walter Benn Michaels has argued in *The Gold Standard and the Logic of Naturalism*,[28] gold, considered as money or as metal, provokes desire in a variety of ways in the novel but always in connection with its representative powers. In this sense, gold is the source for endless possibilities of exchange that reverberate beyond monetary economics; it represents in miniature the desire in westernism for infinite possibilities of regeneration—a relationship dramatically expressed in the Gold Rush. In European-derived cultures, gold is what might be called the ultimate signifier: it can mean whatever you can substitute it for, and you can, theoretically, substitute it for anything. By symbolizing such potential, gold functions as a standard, an authority whose value is self-evident and determines that of other things for which it can be exchanged. Thus it circulates through *McTeague* as the mark of meaning itself, an extended metaphor for the system of references and associations that constitute the very process of narration. But within the narrative economy that it engenders, gold comes to participate as simply one of the many elements that perpetuate desire.[29]

Gold, the valuable stuff hidden in the earth, had no inherent worth or in any case very little practical use in Norris's time. In its culturally determined capacity to be exchanged for anything and in its lack of inherent value, gold demonstrates the principle that things in themselves signify nothing but take their price from the values of other things for which they may, for whatever reasons, be made to substitute. This frankly semiotic lesson that gold offers is rehearsed regularly through *McTeague* and demonstrates Norris's peculiar habit of playing with signs, marks, the hoaxes in words, and the trompe-d'oeils in pictures, as if the signifier itself were the object of his interest and ridicule.

On the other hand, late-nineteenth-century literary representations of gold have much to do with its material form. Embedded in the earth, it is the object that the miner desires to touch and toward which his search is directed. The abstract issues of signification and meaning leave the rock cold, in an orthodox naturalist sense; but just as naturalism creates its own romanticism in order to repress it, gold's authority is diminished by the very fact of an argument in the free silver-gold standard debates of the 1890s, only to retain its mythical value in the nostalgic adoration of a once stable convention. The lack of inherent value noted above is one thing; but the momentum of gold's value-in-itself, accumulated through long centuries of European economics and iconography, ensures its respect in the face of its arbitrary value. Gold is an emblem of pure essence, highly placed, tangible, and signifying nothing beyond itself.[30]

The stasis and internal location of gold considered as a material entity, as well as its arbitrary worth, secure its value as an icon of stability. Its status as essence, as the deep and final thing in itself, as the gold-standard argument would have it, rests on a notion of inherent truth to the values that conservative politics placed on its own valuation of gold. The status as capital signifier emerges from this notion of stable worth but also eventually makes evident the arbitrary nature of this notion, since gold can be substituted for virtually anything. This position would be cannon fodder for the free-silver argument; but in Norris's and London's works that feature money and mining as dramatic material, both notions of gold as matter and as signifier are in play. It is as if the gold served to reflect its own general cultural value as well as the peculiar desire of the miner or miser. And it also matches the ambivalence in Norris's work about the nature of the artistic signifier: would it incessantly conjure up another metaphor like itself, or was there some nugget of stable value and meaning about the West, waiting to be properly represented, that his literature was "prospecting" for?

This account of the perception of gold as model signifier and pure matter is repeated in the function of the mute true West and its "Life" as source in Norris's aesthetics of literary representation. In both of these relationships, the privileged authority that speaks for its own value is sought as parent for the production that follows it. But as causes of desire, these objects take their places within the narrative economies they engender rather than remaining outside as privileged forebears. Thus, the idea of the unmediated true West is embedded in Norris's landscapes—urban and wild—and in his character descriptions, as a source that cannot quite be "captured." Nonetheless, in both cases the seeker studies and courts the origin in an attempt to be faithful to its value, but succeeds instead in taking possession of the idealized source for something different.

McTeague's division between the two very different dramatic situations of the urban-domestic and the wilderness scenarios provides certain characters with alternate levels on which to act out their avarice. Given Norris's general and overt emphasis on what he tries to know in an immediate way as "Life"—the rough and raw realism of the West— we might reasonably consider the two situations as separate fields of value-determination that the novel compares. The late mining sequence, for example, takes the problem of greediness back to money's source in the bowels of the Sierra Nevada, the place of McTeague's own origins. Mining itself, a more blatant way of pursuing gold than the complicated mechanisms of urban social exchange and the guile of the bank, is presented here as if it were a more primary and simple model by which to study the relation of the human psyche to the metal it has made precious. In this scenario the relation is, more properly speaking, greed, the desire for something one does not yet have, than avarice, or the tendency to hoard, evident in the behavior of Trina, McTeague's wife, concerning her coined gold.

About halfway through the novel, after McTeague has murdered Trina and returned to the Sierra, he becomes partners with the prospector Cribbens. Before they set out to find a claim, McTeague and Cribbens discuss their differing approaches to mining. Cribbens has been exposed to a lot of talk on the subject and has made himself something of a geologist by reading about it and prospecting in a rather "scientific manner": "Shucks . . . Gi'me a long distinct contact between sedimentary igneous rocks, an' I'll sink a shaft without ever seeing 'color.' "[31]

McTeague denies the value of any theoretical approach and simply responds, "Gold is where you find it." The difference between the two approaches centers on the issue of interpretation. Cribbens's idea requires that the prospector read the landscape for indications of material that cannot be seen on the surface. The contact of igneous and sedimentary rock signifies the possibility of quartz, which is in turn a clue to the invisible presence of gold. McTeague thinks that such codification of the ground is useless: one might find gold at such a point, and one might not. The dentist "clung to the old prospector's idea that there was no way of telling where gold was until you actually saw it." Rather than proceeding by Cribbens's conventions, which not only ascribe a certain meaning to the terrain, but create that meaning in Cribbens's almost sentimental fondness for the terms of his theory, McTeague will simply take things as they come and avoid such a representative approach to the land.

His slogan, "Gold is where you find it," suggests the ideal, spontaneous realism of "Life" in Norris's aesthetics of fiction; and after all, it too is a theory founded on a kind of perceptual realism. McTeague is a dumb hero, and the simplicity of his method here is entirely appropriate to his character. Nonetheless, the character utters Norris's realism; and Cribbens, the more intelligent of the two, is made to seem at moments more interpretive, or conscious of style and design, than the author's aesthetics would overtly approve.

The language of Cribbens's theory, with its incongruous combination of slang and scientific rhetoric, is also an instance of Norris's habit of parodying the Western speaker. So we have the impression that Cribbens's stylized methodology is a violation of the pure Western experience embodied in McTeague's aphorism, and that his character is something of a joke. But several pages later, Cribbens's description of the correct context for gold matches precisely the geological configurations of the spot where their discovery occurs. The argument, however, is still unsettled since all we have here is one incident, and certainly McTeague's tautology cannot be denied.

The parody of representation posed in Cribbens's prospecting echoes the general anxiety about writing that appears in much of Norris's work. A method like Cribbens's is certainly useful, although Norris would rather sanction the immediacy of McTeague's idea by enacting it in writing; that is, by simply recording what is there in the Western environment as it comes to him, without any literary design. To do so would be to let the stuff of life speak for itself, and thus true West might somehow be conjured on the page. But such an idea is a writer's fantasy.

The kinds of rock at issue in their discussion, igneous granodiorite and sedimentary slate, are, respectively, indigenous (or internal) and foreign (or external) to the specific location where they lie, and the product of this interaction is the gold—the essential meaning behind the geological signifiers in Cribbens's interpretation. Against this neat equation, Norris's aesthetics, fighting to diminish the internal, projective vision of the convention-filled writerly imagination, attempt to register a primarily external impression of the real. The image of the two kinds of rock—igneous, more or less inherent to the spot where it is found—and sedimentary—which has in a sense settled or slid in from elsewhere—stands as a neat little code for the ideal production of meaning, a meeting of subjectivity and objectivity that is not, after all, pure subjective hoax.

The issue of signification and meaning is played out in the treatment of the landscape as a text to be interpreted or not to be interpreted, in the same vein as the discussion of the value of gold. Norris's persistent anxiety concerning the propriety of writing suggests a distrust of the signifier and a wariness of any mark's pretense to "stand for" something else. But the distrust seems to eventuate in a perverse fetishizing of the signifier as such, and the same lack of background or reason for the obsession in Trina's, McTeague's, and the junk dealer Zerkow's lust for gold.

The concern with signification in Norris's novel makes itself known in the collection of photographs, emblems, certificates, coins, signs, written announcements, and so forth. But the steady pressure of McTeague's angle of vision in the narrative perspective suggests the thinness of the entire story itself—that is, its status as an elaborate emblem surrounding the arch emblem gold, whose referent to some reality is sheer illusion. There is something solipsistic and degenerate in the narrow channel of McTeague's point of view, which to a great extent controls the narrative scope; elements of story are chosen from the realm of possibilities by McTeague's position. The psychology of Norris's work is in its narrative structure: its angling and its paced repetitions, which function as rhythmic obsessions.

In following the narrow pathways of McTeague's understanding, the narrator often mimics his piecemeal comprehension. The process of his degeneration leaves McTeague with less and less clarity, and his diminishing mentation is somewhat echoed in the narrator's voice. By the time McTeague has left Trina, the story's information tends to emerge in a more circumscribed manner. The narrator openly withholds explanations of the meanings of events and conditions, and as the reader is led from one traumatic moment to the next, the absence of sympathetic commentary results in parody. For example, the fact that Trina's fingers have been amputated as a result of McTeague's having sadistically bitten them over and over again is treated by the following comment: "One can hold a scrubbing-brush with two good fingers and the stumps of two others even if both joints of the thumb are gone, but it takes considerable practice to get used to it" (271).

The novel's refusal to provide data that would eliminate such gaps in information has a fragmenting effect appropriate to naturalism's anti-humanist ethos. Common subjectivity is constructed as atavistic at the same time as the writer's style is projected as avant-garde and cleverly situated on the edge of fin-de-siècle modernity. But Norris also appears to be resigned, in a decadently humorous way, to his own lack of confidence in explanatory narrative logic; that is, in the ability of literary representation to honor its ostensibly social and psychological sources. This doubt is not a unique component of Norris's imagination, but rather a common symptom, so to speak, of the conundrum pervading late nineteenth-century Euro-American intellectual circles concerning the representation of the real.

In *McTeague* the informational gaps suggest that objects do not safely signify anything: they simply reflect each other and do not refer, with realistic integrity, beyond this play. But to say this is also to imply the simultaneously sad and humorous tone Norris's naturalism imposes on its meaningless conditions, and this in itself is a fairly powerful referent. The author's effort to depict the hard materiality of human life in a direct and uncompromising light is, like McTeague's uncompromising tautology that gold is where you find it, an ideal. The thematic engine of the novel reverberates around this point, and thus the focus regularly shifts from "the object as in itself it really is," in Matthew Arnold's terms, to a kind of self-conscious, intratextual romanticism in the effort to recognize its source.

Chapter 6

Jack London and the Politics of Evolution

Deep in the forest a call was mysteriously thrilling and luring, he felt compelled to turn his back upon the fire and the beaten earth around it, and to plunge into the forest, and on and on, he knew not where or why; nor did he wonder where or why, the call sounding imperiously, deep in the forest.
—JACK LONDON, *The Call of the Wild* (1903)

JACK LONDON, LIKE Frank Norris, situated many of his naturalist Westerns in California and other sections of the West; but his first imaginative geographies were set in the North, far from his Bay Area home. London's Klondike fiction serves here as an alternative to the literature of the continental West in the postfrontier era. Indeed, for London the North was an exotic frontier zone that recalled the wild West, which his own regional culture still anxiously claimed as its source and spirit. In taking the Klondike for his given fictional environment, London left aside the tensions between urbanity and Western tradition in "lower" Western areas. Leaping north, beyond the strains and ironies of Berkeley and San Francisco, he found a plentiful source for naturalist fiction and, however much he did or did not intend it, for Western romanticism in the harsh landscapes of the Klondike.

Later he would turn his attention back to the Bay Area as a setting, and the same rivalry between the two modes would emerge in the urban environment just as it had in the northern wilderness. In the case of *Martin Eden*, the central character seems to act out the dramas of self-emplacement in San Francisco that London had experienced as a young man. Rather than undertake a biographical reading of that novel, however, I use the central thematic rivalry of naturalism and romanticism as a context for analysis. Although London's westernism paid more emphatic attention to overtly political and social issues than Norris's generally did, London like Norris engaged the vocabulary and the literary principles of naturalism to construct a revisionary interpretation of the late-nineteenth-century West. The discourse of the closed frontier is more implied than openly expressed as a textual concern in his work, but the Klondike and other stories beg the question by powerfully imagining a variety of returns to the romantic origins of a mythically wild West.

BEFORE TURNING TO THE subject of London's Klondike fiction, it will be helpful to take a brief look at his Bay Area beginnings and at his intellectual preparation for writing fiction. London's working-class identity was crucial to his various public images, and it contributed extensively to the reputation he fostered as a self-made Westerner. The hard work and hard knocks he had famously survived were always part of his public persona, and his character accrued all the more mystique for having been touched by want and punishment, for having endured a mean, scrappy, and often dangerous youth.

London's inauspicious beginnings stood in dramatic contrast to the recognition and relative wealth that came to mark his adult life as a writer.[1] His continuous invocation of that background in self-representations long after it had ceased to materially control his life constituted a remarkably sustained performance of himself as one who knew the real West by virtue of having worked and suffered in it. Frank Norris's posturing as a literary man-of-the-West pales by comparison with London's self-design as a working adventurer.

Oakland was a tough place in the 1890s, a haven of oyster pirates and wharf gangs who seemed to be living out the promises of the town's origins as a community of hard-nosed, trespassing squatters. Incorporated in 1852 as a city by its first mayor, Horace Carpentier, who was later denounced as a land thief and "shyster" by his constituency, Oakland was by London's time still a "raw mess." As his biographer Andrew Sinclair put it, in the Oakland of that time, "nothing was further from achievement than potential."[2]

San Francisco, on the other hand, was the site of possibility and emblem of the national adventure in which London saw himself participating. As a poor boy from the other side of the Bay, his early relations to the city were marginal. His family moved several times in the area of San Francisco Bay as work and money demanded, but they never had the opportunity to live in the metropolis itself. Even when he could have afforded to, London did not opt to live in San Francisco but instead made his home across the Bay at Glenn Ellen.

The dramatic outline of San Francisco and its status as culmination of the march of U.S. empire crashed to the ground in 1906, with the great earthquake and fire. By that time, several of London's stories had appeared in San Francisco publications, and he was a recognized figure in the city's literary and political circles. *The Sea Wolf*, published in 1904, gave him a national reputation, and with this came a yet more integral place among San Francisco's intellectuals. His description of the earthquake for *Collier's Weekly* narrated the utter demise of the city that had once stood apart from but finally embraced him.

His home was still across the Bay when the earthquake hit on the morning of April 18, 1906. He witnessed the destruction from the distance of his ranch. Shortly afterward, he was in the city itself, touring its ruins. The pinnacle of the West was in ashes: "Not in history has a modern imperial city been so completely destroyed," he wrote. "San Francisco is gone. Nothing remains of it but memories." The "lurid tower of fire" that consumed it was visible, he claimed, from "a hundred miles away." The contrast that he developed between the city's prequake sophistication and the aftermath of smoke and rubble hinged on "thirty seconds' twitching of the earth-crust." The indifferent power of nature to smash "all the cunning adjustments of a twentieth-century city" was stunning.[3] For all of London's eulogizing of the lost grandeur and sympathizing with the fear and panic, his description of the scene bespeaks a fascination with the raw force of nature to demolish everything, and with the stoic behavior of residents as they left their homes and possessions to escape the fire. These processes have a far stronger impact on London's account of the event than does the sadness he evokes for what has been lost.

London's education was as self-made as his public character. It consisted largely of reading on his own, getting advice from acquaintances who had more conventional academic training, and debating ideas with friends and fellow wanderers. Only for brief periods—a year in high school, a semester in college—was he attached to mainstream educational institutions. Probably the most important source of learning for him was the Oakland Public Library, where he began borrowing books during grammar school. The library supplied him with the texts of many influential writers of his day, particularly Karl Marx and Herbert Spencer, whose works he began reading in 1895. Their ideas would be central to virtually all of the fiction and prose writing that London produced, as would selected arguments of Darwin, Fourier, and, later, Nietzsche.

But these are only a few of the writers whose ideas London was trying to consume; Andrew Sinclair writes that at the time, he was "reading almost at random through the shelves of the public library, trying to cram into his mind the knowledge of every subject under the sun" (31). The peculiar ideational mixes he assembled from these writings were alternately egalitarian and deeply reactionary, romantic, and deterministic; and they permitted him to take more than a few positions in between. The intellectual subject that London became was in many ways a gallery of turn-of-the-century popular social and political discourses, rather than one informed predominantly by fascism, socialism, or any other single ideological formula.

In the fall of 1896, after cramming for the entrance examination, London entered the University of California but stayed for only one semester and received grades of "Incomplete" for the three English courses in which he enrolled. One of these was composition, but unlike Norris's "Freshman Themes" course, which was based largely on readings in classic English literature, London's was a study of nineteenth-century science writers, including Darwin, Huxley, and Spencer. In 1892 he had taken a university extension course in Oakland taught by David Starr Jordan, who became president of Stanford University and was a key proponent of social evolutionary thinking in California.[4] Thus, the writing course that London took in 1896 appealed to an already developing interest in theories of natural selection and the concept of "survival of the fittest." In 1899 he wrote that Jordan was, "to a certain extent, a hero of mine,"[5] even though he later repudiated the politics of Jordan's work.[6]

Jordan viewed California, his adopted state, as an exemplary place for the individual and communal development that he thought America capable of generally. Its magnificent natural landscapes, he felt, should foster especially strong and vital human beings, and their society should be a model of balance and adaptability for the rest of the nation. But Jordan's ideas of social evolution required the denunciation of much that was actual in the California of his time. Contemporary regional culture, he felt, was still too oriented toward what he called "the possibility of the unearned increment," a hope for financial profit without having to go through lengthy processes of work and worry to achieve it.[7]

According to Jordan, this attitude had to change before California would be all that it could be. The continuous influx of immigrants presented an obstruction to progress as well, Jordan thought, since foreigners often came with hopes for the "unearned increment" and kept such unworthy ideas alive among the rest of the populace.[8] Although Jordan was something of a California Brahmin and thus represented the elite class of owners and managers who constituted the enemy Other to many of London's fictional working-class heroes, his evolutionism and his attitudes toward foreigners strongly affirmed those of his student. He did not, however, share London's overt racism; there were plenty of other available sources for that in intellectual and academic discourses of the time, even if London had not been sufficiently versed in it before his university studies began.[9]

London's childhood poverty, together with what he learned during his sojourn with Kelly's Army of the unemployed in 1894 and at the Erie County Penitentiary where he was imprisoned briefly for vagrancy the same year, fostered his perception that American society was built out of gross inequalities. In 1896 he decided to join the Socialist Party of Oakland. In these identifications with the proletariat, his thinking was very different from Jordan's. But at the same time, London's evolutionism suffered little from his affinities with socialism. The language and ideas of Herbert Spencer, so readily adaptable as apologies for rampant capitalism and imperialism, seemed to remain central to London's political imagination, regardless of other, sometimes antithetical, political and social positions he took.

Evolutionism affirmed not only his rather obsessive interests in physical strength and mental adaptability, but the intense individualism that was often attached to those interests and that usually contradicted the ethics of selflessness and devotion to the group that he claimed were equally important to him. London's interpretation of Spencer's key narrative of development—that discrete and homogeneous forces eventually become complex and heterogeneous[10]—emphasized both ends of the formula, such that his wilderness characters draw their strengths from a kind of primitive, isolated mentality that is as necessary to adaptation as the acquisition of social instincts and the recognition of environmental limits. Thus, they operate alternately as figures of naturalism and romanticism in a fiction that tries to assert the primacy of both visions of the power of American subjectivity.

After London joined the Socialist Party, he quickly became one of its most avid and vocal members. Reading Marx, John Ruskin, and William Morris, delivering soapbox speeches, carrying on heated debates with both converted and unconverted friends, he gradually furnished his street sense of socialism with the intellectual ammunition and rhetorical skills that made him seem a real asset to the party. Shortly he acquired the nickname of "Boy Socialist of Oakland." His precipitous ascent within the group and his fast comprehension of the theoretical underpinnings of the party's activities ironically seemed to foster in him a sense of his individual strength and ability to succeed, as much as they did a native respect for revolutionary socialism.

A representative statement of his efforts to reconcile natural selection and revolutionary politics is found in a letter to his friend Cloudsley Johns in 1899: "The race with the highest altruism will endure—the highest altruism considered from the standpoint of merciless natural law, which never concedes nor alters. The lesser breeds cannot endure. The Indian is an example, as is the black man of the Austrailian [sic] Bush, the South Sea Islander, the inhabitant of the Sub-Artics, etc."[11] Nature's radical egalitarianism does not apply to "the Indian" or the "the black man." A few months earlier, London had written to Johns, "I cannot but hail as unavoidable the Black and the Brown going down before the White" (61). The weakness of "the Black and the Brown" goes unexplained, and London positions these groups as recipients of natural law on whom the merciless energy of natural process is always visited. Since the Blacks and the Browns, the Indians, Australians, and Sub-Arctics "go down" before the whites, the whites tend to figure here as the agents or representatives of "natural law." In much of London's fiction, Anglo-Saxons are construed as a race that can soar to the highest altruism but that also embodies the disinterested power of material necessity itself.

The combination of love and indifferent viciousness in this account of the essential white subject is apparently not a problem for London; his way of resolving it is to portray altruism as the product of hard work and sacrifice and to reserve these practices for working class white characters. Their strength and worthiness are shaped by comparisons with the marginal Others who help or resist them, and who, in this sense, serve the narrative economies that give such whites form.

London's racist sentiments get dramatically elaborated in his fiction set on the margins of U.S. territory. Largely divided between the frozen, white north and the fetid tropics of the Pacific, these settings are typically populated by characters represented as racial others to Euro-American and English visitors. The whites are drawn by opportunities for adventure and by the enchanting chaos of a wilderness far from the overly civilized and domesticated United States. Their failures and successes depend on their abilities to adapt and survive in the face of great adversity, by means of the cunning and violence that the wilderness scene elicits. Altruism is reserved for fellow whites, and particularly for strong male characters of the sort that London often refers to as "the blonde-beastly type," a term he took from Nietzsche and revised for his own purposes.[12] Camaraderie and selflessness are the proper ethics for survival in the treacherous natural world, which includes Athabascans and Solomon Islanders as well as forests, jungles, ice traps, and diseases.

But weakness is often wrapped in the features of white male elites as well as of women and Indians. They display all that the working-class Anglo-Saxon male does not want to be in the wilderness scenario. Their presence is thus crucial to the construction of this tougher "type," whose strength would be difficult to articulate without the negative comparison, or without the opportunities provided by weaker characters for the exercise of his powers.

In London's fictional ethic, working-class Euro-Americans who share their strengths for the benefit of the group, like a pack of wolves, will overcome whatever stands in the way of their destined achievement. Failure is its own, natural punishment, but success is not so much a reward as it is the probable outcome for whites in their encounters with "the Black and the Brown."

LONDON'S EARLIEST PUBLISHED fiction was set not in the Bay region but in Alaska and the Yukon Territory, where he had traveled in 1897 to take part in the Klondike gold rush. The sense of adventure and risk that was so much a part of romantic westernism and that was remembered so avidly in the discourse of the closed frontier was an important motivator for those who went to the Klondike, including London. Among the significant alternatives to the Bay Area that the "frozen north" offered as a setting was its capacity to function as a belated wilderness where the dramas and dangers of an earlier westernist imaginative geography could be replayed.

London's frozen north is a silent world, utterly empty of civilization. As such, it sets in motion a naturalist game of survival for London's thinly drawn characters. The lack of the most simple amenities and the constant threat of death are structural givens; they reduce the Klondike environment to a field of figures for an unshaped and unvoiced Nature. But for all of its unavailability and indifference to the human subjects whose fates it determines, the silent pressure of nature manifests as a brute, inimical companion, and thus acquires the presence and agency of an unnamed, mystified character. Its existence is so powerful that it stands in antagonistic relation not only to characters proper but to the narrating voice of the fiction. The landscapes image this force in the stretches of blank, white surface and dark, wooded depths. These material elements of the stories' ground not only recall the testing environment of former frontiers, but they imply as well other material determinants of character and narrative trajectory—economic, biological, and social factors that the Klondike adventurers bring with them from home. In projecting a nature too fierce for human comfort and too alien for romantic transformation, the brute elements of landscape speak for a range of limits on human action and experience that London both believed existed and nevertheless continuously imagined his characters overcoming.

The implication is strong that the pursuit of redemption or reward at the end of the trail is a fool's errand. Nevertheless, this emptiness gets "discovered" and, in a variety of ways—however minimal—mapped by its visitors so that negotiation of the dangers becomes possible. This, of course, depends on one's capacities for reading the landscape, disciplining one's emotions, and hardening oneself to reactions the landscape necessitates. Those who make it do not always do so by virtue of their own strengths or abilities; often it is chance that permits their survival. But those who pass the test are, after all, enlarged by the experience, even if it means that they become as cold and elemental as the landscapes that reshape them. In the end, London's Anglo adventurers often develop romantic mutualities with their Klondike surroundings and find regeneration in the classic, westernist manner. The spareness of the northern landscapes ensures the spareness of character and plot; and all of these elements work to present the most simple and concentrated forms of late romantic westernism.

"The Wisdom of the Trail," one of the Northland stories that London published shortly after his return from the Klondike, is in many ways a representative text of the social dynamics of London's belated frontier West. At the risk of invoking once again what may be an overused set of analytic categories in contemporary literary discussion, I want to address the relationships of gender, race, and class that London establishes in the story and that can be understood as symptomatic in his work. Because of London's own polymorphous politics, in "The Wisdom of the Trail" these relationships are quite complicated; but the ideational thicket is significantly intensified by the highly unsettled and continuous encounter between naturalism and westernism in almost every aspect of the story.

The Indian character of Sitka Charley, who appears in several of the Klondike tales, is in "The Wisdom of the Trail"[13] a vehicle of native lore and a faithful conduit of white interests and knowledge. His acquaintance with white culture goes back to his boyhood, but he is still alien to it and in awe of white power. Slowly over the years he has come to comprehend "the honor and the law" as keys to the acquisition of authority in that culture. The length of time he has taken to learn this is only natural, though, for, "the aboriginal mind is slow to generalize, and many facts, repeated often are required to compass an understanding. . . . Being an alien, when he did know he knew it better than the white man himself; being an Indian, he had achieved the impossible" (325). Sitka Charley is thus introduced as a brutish creature who has, romantically, overcome what for him are biological and genetic obstacles to learn "the honor and the law" of the whites. Whereas the other Indians in the party are alien and cowering, Charley serves as the perfect foreman to Captain Eppingwell's expedition. In doing so, he makes it possible for white culture in the West to extend itself geographically at a moment when it presumably cannot do so in any other way.

The 1897 Klondike gold rush in which the story was set opened a frontier to Euro-American exploration well after Turner's pronunciation of the end of such a possibility. It had a short-lived history, and very little gold was taken from the region, in comparison with money spent on transportation and outfitting. It can thus be understood, like expeditionary events that were connected with the Spanish American war, as something like a replay of the conquest of the wilderness for Euro-American men, particularly those who were already living in the West at the time gold was discovered in Dawson City, Alaska.

Certainly expansion continued in connection with the Spanish American War, but in 1900, when London published the story, the matter of extracontinental imperialism was a topic of extensive domestic debate, and although the United States had already established a military presence in Cuba, Guam, and the Philippines, there was not a general consensus that the nation's future would include new, extracontinental frontiers in a new colonial empire.[14] Prominent political and commercial figures in the U.S. who publicly took part in this debate commonly referred to it as a matter of national identity. The questions raised by this debate impinged not only on images and meanings of a national culture, which until recently had been able to draw on the strength and endurance associated with the Euro-American frontier; as Donna Haraway, Mark Seltzer, and Amy Kaplan have persuasively argued, these questions also complicated public representations of U.S. masculinity, insofar as national identity was an important component in the construction of male subjectivity.[15]

Without rehearsing these arguments, I want to note that the celebrations of masculine vitality for which London and Norris are famous

can be quite easily and reasonably understood within these terms—
that is, as anxious assertions of a potency that can only be imagined as
the proper condition of Western and U.S. character generally. An
alternative to the reproduction of selfhood in the framework of empire
would be the influencing of colonized character on the model of the
master—not after the colonizing moment but at the point of exhaustion of the empire's reach. Frantz Fanon's map in "The Pitfalls of
National Consciousness" of the dynamics of "national character" formation in recently expired colonial situations has some purchase in
the case of London's Sitka Charley.[16] It is in the reconstruction of the
person of Charley and other indigenous persons like him that the story
envisions the extension of U.S. cultural authority, more than in taking
possession of the landscape and of its mineral contents. Thus, it makes
sense to understand the cultural conversion of Sitka Charley in terms
of a substitution, whereby earlier mechanisms for the reproduction
of national ideology in conquest and expansion are replaced by
the making of his indigenous character to resemble that of a metropolitan subject.

If Charley's character is designed by London according to naturalist theories of social determinism, he is also a figure of romantic strength.
The entanglement of naturalism and Western romanticism becomes
most explicit in Charley's speech patterns. His archaic Anglo diction
sounds remarkably like that of Cooper's Natty Bumppo of *The Last of
the Mohicans*, and the resemblance slides from the scout to that novel's
major noble savage and faithful guide to the whites, Chingachgook. So
closely does Sitka Charley resemble the Cooper model, with his stoic
adherence to the repeated code of "honor and law," that he has con-
tempt for other Indians who do not respect it. Given this romantic
stature, Charley has the promise of imagination, complication, and
ambiguity, all of which traits seem to strain against the limitations of
his being as seen by the codes of naturalism. But insofar as "honor and
law" are standards of Enlightenment rationalism, it is his long resistance to inculcating them that would more properly seem to constitute
Charley's romantic being.

London nevertheless insists that the strength and charisma in
Charley's character lie in his adaptation to the values of the colonized
environment. Thus, it becomes evident that the story's sense of this

code is that it is not peculiar to the whites, but rather has transcendent value for all human communities if they can but progress, in evolutionary terms, to the perception of its natural propriety. "Honor and law" are simply those achievements that mark the end point of natural selection. Even if they work to favor the plans of the whites, they sustain what is best for everybody and emerge from nature as a "force" of evolution rather than as instruments of very human power.

Adherence to this code in "The Wisdom of the Trail" is represented by conscious rationalization and a lofty regard for the expedition community and its goal, as opposed to action based on animal desires and the satisfaction of immediate, private needs. The latter is evident in the cowardly Indians who, hungry and cold, continuously disobey Charley by stealing fuel and food. However much punishment is promised, they cannot manage to alter their skulking behavior. The demands of law and honor are placed in opposition to the needs of the body. The ability to perceive a system and have confidence in its morality stand against isolated desire, mistrust, and concern only for the moment.

Charley's identification with the law and honor is particularly evident in his regard for Mrs. Eppingwell, whose intention to accompany the expedition at first elicits from him a refusal to participate in it. But her petition is too strong for him to deny:

> When she came to him with her wonderful smile and her
> straight clean English, and talked to the point, without
> pleading or persuading, he had incontinently yielded. Had
> there been a softness and appeal to mercy in the eyes, a
> tremble to the voice, a taking advantage of sex, he would have
> stiffened to steel; instead her clear-searching eyes and clear-
> ringing voice, her utter frankness and tacit assumption of
> equality, had robbed him of his reason. . . . He knew why the
> sons of such women mastered the land and the sea, and why
> the sons of his own womankind could not prevail against
> them. (327)

Mrs. Eppingwell's simple, undesigned presentation of her position is what persuades Charlie to stay with the expedition. As wife of the party's leader, she speaks for the best in her husband's project and the culture in which it emerges. The phrasing of London's description of her rhetoric—"straight clean English," "to the point," "clear-ringing," and "utter frankness"—speak to the naturalness and honesty of her proposition. Each of her words and gestures, London would have us think, attests to the fact that her request comes from no particular interest but simply reports what is true and right. As representative and vehicle of reproduction of the white culture that supports her, she convinces Charlie, representative of the best in his society, to do something that he very distinctly does not want to do before she comes to lobby him. Her words of presumably ungendered rationalism, and of what is irresistibly real, account, in London's logic, for her power. In this sense, the encounter between them is a miniature of the archetypal relation between whites and Indians generally in London's Klondike fiction.

But there is another dimension to this exchange that complicates the icon of imperial persuasion that the meeting seems to formulate. Although Mrs. Eppingwell clearly serves as the wife of empire, London tries to make the case that she is her own woman. Her "tacit assumption of equality," straightforward speech, and direct gaze position her as one who conceives of her desires as genuinely her own and who is confident of their legitimacy. At the same time, her concern for the group at large marks her as one of London's strong, selfless "types," who lose neither perspective nor a sense of priorities in their own problems and desires.

The respect that London pays to Mrs. Eppingwell, like that he accords to select wilderness women in other Klondike stories, is in some ways based on her resemblance to the male characters whose efforts she supports. But rather than simply being one of them, she is inherently different. This is not to say that London was particularly interested in feminine difference, but that he found it aesthetically useful in constructing female characters who could fit the role of the "man's woman"—a privileged figure in Norris's fiction as well—who could stand up to the codes of masculine behavior in situations that called for exceptional skill and bravery. Like them, London made the most of the ability of such women to meet and mimic, in spite of her difference, the model of the male natural aristocrat. In this sense, she is an ideal metaphor for the male culture to which she belongs.[17]

Yet London extended such romantic sameness to select indigenous characters, and to dogs as well. As Others to the white male model, these creatures are, for all of their strength and bravery, inherently confined to the limited scope of knowledge and behavior that comes with survivalist conformity and imitation. In that sense, they illustrate central tenets of naturalist determinism. But their racial, gender, and species differences were the precise keys that London used to dramatize their efforts at romantically overcoming such limits.

It cannot be denied that in London's fiction feminine worth is often downplayed and that women are sketched largely as, at best, hearty helpmates to their men. Just as often, they appear as weak, or dim-witted, ineffectual creatures. Mrs. Eppingwell is in a sense both, for she is also striking to Charley because she is "tender and soft," her feet "born to easy paths and sunny lands, strangers to the moccasined pain of the North." Her nobility is thus always understood in comparison with another kind of woman that the story envisions she might have been: the coy, seductive, and whining creature that Charlie is surprised to find she is not. In spite of her differences from such a model of femininity, she is always evaluated by the narrator as if she stood directly beside it.

Mrs. Eppingwell's complex representation is in several ways matched by that of Charley. He is the stoic figure of rigid, ethical correctness, his function always to uphold the white law; and yet a more indigenous being is somehow always present in the margins of his character. The ambiguity in this portrait is central to the story's dramatization of cultural and gender differences. The always possible, opposite term to his stately character appears in the disobedient Magua types, Gowhee and Kah-Chucte, who in the end are shot by Charley because they cannot adapt to his model of behavior.

In fact, we can readily see that Mrs. Eppingwell, like Charley, is mistaken in believing that her "own" voice is so, since she is clearly an attendant in a project that privileges Euro-American men. Mixing a sturdy romantic individualism with the determining effects of the social, Mrs. Eppingwell mirrors Charlie, rather than acting only as ambassador of the expedition. Even though London pictures Charlie as more retrograde in his sexual politics than any of the whites, he makes Mrs. Eppingwell resemble him all the more closely, in that they both believe the ideas and policies they support are of their own choosing and work to their best advantage. Both of them are, after all, "determined" by the "force" that London conceives of as disembodied and irresistible but that is patently a mystification of his own authorial powers to create and move these figures—in the manner of the white, male agents of the story—from an unquestioned distance.

The battle between naturalism and romantic individualism is won by naturalism in the case of Charley and Mrs. Eppingwell, and by romanticism in the case of London and the expedition officers of the story. In overcoming their limits, Charley and Mrs. Eppingwell are figures of romantic drama, but in being so they relinquish their differences in order to "adapt" to the dominant model of frontier heroism. The story thus conducts an evolutionist judgment of culturally different people according to the same scale of values. The product is a text that complicates the picture of life on the frontier by converting the romance of strangeness into a story of the transforming effects of the familiar forms of civil behavior and by introducing the modernity of naturalist evolutionary theory.

But rather than replacing romanticism with a scientific, object-oriented representation of life in this particular final frontier, the story is part of an epic of national romanticism, in which the Cooperesque Indian and the capable woman graciously serve the course of empire. In doing so, they become versions of the lyrical European masculine subject who tames the chaos of the wilderness. The question remains as to whether this makes them open-ended subjects who stand to experience all the various adventures possible to Euro-American male subjects; or ciphers limited to imitations of what they perceive in those models, literally from the outside.

The competition of determinism and romanticism keeps going, one term continuously upsetting the other and at the same time lending it viability. Insofar as romanticism is seen as a form that imagines subjects as to some degree self-generated and highlights their models of perception, speech, and action, it would seem to stand in diametric opposition to naturalism's deterministic account of the human and nonhuman world. But if naturalism can be understood as an argument for the cultural construction of subjects according to the limited variables of a given ideological system, then its incorporation of romance as a likely mode for Western characters to follow might be seen as simply logical, given the continuous significance of romanticism in American thought.

PERHAPS LONDON'S MOST famous book is *The Call of the Wild*, a best-seller since its original publication in 1903 and still described by some readers as his greatest accomplishment.[18] Although to my mind such commentary exaggerates the book's worth, it does point to the oddly enduring popularity of London's more polemical adventure writing. Unlike "The Wisdom of the Trail," which manifests its racial ideology through dramatic action, *The Call of the Wild* spells out its peculiar brand of evolutionism in a series of small lectures. The rhetoric of the empirical lesson operates in counterpoint, however, to a kind of genetic mysticism to which the novel is strongly attracted; scientific realism conducts the central action toward a romance of isolation and primitiveness that ends in an image of Buck singing "a song of the younger world."

The book focuses largely on survivability in the context of a given physical environment rather than within a system of human relationships. Its central character is, after all, a dog, and the narrative engine is the dog's "development" from being a civil house pet to a wild animal. Judged by the evolutionary scale that the novel depends on in order to situate its characters' relative strengths, this development is actually regressive, since Buck loses his sense of the more complex rules of canine behavior demanded by the well-to-do California ranch life where he first appears. London stipulates this ambiguity quite specifically: "His development (or retrogression) was rapid" (22). Rather than proceeding to a more integrated place within the heterogeneous and enlightened forms of Euro-Californian life, he becomes isolated, a loner whose existence appears to be determined by no more of a system than what comes with the regularity of bodily desires. But Buck also acts to assert and reassert his status as strongest of the strong, meanest of the mean. His career as a character thus takes him far from the sanctuaries of modern human domesticity and back, across a frontier of time and history "into the primitive," as the first chapter is titled.[19]

Here Buck retunes his senses so he can hear, smell, and register in other, less humanly known ways the data of life in the wilderness. As an

animal, he has the advantage of not being caught up in the issues of free
will and self-determination that commonly preoccupy human figures in
more overtly romantic Western writing. In this restricted form of being,
he seems designed to demonstrate for London the biologically real
processes of development and survival for a given creature in a given
environment.

Although London makes some effort to work within the realm of
conventional wisdom about what is possible for canine mentality, nevertheless his hero seems in most ways to substitute for an ideal Western
human. As the helpful pet of a wealthy family, he has the status of a servant, a strong, white servant who is morally better than the Mexican
gardener who steals him. Even as a dog, he takes the role of London's
favorite type, the Euro-American working class male. The kind of character that he becomes in his journey into the wilderness is in many
ways an example of the toughened survivor whose strengths are honed
on the frontier in Frederick Jackson Turner's essay on Western history.
The culmination of his progress in a mystic howl is, in a sense, the dis-
tillation of pure masculine vitality, which London images as animality
developed to a finely managed viciousness that sustains his arch individualism, divorced from social being.

The allegory of return to the conditions of old frontier life becomes
more and more palpable through the course of the novel, particularly as
it becomes evident that Buck is not erasing his domesticated self in the
process so much as he is putting it aside while he develops a more
romantic subjectivity. From the moment the novel opens, with the
patently absurd comment that "Buck did not read the newspapers, or
he would have known that trouble was brewing," to the many dreams,
fears, and other psychic experiences that follow in the elaboration of
his character, Buck is divided, complicated, and submitted to the sort of
internal dialogues that a romantic human character might experience
in his situation.

These psychical processes are described by the voice that narrates
Buck's story as part of the analysis of his regressing character, but the
analysis invites a very familiar, lyrical elaboration of frontier subjectivity. Even as Buck is required to adapt to a new environment in order to
survive, and in the process to illustrate a key concept in naturalist
theory, he can only do so by using the innate animal qualities with

which he was born. London's description of Buck in this situation as one who is "reborn" only partly resolves the contradiction that has already emerged between the idea that the dog adapts to his new environment and the idea that he exercises inherent abilities that have long lain dormant. Buck's basic instincts are, after all, understood as kinds of knowledge that come from the most elemental sources of his being—a development made possible by his isolation in nature.

The development of retrogression in Buck from pet to animal begins as he awakes from his inaugural night in the Northland, terrified with the sense that the walls of his snow bed are pressing in on him like a trap. The fear that entrapment provokes "was a token that he was harking back through his own life to the lives of his forebears" (18), London writes, and this recollection becomes a motif in Buck's characterization through the remainder of the book. His training has never brought him into contact with traps, and so the fear specific to that experience can only come from some unlearned source within him. It is not his quick intellect that tells him to be afraid, but a form of knowledge that he shares with his ancestors and that comes to him as a strange kind of memory.

The vehicle of this memory—the material that contains it, the place in the body or brain where it is stored—is not specified; and although one of the book's most evident projects is to shape Buck's character and history in terms of what London thought were material and scientific principles, the dog's intensifying connection with his ancestors' knowledge and behavior fosters in him an insidiously mystical quality.

This quality is insidious because London professed in much of his occasional and critical writing to have no inclination toward mysticism or spiritualism of any sort. His mother and his presumed biological father had both been spiritualists and had earned money conducting seances and reading astrological charts. As several London biographers have suggested, his obsession with scientism was not only inspired by contemporary intellectual discourse but by his fierce rejection of his parents' occult practices.[20] Nevertheless, the call of the wild to which Buck responds is an ineffable thing that is never described in terms of physical composition or material nature of any sort. Rather than some quantifiable entity, it is an elusive voice, audible only to Buck and, presumably, other select creatures: "Deep in the forest a call was sounding, and as often as he heard this call, mysteriously thrilling and luring, he felt compelled to . . . plunge into the forest, and on and on, he knew not where or why; nor did he wonder where or why, the call sounding imperiously, deep in the forest" (62). The call reaches Buck's senses unimpeded, and he comprehends it without translation of any kind. Although this comprehension will eventually provide him with the means for "reading" the data of the forest as if they offered messages, no such symbolic or linguistic order is implied in the delivery of the call itself. Without symbolic mediation, it has a kind of mystical power to permeate its object; in other words, the recipient can absorb the call without having to "read" anything.

London explains that as Buck's primitiveness increases, he perceives, determines, and responds to the phenomena of the wilderness almost simultaneously, since the "intervals of time" between these actions are "infinitesimal" (78). Such a process would also seem to describe an (impossibly) ideal literary realism that could effectively transfer data from a writer's to a reader's imagination in some utterly pure form of communication. As in the case of Vanamee's extrasensory perceptions in Norris's *The Octopus*, the mediating effects of language and imagery, which translate into meaning, are minimized so understanding is direct; perception contacts its object without risking the distracting or misleading mechanisms of representation. Rather than interpreting what confronts him and deciding what to do in response, Buck assimilates all that the environment is, instant by instant.

Norris's Vanamee and McTeague develop what their author calls a "sixth sense" under the weight of an intense passion—in Vanamee's case love, and in McTeague's fear; but that sense is more emphatically understood to flourish because of the very raw, virtually prehistoric conditions in which the characters are situated when it emerges. The absence of civil structures and human relationships in these situations allows the peculiar form of perception to expand, since there are no social limits to its actions. Buck's perceptions are equally sharpened by the absence of human society, but they are an effect of his having been literally called by the wild, or, more appropriately, recalled by it, since "the wild" is a temporal frame as well as a category of nature, a past that in some way belongs to him but of which he could not be aware under the conditions of civilization.

London makes no attempt to describe the way of knowing and behaving that the call of the wild makes possible in terms of an empirical, material process; like Buck's strange memory, it is simply "stamped into the heredity of the breed" (22). The peculiarly abstract formula conceives of this "stamp" as existing without change through time, from the earliest generations of dogs and humans to the latest, nineteenth-century survivors.

The theories of Caesar Lambrusco, Joseph LeConte, John Fiske, and other well-known evolutionist thinkers of London's time work with similarly ahistorical, essentialist notions of human subjectivity in their shared view of the atavism always possible in any personality and always capable of drawing more evolved strains of the psyche into retrogressive states. But their ideas always situated the two modes in opposition to each other, as antithetical tendencies, the baser of which never changes. For the higher mode, change is a central feature, essential to development and continuous existence. London's revision of these theories situates the bestial as the best, as the result of immersion in the wildest and least integrated modes of being. Here, as elsewhere, London reverts from the celebration of civilization, as in "The Wisdom of the Trail," to a powerful romance of the wildness of unmediated vitality as the privileged vehicle to the "highest" modes of being. With such a transcendent quality attached to the concept of its title, the novel proposes some very metaphysical ideas that strain heavily against the scientific realism in the articulation of Buck's character.

The dog's individuality increases as he makes a name for himself through various feats of valor, and his reputation spreads "through every camp in Alaska" (64). As Buck feels an increasing urge to disappear into the forest and to leave behind forever his association with humankind, autonomy and individuality accumulate. But in one respect the romantic subject that he has become is compromised as it merges, in dreams and trances, with the ancestors whose codes he mystically remembers:

> He linked the past and the present, and the eternity behind
> him throbbed through him in a mighty rhythm to which he

swayed as the tides and seasons swayed. . . . Behind him were
the shades of all manner of dogs, half-wolves and wild wolves,
urgent and prompting, testing the savor of the meat he ate,
thirsting for the water he drank, scenting the wind with him,
listening with him and telling him the sounds made by the
wild life in the forest, dictating his moods, directing his
actions, lying down to sleep with him . . . and dreaming with
him and beyond him and becoming themselves the stuff of his
dreams. (62)

In these moments, Buck shares existence with the shades of earlier
creatures whose forms anticipate his own, but whose senses *are* his.
Their participation in his every act and perception multiplies his subjectivity and, insofar as he is just like them, dulls his distinction. The
passage literalizes the idea of the determining force of inheritance; and
the scene dramatizes a central notion of much evolutionary theory, that
individual beings count for little in the long run of a species history,
since it is the general type that survives and matters.

But it is nevertheless clear that London romanticizes Buck's relation to the ancestral shadows. The litany of their continuous presence
describes an intimacy and a profound identity between the dog and the
ancient creatures. They account for his love of the wilderness and are
the means by which he is enlisted in the natural world as one of its elements, related to the forest in the same mystical way as he is to them.
The spectral scene puts Buck into direct contact with his aboriginal
self, and thus allows him the ideal Western wilderness experience.

Here, under the banner of literary naturalism, we find again the
narrative of return to the most fundamental levels of being that the old
frontier journey had promised and that the Klondike offered once
again. The Alaskan gold fields, London seems to argue, are where the
purest life thrives, without relation to civilization. In *The Call of the
Wild*, as in many of London's Klondike stories, the terms of naturalism
and of Western romanticism collide and yet host each other. A representative moment occurs when Buck meets an actual wolf and finds
that he is able to befriend this brute version of himself. As he runs with
the newly acquired comrade, described as his "wood brother," the instincts
of ancient eras flood Buck's memory: "Old memories were coming upon
him fast, and he was stirring to them as of old he stirred to the realities

of which they were the shadows. He had done this thing before, some-where in that other and dimly remembered world, and he was doing it again, now, running free in the open, the unpacked earth underfoot, the wide sky overhead" (76).

The lyricism of Buck's evolution, like the mystery that London ascribes to the environment, competes effectively with his scientific vocabulary to dominate the book's tone. But the ideational framework of the novel is supported by both modes, and whether London is speak-ing as a naturalist or as a romantic Westerner, his vision of the wilder-ness is of an ideal, primitive, "White Silence," to use the title of another Klondike story. This title condenses the color of the story's landscape and the skin shade of its central characters, for whom the emptiness of the snowfields mirrors both the raw possibility of the Alaskan frontier and the fierce silence of its unevolved constitution. The values of regeneration that the Klondike fiction articulates are values for the white, hard-working characters whom nature—that is, London—favors. His science is a strange blend of romantic mysticism and evolu-tionary theory that concentrates nature into a deadly morass, best encountered with a mind oriented toward other realms and times other than the material present.

IF LONDON WAS UNSUCCESSFUL in his efforts to construct the narrative of *The Call of the Wild* in terms of the material implications of biologi-cal reality, he did manage to portray the environment and society of the Alaskan goldfields in a way that avoided some of the anxieties of Norris's Westerns. London's frontier characters move about in the wilderness that he had experienced in the Klondike, a genuinely rough and highly uncomfortable scene that, to be endured, demanded patience and intelligence as well as physical and psychological strength.

Norris's brief assignments in South Africa and Cuba to report on the Boer uprising and the Spanish-American war were the closest events in his life to any sort of frontier experience, and it might be argued that he found the materials for his Westerns in those environ-ments as much as he did in California. The ironic tones that expressed Norris's ambivalence about the belated frontier culture of the1890s, as evidenced in the Western stories discussed in the chapter 5 and in *McTeague*, resulted in an often simulated and "literary" West. London's work, by contrast, has little of that ironic play and is not so preoccupied with representation itself as an issue as to challenge his efforts at hard-core realism.

Norris's concerns with aesthetics and London's with materialism go a long way to account for these differences. London's interest in the working man and his overt socialist politics were not as dominant at the time he wrote "The Wisdom of the Trail" and *The Call of the Wild* as they had been before he went to Alaska. But the residual effects of those interests, added to his intense and idiosyncratic brand of evolutionism, put a demand on his fiction to fill the space of the Western scene with substantial, material dynamics of character and environment. But the theories and polemics that overtly controlled his perceptions compromised his efforts to construct a replica of these dimensions. Rather than a stark, material place, the Klondike becomes an extended analysis, a topographical argument.[21] Far from being depicted as a field of being in its own right, nature, following a distinctly romantic tradition, absorbs and reflects the ideas and emotions of a narrating sensibility.

London's Klondike fictions, like Norris's Westerns, used the frontier as an image of primitiveness in which to elaborate ideas about modernity. The contrast provided clarity, but, more important, the quality of rawness in the frontier image did the rhetorical work of naturalizing whatever the text's attitude toward modernity was. Serving as the mark of originary, proper being, the frontier made everything that was not a part of it appear belated, compromised, and unnatural—except the author's own understanding of the differences between the originary and the synthetic. This perspective was sanctioned by what Norris and London each thought was his affinity for the old West, and, like Boone and Lewis, they appointed themselves spokesmen for it. For London, the bodily connection to the physiology of the Klondike frontier reinforced his self-identification as an inheritor of a heroic westernist subjectivity. Norris, more distanced from the material terrain of natural landscapes, saw himself as a part of the West by virtue of his familiarity with local language and custom. For both of them, however, the iconic image of the frontier worked to gloss their authorial attitudes as natural. And its legendary, elemental vitalism metonymically pointed to the literary vitalism they both so fiercely desired to produce.

JACK LONDON'S NOVELS dramatize ideas that seem to systematize and theorize what might otherwise appear as an incoherent social fabric and, in Henry James's phrase, "a world of wanton fable." *Martin Eden*, published in 1909, presents an awkward, working-class San Franciscan who is introduced to a circle of glamorous socialites and intellectuals. The aesthetic objects and theoretical paradigms that occupy their attention begin to dramatically influence Eden's speech and self-representation shortly after his introduction. Converted, to a degree, to the styles and discourses of an elite social class, Eden nevertheless demonstrates for London the dynamics of class difference and of intellectual debate current in the fin-de-siècle Western city.

The Berkeley-trained Morses are both embarrassed by and drawn to Martin Eden, the representative of romantic labor—in this case, labor of the sea rather than of the ranch, but a working-class Westerner nevertheless—whose environment and milieu are passing in the long run of cultural survival. But rather than let Eden's type slip in to the hazy past or become material for nostalgia and pity, London takes him through a rigorous course of social and intellectual development that strengthens him beyond the bourgeois capabilities represented by the Morses.

Eden's energy and ability in acquiring intellectual knowledge are self-generated; but they are boosted by what the novel presents as his great advantage over the Morses, his experience. He knows life, both working life and the social life of the crowd. This knowledge equips him with a capacity for practical critical analysis that eventually leads him to abhor the hot-house intellectualism that initially confuses and fascinates him. The highbrow discourses of the Morse family are finally treated as images of linguistic specialization that have no functional relation to social dynamics beyond the parlor or ballroom. Eden's authenticity and experience, by contrast, indicate that he possesses the elusive "life," the presumably unmediated, unconventional spontaneity of Norris's Western heroes. Although he loses this quality in the smoke of love and bourgeois social glamor, he regains it in the end, doubled with self-consciousness.

Eden's great inspiration, which lifts him beyond the fumbling difficulties of social climbing, comes with his discovery of Herbert Spencer's

First Principles. The novel's descriptions of Spencer's theories are offered
in a breathless, excited fashion that mimics Eden's eager consumption
of them. He is so impressed with the arguments of *First Principles* that
he takes them on as informing ideas for his own intellectual and social
development. Soon he is systematizing everything he sees and hears
according to Spencer's themes. Rather than training his mind to an
ideally Spencerian heterogeneity through reflective and patient mental
operations, however, Eden is converted from an initially brutish working-class character into a stick figure of the most driven Nietzschean
individualism. His critique of socialism makes it plain that London had
fairly well passed through that stage of his political life by the time he
wrote the novel. The celebration of Eden's strength and genuineness
depend heavily, however, on his characterization as a lower-class sailor,
one of the masses. His drive to learn and to write are aspects of a naturally capable person whose starting conditions are London's testimony
to what he construes as the independence of natural intelligence. The
Morses, on the other hand, are presented as agents of bourgeois decadence, too weak and conventional to take full advantage of the knowledge readily available to them.

In bringing Eden through this career, the novel goes a long way to
sustain his favored position as representative of the quintessentially real
and the quick of Western life. But his extensive engagement in books
and ideas brings him deep into contact with the vocabularies and intellectual discourses of the time: Eden and the characters Norton, Strawn-
Hamilton, Perry, Kreis, Brissenden, and Judge Blount mouth the issues
at stake in and the vocabularies of monism, socialism, spiritualism,
"psychology," and democratic individualism. This display does not so
much conduct an argument to its conclusion as it reviews the options
available to Martin Eden for informing ideologies of his own thought
and behavior. Initially he does not take their measure in terms of their
experiential plausibility but in terms of their discursive power—in
effect their poetic persuasiveness. London's final choice of arch individualism as Eden's pocket philosophy attempts to recuperate some of the
authenticity and integrity of his unrehearsed, untheorized self, since it
stresses spontaneity and unsystematic responding to the world. But
such individualism is as much a program as any of the others, and the
spontaneous, disinterested experience central to it becomes ever more

elusive as a representable element in Eden's character. He emerges on the other end of his attraction to the Morses with his unconventional vitality supposedly intact, bolstered now with the power of ideas; but the self-consciousness that they provoke and the impulse to theorize leave Eden constituted entirely by reflections and abstractions, never simply "himself."

London makes an effort to curb these romantic turns, though, by presenting the reflections and abstractions that make up Eden's mind as polemical thoughts and arguments rather than as dark nights of the soul. *Martin Eden* is preeminently a novel of ideas: characters wear their ideologies like costumes and conduct long arguments about their relative advantages. Surrounded by a smorgasbord of fin-de-siècle intellectual discourses, the argument for individualism stands in relief as the novel's most weighted and favored mode. But its aspect is coarse, hard, ruthless in its driven need. The romantic individualism of midcentury poetry and fiction is flattened in an odd hybrid of scientific and metaphysical revisions. Whitman's multisignificant leaves of grass are turned into metaphors of evolutionary becoming, as Eden explains to Ruth: "The grass is more beautiful to me now that I know why it is grass, and all the hidden chemistry of sun and rain and earth that makes it become grass. Why there is romance in the life-history of any grass, yes and adventure, too. The very thought of it stirs me. When I think of the play of force and matter, and all the tremendous struggle of it, I feel as if I could write an epic on the grass."[22]

Martin Eden's aesthetic sensibility here is given not as an idiosyncratic set of desires and talents but as a form of knowledge available through science and theory. The allusion to Whitman recalls the poet's elaborate celebration of individualism, but London takes the possessive, voyeuristic superiority of Whitman's vision and affirms the power of the transcendental subject to appropriate persons and objects that enter into his sight.[23] It is the individualism of the superman that caps Eden's intellectual development.

London's revisions of mid-nineteenth-century romanticism include as well a more systematic version of Edgar Allan Poe's "Eureka" in Eden's Spencerian text, "Ephemera." These, as well as various loosely articulated allusions to Emerson and Thoreau, are worked into his theories of militant individualism as the marks of the evolutionary survivor. But all such efforts in *Martin Eden* to schematize romanticism recede, finally, back into their original forms with fewer revisions than the novel seems overtly to propose.

Nevertheless, Eden has remarkable powers of visualization that give him an advantage over the others. Clear and detailed scenes from his past emerge into consciousness, and these aid him in contemplating and categorizing situations in the present. When Arthur Morse introduces him to his sister, the sound of his own name, "Mr. Eden," sets off a chain of images, memories of other moments in his life when he was addressed by his name. The images are rich in detail, and his memory at moments like this becomes variously "a vast camera obscura" (560), "a kaleidoscope" (567), a "flashing, dazzling palimpsest of imagery" (695); it makes him feel he is "gazing into a kinetoscope"(678).

The intense clarity of these visions is both illuminating and distracting, since they catch him off guard, often in the middle of conversations and social situations, with the effect of retarding his responses to the scene at hand and further distancing him from the people who already consider him an outsider. But the direct perceptions and acute feelings which the memory-images initially stimulate are compromised by the elaborate aesthetic designs that increasingly draw his attention. This appreciation accumulates to such a degree that Eden begins to conceive of his present activities as pictures as well. Remembering himself as a "youthful hoodlum" who followed the behaviors of the crowd, his vision suddenly shifts to another image of himself:

> The stiff-rim and the square-cut vanished, being replaced by
> milder garments; the toughness went out of the face, the
> hardness out of the eyes; and the face . . . was irradiated from
> an inner life of communion with beauty and knowledge. The
> apparition was very like his present self, and, as he regarded it,
> he noted the student-lamp by which it was illuminated, and
> the book over which it pored. He glanced at the title and read,
> "The Science of Aesthetics." Next, he entered into the
> apparition, and himself went on reading "The Science of
> Aesthetics." (793)

Seeing himself in a picture, Eden follows the conventions of pictorial composition to construct an appealingly romantic image of a student reading late into the night. While the title "The Science of Aesthetics" seems to be taken from an 1872 study by Henry Noble Day,[24] it is highly suggestive of Spencer's philosophical vocabulary and his method of schematizing emotional as well as intellectual experience into categories of analysis, or conventions. Eden's intense self-consciousness in this "vision," the recognizable type by which he images himself, and the currency of the argument that the book propounds, all conspire to portray him as a conventionally minded thinker, especially in his most romantic moments. In trying to make his character transcend the conventional by posing him in such supposedly peculiar moods, London calls on images readily available in late-nineteenth-century American intellectual and artistic culture.

What London may be said to effect through the figure of Martin Eden as writer is an account of his own efforts to paint these visions that flashed unsummoned in the mirror of his mind. Ekphrasis becomes one of London's rhetorical modes in the story, as his repeated verbal representations of visual art forms, including the "pictures" of Eden's memory-visions, attempt to compensate for the mediated, belated nature of his medium throughout—language. Eden discovers that his ability to express—to paint—these visions is precisely the achievement of the great writers whose works he studies. Eden "saw noble and beautiful visions," but, like a dog, "he could only wine and bark" (637). At the same time, "he had a basic love of reality that compelled him to write about things he knew" (638). The real expression of what he sees can be accomplished only through study, through the acquisition of knowledge—general, European knowledge—which he tropes as a chartroom through which one is led by a teacher who can only point out the markers, not generate the matter charted.

Following the course of his own metaphor, Eden sets out, after an extended period of reading, on an expedition to the Solomon Islands with a treasure-hunting schooner. His adventure is productive of several essays and poems, although the practical purpose of the trip is to find treasures. The two practices of writing and searching are mutually productive, and they come to substitute for each other in such a way that writing appears as a search for treasure and a version of the "pearl-diving" of Eden's essays. The realism that he seeks in the expression of his richest thoughts is something to be achieved after a process of mining the sea.

McTeague's adventure in the Panamint, searching for gold, and Eden's in the south seas for pearls and treasure, are both fictional expeditions that set out from an overly civilized San Francisco to a yet-wild frontier that can be tapped for wealth and personal regeneration. But these mining processes are equally metaphorical for the essence, the real, the "treasure" of deep meaning in expression. The literary function that such mining serves, though, compromises in advance the spontaneity, the discreteness, and acute realism of the Western venture. In the middle of the effort to coin the truth in words, McTeague and Eden move through the phases of their brutelike "natures," as if contact with true West had brought them into contact with the most basic, animal level of self. But the civilized world coaxes the brute into emergence as well—in the case of McTeague to greed and murder, in the case of Eden to fascist individualism and suicide. The naturalist character in the American West is evidently both the servant of an evolutionary ideology and the hero of a belatedly romantic adventure.

Chapter 7

Stephen Crane's Literary Tourism

*This man has been reading dime novels, and he thinks
he's right out in the middle of it—the shootin' and
stabbin' and all. . . . It isn't different there even—not in
these days. But he thinks he's right in the middle of hell.*
      —STEPHEN CRANE *"The Blue Hotel"* (1898)

THROUGH THE WINTER AND spring of 1895, Stephen Crane traveled in
the West as a roving correspondent for Irving Bacheller's newspaper
syndicate. From Nebraska to Mexico, he reported on what has been
referred to in critical commentary as the "last of the authentic and tur-
bulent West."[1] It is doubtful that Crane himself saw the West in this
way, for his representations of it treat notions of authenticity with a
good deal of self-referential irony. Turbulence as a style of action has a
place in his textual West, but it is as often a matter of awkwardness in
manners and ethics as it is of violent physical exchange. But whatever
forms turbulence takes in Crane's Westerns, its dominant feature is its
containment—its boundedness and the social controls that finally
frame it within a very closely studied intersection of time and space.

For all of the irony that Crane so interestingly produced in his literary snapshots of Western regional life, this quality of confinement
simultaneously provokes a sense of nostalgia for the kinds of action and
the manners he imagined to have been characteristic of an earlier
Western lifestyle. Pictured as receding farther into the horizon of the
past with every social exchange, Crane's portraits take up what might

be called a habitual nostalgia in Euro-American accounts of the West. Thus, like Norris and London, Crane inflects his naturalism with an acutely romantic tone. But unlike them, Crane was very much a visitor to the West. Not the least important implication of his New Jersey background was the sense of mobility that it meant for him in relation to the West and westernism. For all of his attraction to adventure, romance, and wars, he could always go "home," to a place where such a thing as regional identity was so taken for granted as not to be a topic of discourse. And he could take his leave of the West without having to account for himself for doing so.

A child of the suburban and rural environs of New York City, Crane's knowledge of the West had come mostly from literary representations. His sense of the frontier tended to begin with rather schematic situations, and much of his writing on the West, journalistic as well as fictional, is organized by cartoonlike binary relations between wilderness and civilization, open and closed societies, and so on, however much the effect of his work was to complicate these very oppositions.

Crane grew up in a devout Methodist household. His father was a minister, and his mother was the daughter of a minister. But the family was as bookish as it was pious. Both his parents wrote for religious publications, and his father founded a school whose curriculum he shaped to his own ideas. Although Crane clearly followed his parents' literary inclinations, he seems to have distanced himself from most of what they stood for. Getting away to the "wilderness" of New York City, where he first worked as a professional writer, and to the American West, can be understood in part as efforts to find more dramatic and exotic environments than New Jersey and upstate New York religious communities offered.[2]

He was largely self-educated: his college career was brief and unremarkable, with a semester at Lafayette College in Easton, Pennsylvania, in 1890 and another at Syracuse University in 1891. Rather than study, he wrote newspaper reports—for the New York *Tribune* while at Syracuse and for his brother Townley's news bureau at Asbury Park during the summers. In this work Crane already positions himself as a writer with an affection for the life of the streets, hotels, and newspaper offices, as if these were fundamentally different from the more conventionally "literary" materials offered in his college English courses.

In these early journalistic exercises, Crane wrote about people of other classes and social milieus: prostitutes, criminals, and wealthy socialites. This interest in societies other than his own early on prompted his penchant for literary tourism, for watching and sketching strangers from a distance, fascinated with the terms and meanings of their differences. From the start, his writing demonstrates a particular interest in the sordid and the scandalous. His articles on high society, for example, were full of gossip, and the crime reports turned up every detail to suggest the danger and grime of criminal underworlds.

Later, living in New York, Crane watched the street life and poverty of the Bowery at close hand. But he was not just "touring" in the Bowery, even though his more well-known writings from this time are titled "Experiments." He shared the poverty of the bums, stood in bread lines with them, slept in flophouses. The editors of the most recent volumes of his correspondence nevertheless assert that he "never formulated convictions about the causes of social injustice. His aesthetic aim was to set forth reality as objectively as possible, and he considered preaching 'fatal to art in literature.' "[3] Given his apparent affinity for irony, this might be true, but the regular attention to poverty and to squalor in Crane's work involved more than a cynical, lurid, or aesthetic interest in "realism." While Crane's attention may have often shifted in the New York City sketches from the larger picture of social conditions and the structures of urban life to minute details of clothing and facial expression in his characters, these shifts do not mean that his interest was in some final and ineluctable way aesthetic at the expense of the social.

In any case, his reporting from Mexico during the 1895 trip gives both a fairly explicit sense of his politically articulate perception of the city of Mexico and a fairly explicit critique of the exoticizing views of Mexico held or projected by most American tourists, and presumably by writers whose orientations were largely aesthetic. The former is evident in "The Mexican Lower Classes," the latter in "Stephen Crane in Mexico." None of this means, however, that the content of those perceptions was thoroughly mapped out or without contradiction. The intention on Crane's part to give representation to the larger, international social picture is obvious, but the development of his logic is not utterly viable. He concludes his observations about the differences between Rockefeller and Huntington on the one hand and poor Mexican peasants on the other by declaring first a kind of moral egalitarianism between them. This shifts to a sense of moral superiority on the part of the author, and, implicitly on the part of the peasants as well in comparison to the great businessmen. He ends the discussion by describing his perception that "their faces have . . . a certain lack of pain . . . I can feel the superiority of their contentment."[4]

Crane was also aware of the debates over the public domain, and his writing speaks very much to the questions implied in Turner's argument about the future of everyday life in the West. Thus, while his position as tourist allowed for a certain openness and a comic tone in fictional representations of Western life in the1890s, his sense of the gradual easternization of the region included a view of the future in terms of the forms of civilization with which he was most familiar. His desert towns and plains landscapes are sketched with a patina of darkness that announces the already operative mechanisms of the stable social orders and exchanges that would come with the development of the West. In this sense, his tourism is arguably not strictly a matter of aesthetic consumerism in relation to a foreign culture, but is inflected with an active and critical social sensibility. His sense of the West as a not-quite-completed sector of mainstream U.S. civilization allowed him to identify with the region to that extent; and the romantic notes in his Eastern literature thus speak to a wishfulness rampant with contradictions.

The fiction that emerged from his experience of the 1895 tour dramatizes the idea of the end of the West in terms of a naturalist perspective inflected with irony, comedy, and nostalgic romanticism in the portrayal of frontier character and community. From "A Man and Some Others" to "The Bride Comes to Yellow Sky" and "Twelve O'Clock," Crane sketched the West as a zone still edged with mystery, but not the mystery of an uncharted territory. Rather, the mystique of his West is in its unmapped sociality that fostered liminal perceptions and self-conscious actions. In Crane's hands, the Western turns sociological, so that it is not a story of land, or "wild" life, but of a curiously half-formed culture.

Four of the finest works in this series, "The Blue Hotel," "The Bride Comes to Yellow Sky," "Moonlight on the Snow," and "One Dash—

Horses" deploy Crane's much-noted fictional impressionism to thematize the confusions of regional culture in the post-Turner West. In addition, his sometimes parodic representations of supposedly typical Western life in these works convey the awkwardness of the moment and of the strangely half-coded situation.[5] In making his characters aware of their own images and perceptions, Crane intensifies the self-consciousness evident in Norris's characters to such a degree that identity and behavior become topics of discussion and analysis among the stories' personnel. At the same time, plot presents a contest of plots that offer competing sets of expectations and actions.

Like Norris, Crane represents the end of the American West in the tones of literary naturalism that seem to shut down any notions of open-ended horizons or of romantic regeneration in the Western setting. "The Blue Hotel," "The Bride Comes to Yellow Sky," and "Moonlight on the Snow" evoke a sense of sadness and loss, even as they satirize the human figures that anachronistically voice and act out the central ideas of the "old West." Crane does not script this loss as an emptying out of meaning in the styles of Western life; rather, he expresses it in the prevailing sense that these meanings and styles cannot be reproduced. His stories seem to pose a set of questions about whether or not Western style can be revised amid the general social developments of the time so that it will include domesticity and specification without effectively disappearing.

Doubts about the possibilities for such meaningful revision are registered in terms of temporal limitation as well as spatial claustrophobia, and what remains of the "passing West" is framed as a rarefied, and thus more highly valued, cultural commodity. The horizon of Western landscape presents a familiar image of opportunity and possibility, but the image is openly compromised by its signification of social responsibility in "The Bride Comes to Yellow Sky"; of the claustrophobia imposed by a snowstorm in "The Blue Hotel"; and of real-estate speculation in "Moonlight on the Snow." Elements of the old codes inevitably remain, and Crane effectively stages their inappropriateness. At the same time, however, he treats other aspects of those codes as if they were current and still useful. Questions fill the air, and the thin characters are gradually inflated with dimension as they wonder what to expect, what to think of themselves, what to say and do in a region without a coherent ethos.

"THE BRIDE COMES to Yellow Sky," like several of Norris's Western sketches, is organized by a fragile opposition between East and West, in which the two directions are so interdependent for their respective meanings that their division becomes quite tenuous. The absorption of the West by an Eastern cultural agenda is imaged at the outset of the story, as the train carrying Jack Potter and his new bride flies westward from San Antonio on the way to Yellow Sky. Viewed from the windows of the fast-moving parlor car, the dry landscape, with its mesquite and cactus, is "sweeping into the east," sucked into the vortex of modernity indicated by the speeding train.

The contrast posed in the story's allegory between the domestication of male anarchy in the figure of the married Jack Potter and the clumsy continuation of it in the figure of the gunfighter Scratchy Wilson makes the latter's lifestyle appear all the more fantastical, however appropriate it may once have been. In the tradition of Yellow Sky, Potter is the only character who can effectively neutralize Wilson; and his ability to do this derives from the same authority that his figure elicits from the calmer townspeople. But Potter has upset this tentative balance on which his character as Western hero depends by going East, to a city, to get married; and by bringing his bride back to Yellow Sky.

In many ways the more fraught contrast of Eastern and Western modalities in the story appears in the confrontation between the bride and Wilson. The heavily coded image of Wilson bears all the insignia of the Wild West, the violence, lust for adventure, rough speech and manners common to popular conceptions of frontier character. In all of this, he presents a precisely antithetical figure to Mrs. Potter, whose dress and comportment advertise her position as a model of civilization. But Wilson's New York shirt and New England-style boots betray the reach of Eastern influence in the commodities of daily life in Yellow Sky; and the bride's gentleness is itself a form of power for her, in that it expresses the newly important ethics of domesticity and regularity in the West, as elsewhere. In the Eastern details of Wilson's apparel and the power of the bride's manners, the antithetical relation between them weakens, and the emblems of regional difference that they might have once provided are thus qualified and confused.

The figure of the bride loosens another familiar framing of the basic dichotomy, that which contrasts feminine civilization and masculine frontier. The bride disturbs this opposition by bringing with her the phallic power of progress, demonstrated less in Western expansion at the end of the century than in the vertical erections of city architecture and the consolidated municipal and corporate energies that they commonly represent. The bride's person serves as a site where the ideologies of East and West, of civil order and free-sprung liberation in the New World forest, meet. Once she has arrived in Yellow Sky as representative of her husband, she is positioned at the apex of the two cultural environments, in a sense transcending both but effecting a face-off between them.

The bride's peculiar presence as a neat, well-pressed woman at the tough marshall's side is the center of a series of oppositions that reverberates beyond and back to her as emblem of civilization in the frontier. This action is epitomized in the face-to-face encounter between her and Wilson that arrests the usual recognition between East and West in which difference is established.[6] Her "plain, underclass countenance . . . drawn in placid, almost emotionless lines," her seeming emptiness as well as her silence, presents less a character than a screen; neither Wilson nor Mrs. Potter recognizes the other, nor offers any signals of communication.

Surprised by the bride's sudden appearance and finding her thus incomprehensible, Wilson recoils from her and is thrown back on his own devices. The limits of his knowledge and perspective quickly reshape his character from that of a wild man to "a simple child of the earlier plains." But his retreat simultaneously suggests a sudden maturation, as he puts away the guns and shuffles off, in recognition of his inappropriateness. Marking his retreat with the famous "funnel-shaped tracks in the heavy sand," Wilson draws an image of the passing of time and of the viability of his type. Thus demoralized, he is simply another citizen, tamed by the culture of Potter and the bride which challenges him more effectively than the gunfight he expects to find.

Not only does the bride's presence impose a new kind of authority on Yellow Sky, but her power of intimidation is bolstered by the sense the story seems to offer that the mysteries and dangers of San Antonio include her, as she stands "face to face" with Potter, presumably luring him, like the city does, into transgressing "social hedges" established by Yellow Sky.

HER EFFECTS, LIKE THOSE of her city on him, are phrased in language once reserved for elements of a more remote, disorganized West: "Face to face with this girl in San Antonio, and spurred by his impulse, he had gone headlong over all the social hedges. At San Antonio he was like a man hidden in the dark. A knife to sever any friendly duty, any form, was easy to his hand in that remote city. But the hour of Yellow Sky—the hour of daylight—was approaching" (789). Recalling the grim jungle of New York in Crane's *Maggie, A Girl of the Streets* and other works, San Antonio's density is the setting for a kind of anonymous violence and anarchy once reserved for narratives of the wild frontier. San Antonio is as dangerous as the riskiest areas of Comanche country that once stretched from the Arkansas River to the Rio Grande. If the contrast between city and country in "The Bride Comes to Yellow Sky" reverses for the moment the usual relation of frontier life to the dominant culture so that the frontier appears the more tame and passive location, it is only because the West is slower to receive the currents of urban and industrial dynamism that will eventually overtake it. For the meantime, it retains a quaintly comical and somewhat appealing ignorance of what the narrative perspective displays in its larger panorama. While Potter can act in San Antonio like some sort of urban guerrilla in relation to proper social form, he will not match Scratchy Wilson's cowboy violence on the streets of Yellow Sky. So it is a moment when the West is just beginning to "grow up" that Crane imagines in his story, before the grid of mean and dangerous cities are imposed on it and after its older forms of violence have been recognized as inappropriate. Yellow Sky is drawn in a shrinking space and a pinched bit of time that momentarily preserve its naivete. As Potter contemplates the "crime" he has just committed in San Antonio by marrying, he imagines the responses of his fellow citizens, for "he was bringing his bride before an innocent and unsuspecting community."

The defamiliarizing effect of the bride's presence and the shock of recognition that it initiates in Wilson alienates her from readers as much as it does from the other characters in the story. Nevertheless, her opacity has the peculiar effect of acquiring the story's perspective, for all that the fiction seems, at least initially, to be about Potter's psychological experience. As point of view, she stipulates the reader's vision of the story's materials, such that one sees with her, even if one cannot know her well enough to understand her, or to think as she thinks. The visible face offered to view in the central encounter is the horrified face of Wilson, grimacing in response to the woman. In this sense, it is Wilson who is the spectacle, the strange but perhaps entertaining creature whose social place and regional identity are unsettled and marginal. In this condition, Crane's exhausted gunslinger maintains his traditional aspect of living on the edge, outside of civil norms and, rather than simply serving as a caricature of outdated behavior, enacts a version of what will become a long tradition in American narrative, the myth of the last Western.

One can experience from the bride's perspective the sadness, not so much of Scratchy's rejection but of the anachronistic difference of his type in the necessary flood of civilization, and this has some romantic value. But Scratchy's situation also positions him as a generic naturalist brute, driven by "forces" that he cannot know, much less understand. His violence and his ridiculous demands for action from Potter and the other townspeople in the story express the elusive psychical and biological "drives" that feature centrally in the typically lower-class subjectivity of the brute, and at the same time, these drives describe his identity as a cowboy without a frontier. For the brute personality, the drives are in many ways the effects of the processes of urban civilization, as they are for many of Zola's characters. For the cowboy, they are the last outlets of a passing wild life. The two sets of sources and functions of the brutish drives are merged just as the regions that properly represent them are.

As FIGURES IN AN allegory, the characters of "The Bride Comes to Yellow Sky" appear at first to be mere pencil sketches, the stick figures of a melodrama, with barely more dimension than the tracks left by Scratchy Wilson's boots in the sand. Similarly, the figures that Crane draws for "The Blue Hotel" appear initially like ciphers put into play in a series of exchanges that tell another story about the stiffness and awkwardness of social relations in the post-Turner West. In their emptiness, these cipher-characters have little agency and are born along by events that unfold by a seemingly ineluctable logic. The opening section of the story employs a series of passive verb forms that make the players look as if they are receiving more than effecting the story's actions. The only one among them who seems to have any powers of initiative is the hotel keeper, Scully, who, on meeting the train, "work[ed] his seductions" on the others, "performed the marvel of catching" them as customers, and "practically made them prisoners" (799–800). But for all of his entrepreneurial manipulations, Scully is as swept along as the rest by the strange engine of effects soon to follow in his hotel.

Furthering their apparent insignificance, the story withholds most of the other characters' names so that for much of the plot, they function as stock types. The "Easterner" is revealed as Mr. Blanc about one quarter of the way through the narrative, after having been involved in much dialogue and action; the cowboy is not identified as "Bill" until the fight scene in section six; and "the Swede" is never given a less generic label. Scully's son is named "Johnnie," and, like his father, is a very slight sketch of an immigrant on the Nebraska plains.

Once the grounds of the story are laid, the figures are put into play with an implicit hierarchy operating among them: Scully sets the rules of the house; the Swede, the largest and loudest of them all, is next in importance; Johnnie follows as chief antagonist of the Swede; the Easterner is deferred to by everyone, although his contributions are minimal; the cowboy is last of the men in order of intelligence and personal power; and finally the women of Scully's household make only a cameo appearance at the end of the fight scene. Once the initial moves are made among these characters, the story plays out a series of exchanges selected from what seems to be a carefully limited store of possibilities to conclude with the Swede's death.[7]

The card games featured at some of the major turning points of "The Blue Hotel" reflect the story's formulaic procedures and its deployment of stock actions according to conventional patterns. The card games and Crane's coarse stylistic restraints emphasize the almost prefabricated manner of the story and lend a sense that the outcome of the game, like the direction of the narrative, will be determined by the generic limitations, or ruled possibilities, placed upon it. The metaphor suggests not only the limitations of a modern Western world but of Crane's fictional language, as limited in its imaginary reach and stylistic inventions as the world that it presumably represents. At the same time, "The Blue Hotel," like "The Bride Comes to Yellow Sky," is about the frustration of the familiar structures of iconic Western narrative.[8]

The lack of apparent agency in the events that push them would suggest that no predictable conclusion can be forecast, since, however conventional the story's arrangements, their logic is befuddled and difficult to read.

The opposition of East and West in "The Blue Hotel" is a conceptual more than an experiential one, although it shares with "The Bride Comes to Yellow Sky" a sharp interest in the psychology of westernism in its overwhelming contact with modernity. The East here is not so much indicated in the person of the dignified but somewhat cowardly Easterner, Mr. Blanc; rather, it is the figure of the Swede that constitutes the "other" to the frontier environment. The Swede's problem is that he has no real experience of the West. All he knows comes from hearsay, and worse; as the intelligent Easterner observes, "it seems to me this man has been reading dime novels, and he thinks he's right out in the middle of it—the shootin' and stabbin' and all" (809).

The plot set in motion by the Swede's paranoid imagination is thus superimposed on the tale of "The Blue Hotel" by the stock of Western stories circulating in Crane's time out of the publishing house of Beadle and Adam. The illusory West that the Swede stubbornly perceives absorbs him totally, and it might be justifiably said that he becomes the agent of his own classic Western death, at the same time that dime novels constitute his agency.

Upstairs in the hotel, Pat Scully attempts to distract the Swede from his hallucinations by showing him photographs of his children—real people who are members of an ordinary, respectable family, not of a wild West show. But the Swede is not interested; his watch is kept "on the gloom in the rear" of the room, full of paranoiac expectations. Scully's attempt to point to the real in the photographs only makes the scene more uncanny, in that the figures in the pictures, despite their ordinariness and familiarity, seem remote, whereas the Swede, gone far afield into his madness, seems entirely present. Scully's pictures extend the story's realism into the dimension of the hyperreal, which is ironically more distant from realism than the situation at hand; for the pictures have very little to do with Scully's pressing duty to dispell the fiction that is operating in a very real way to the detriment of peace in his house.

Scully's attempt to clean his house of fictional westernism suggests an assumption of a plain and ordinary—precisely a familiar—scene functioning in the West, a civilized mode that, like the presence of the bride in Yellow Sky and the gently-mannered narrator at Bunt's side in Norris's "The Passing of Cock-eye Blacklock," organizes the once wild and natural into predictable patterns. Thus the stories emerge in relatively conventional forms, not only in the ways they are constructed but in what they represent. Crane's "Blue Hotel" demonstrates the loss of distinction between things traditionally understood as Western and Eastern in the demonstratively literary and psychotically stylized modes of the "Western" that the Swede perceives, and in the ordinariness that registers realism in the civilized patterns of Western family life.

The much analyzed concluding section of the story subverts this whole process, however, by changing the terms of action such that, belatedly, Johnnie is represented as having actually cheated. The Easterner reveals this fact and offers an analysis of the event that seems to bear the affirmation of the story's narrating voice. Johnnie's cheating, he explains, initiated a series of movements in which they all collaborated. If they are implicated in Johnnie's deception, either by knowing of it and not challenging him along with the Swede, or by assuming that the Swede is imagining things but not taking it upon themselves to investigate the situation, then they are all moral accessories to Johnnie's act and to the Swede's death. This, together with the intensity of the Swede's fiction-designed vision, suggests that the West— even though, as Blanc reminds us, this is only Nebraska, and thus only relatively the West—is still the home of wildness, riskiness, and danger.

In fact, the Swede has been killed by the gambler simply because he is irritating, and the gambler goes to jail for only three years in recompense for the murder. In response to the Easterner's elaborate theory of collaboration, a more or less conventionally civil way to perceive human relations, the cowboy gets the last word of the story. His "Well, I didn't do anything, did I?" reaffirms the anarchy of Western culture and psychology, even as the question betrays his self-consciousness and recognition of himself as one among others, possibly responsible for something he still does not quite understand. The ambiguity of perception in the story, as in its closing question, precludes any stable sense of accomplished domesticity in a now lost West. The romance and the mystery remain, not only in the psychology of Western character but in the tilting and unreliable codes of behavior.

The limitations of fictional schemes and their nevertheless palpable relations to actual behavior are not only issues raised in the story's rhetorical design, but they feature as central themes for the characters to discuss. In the process of these discussions, the figures in the Palace Hotel accumulate more substance than their initial, cipherlike status affords them. But the single figure in "The Blue Hotel" to be given a full history and psychic depth is the gambler who slaughters the obnoxious Swede just before the story's closure. This figure, the one who knows best how to work the materials of the game, is the one who displays the most sensitivity, the most reality. He is also the coldest, the most powerful character, who has no qualms in effecting what he perceives as the need for the Swede to die: "There was a great tumult, and then was seen a long blade in the hand of the gambler. It shot forward, and a human body, this citadel of virtue, wisdom, power, was pierced as easily as if it had been a melon" (826).

The control that the gambler takes of the situation and the way he determines its direction give his character a rather surprising authority in comparison with the others. His profession, we are told, keeps him always living on the edge of common life, but in control whenever he encounters it. As a master of risk and experimentation, he is never genuinely accepted by those whose fates he might, at will, overtake. Ever situated on the outside, he watches, carefully, and plays the elements of the controlled scenario toward the best conclusion for himself from among those that the game itself will allow.

With these attributes, the gambler lends himself for comparison with the writer—if not Crane himself then the type in general, who works the terms of a code, a game or genre the guidelines of which, although established at the outset, can guarantee no particular conclusion. In a sense the gamblers of "The Blue Hotel" and "Moonlight on the Snow" experiment in the constructions of situations in the manner prescribed by Zola for the naturalist writer in "The Experimental Novel." The elements are chosen from a "stock of available reality";[9] Crane's gamblers deploy certain conventions of action and statement in an effort to control or manage their situations, to achieve some autonomy while blocking the artist's control. These conventions, like those of the card game, are limited, and can be put to use only in specific configurations or they will have little if any effect. Crane's stories play with such schematic narrative designs, which not only mimic the

formulaic patterns of dime novels but of Western romanticism generally. Even with such codified procedures, however, the outcome of the
game still will be to some degree indeterminable.

Although this prescription is patently idealistic in its assumptions
about the possibilities of uninterested literary realism, it does point to a
way in which literary language can, in many ways, develop a life of its
own, as it were, separate from its author's conscious purposes. In this
latter sense the gambler's game initiates the experimental novel; like
that kind of fiction, the game takes its own course and cannot guarantee any particular outcome. To use Zola's words, the talent of each man,
like that of the writer, lies in "the originality, the inventiveness, the
genius"[10] to function somewhere between the biologically and socially
determined situation and the individual sentiment.

IN 1899 CRANE PRODUCED yet another lyrically titled Western, "Moonlight on the Snow." The name does not refer to any natural image in
the story but to the ice-cold irony in the disposition of its central character, another of Crane's elegant and violent gamblers. An exceedingly
smooth talker with impeccable manners and the marks of a fine education, Tom Larpent is "handsome and distinguished and—a devil. A
devil as cold as the moonlight upon the ice" (844). But the diabolical
traits in his persona are not evil in any profound sense; they serve as
antidotes to his gentlemanly profile and constitute part of his charm,
not only as a Western character but as a darkly charismatic figure in the
society of the town of War Post. As the most polished member of his
community, Larpent represents and speaks for the rest of it, even so far
as to direct the procedures of his own hanging. The others are willing to
follow his instructions because he is one of them, a brother in crime
during the twilight days of the rough old West.

Like the gambler of "The Blue Hotel," this one has more dimension than anyone else in the story, and his sensitivity to the thoughts of
others, together with his magnificent confidence, allows him a great
deal of latitude among them. His interest in the proper rhetorical and
procedural forms, his recognition of the irony in the situation, as well as
his professional engagement in creative experimentation once again
tend to identify the gambler with the writer. Larpent's perceptiveness
and his central location within the various scenes of the tale grant him

a privileged point of view, in terms of what he sees as well as the information that his view offers to readers. The comic irony that sustains Crane's attitude toward the material of "Moonlight on the Snow" is a key aspect of Larpent's personality. The disjuncture between that attitude and the far more limited understanding of the rest of the townspeople levels the story's personnel, such that the gambler, and, by implication, the narrating voice of the story, have far more authority and believability than the others.

Nevertheless, Larpent is located very much among them, particularly as he is subject to their extremely awkward and fumbling justice. In this position of being simultaneously above and among the coarser figures of his community, Larpent demonstrates a common aspect of the realist-naturalist writer's relationship to the characters of a fictional text. Larpent's ambivalence in being interested enough to study, understand, and represent his fellows, on the one hand, and, on the other, sufficiently disinterested to condescend to them in mild amusement is mirrored by their responses to him—that is, by their absolutely simultaneous efforts to respect and bring him down, to save him and to condemn him to death. The brutally realistic gambler and the equally, however suddenly, practical townspeople face each other in a comical drama that mixes the romantic affections of brotherhood with the colder relationships that presumably come with modernity and the "development" of the West.

This ambivalence in the voice of the narrator and in the attitude of the central character also expresses the complexity of Crane's tone generally in his representations of the fin-de-siècle West. The comical strains of "Moonlight on the Snow" and the other Westerns are possible for him in part because, as a visitor to the region and to this kind of regional realism, Crane, in a sense, can appreciate at his ease the comedy he perceives. By contrast, for Norris and London issues of personal as well as regional identity are too much at stake in the representation of the West for such comic tones to predominate.

At the same time, however, Crane inflects his comic images with the darker, more cynical tones peculiar to his Northeastern regional realism. The grim, enclosed spaces and tightly circumscribed possibilities for action of the New York City sketches that he wrote just prior to the tour of the West offer classically Zolaesque images of urban life. If for Crane the future of the West is something like the San Antonio of "The Bride Comes to Yellow Sky," which shares some important features with the New York of "An Experiment in Misery" and "The Men in the Storm," then that future includes the looming walls and social fences of his own overly determined region.

But the other future that Crane seems to envision in "Moonlight on the Snow" is the suburbanization of the West, in some ways a more deadening prospect, for this scheme produces the tamest landscape of all. The city, as "The Bride Comes to Yellow Sky" suggests, looks as wild and dangerous as the frontier was once supposed to have been. But Crane's representation of suburban life in *The Monster*, for example, projects a hideously tame, intensely conventional place whose restrictive social codes produce mean and small-minded citizens. Similarly dim visions of suburban landscapes and societies are imagined for Crane's fumbling and comical, quasi-open West. The effects of an anticipated suburbanization in "Moonlight on the Snow" include the alienation of land as a commodity. He points to the shift from geographical to suburban neighborhood designations in the names of the various sections of landscape: "The stern and lonely buttes were given titles like grim veterans awarded tawdry patents of nobility—Cedar Mountain, Red Cliffs, Lookout Peak" (837). The accompanying adjustments to human relations mean the authority of violence is to be replaced with the authority of zoning codes. Crane's nostalgia for the Western lifestyle is evident in his representation of the older relations, which, however much sustained by the rougher forms of authority, allow for a more intimate communication and a sharing of communal identity.

The townspeople's reasons for wanting to hang the gambler for the murder he has committed, and thereby to initiate a form of institutionalized justice in War Post, have nothing to do with morality as such but rather with cashing in on what is understood by everyone as the region's ongoing real-estate boom. In perhaps one of the most explicit fictional references among naturalist Westerns of the 1890s to the idea of the West as an evenly parceled, titled zone, Crane constructs the larger problem of his story as the development of the region by Eastern corporate interests, which he ironically designates, in a kind of faux-allegory, as "the angel of peace." The name points to what Crane sees as the missionizing impulses of U.S. consumer culture and the homogenizing effects of its progress across the West.

When the stagecoach roars into War Post at the moment of the hanging, bearing a new minister from the East and his beautiful, fainting daughter (along with four other newcomers), the idea of the angelic visitation is illustrated in more specific terms. Both of these characters speak for civility, justice, and domesticity; they are, the story facetiously suggests, angels of peace. "The inhabitants of War Post peered at the windows of the coach and saw therein six pale, horror-stricken faces." The driver, in response to the passengers' demands to know what is going on, replies that "he s'posed anybody could see, less'n they were blind." Seen through the frame of the coach window, the two groups make their mutual recognitions, as if by posing as pictures for each other. They are all extremely typed characters, and this fact, together with the predictable nature of their dialogue, enhances the sense that the story is dramatizing the reductive conventions and caricatures on which Crane thought interregional perception was commonly dependent.

Once again, he uses the devices of the dime-novel Western to show how absurd such images are; and at the same time, the story seems to suggest that their real currency in popular discourse is not simply wrong, but productive of the types and actions for which the conventions have set up expectations. At Larpent's direct admission of guilt for the murder of which he is to be hung, the newly arrived minister "waved his arms in a gesture of terror and despair and tottered toward the coach; the young lady fainted; the two little girls wailed." The ministerial gesture, the drooping and crying, all fulfill certain stereotypes of Eastern sensitivity and emotional excess for the people of War Post. This behavior in turn provokes a movement among some of the citizens to kill the coach driver "for trundling up his old omnibus and dumping out upon their ordinary lynching party such a load of tears and inexperience and sentimental argument." The Westerners thus act in accordance with the Easterners' shocked expectations. This comedy concludes with all of the figures frozen together into a kind of panorama: "There were the two children, their angelic faces turned toward the sky, weeping . . . there was the beautiful form of the young lady prostrate in the dust of the road, with her trembling father bending over her; on the steps sat Larpent . . . with a derisive smile, while from time to time he turned his head in the rope to make a forked-tongued remark" (845).

The development of the West, Crane suggests, is conducted by such people as the minister and his daughter, with their projects for a new morality; but he seems to enlist them as participants in the real-estate scramble, their pieties the tools of landscape as much as spirit conversion. The capitalist momentum that includes them is, on the surface of things, a less esoteric factor of social change than its allegorical name would suggest, but one that operates with the same ubiquity and ineluctable force.[11]

The narrative of settlement in Crane's story has gained such momentum, has become such a familiar pattern, that it has made possible the transformation of Western ground into the commodity of an industry. The angel has drawn the changes, and they are followed by a domestic Eastern culture of greenhorns handing over money that War Post, with its continuously unstable daily life, is not getting. Crane's description of this process in the opening of the story emphasizes the contrast between the broad expanse of the landscape and the boundaries being imposed upon it not by actual buildings and fences so much as by maps, signs, and plans. It is as if the text of modernity had been superimposed on the old, iconic setting, in such a way that the materiality of the West as *Ding an sich* is set in opposition to the mere signifiers that indicate what is coming. The more real of these two fields, the story seems to argue, is the latter. At the same time, though, Crane's comical portraits of the dregs of the romantic West suggest that, rather than a metamorphosis from unmediated to mediated landscape, this one results from a transition of the value of Western land within one symbolic order to its value within another.

RATHER THAN ACTING ON any genuine impulses, the characters in "Moonlight on the Snow" have become part of a literary scene that "through some bewildering inner power of its own . . . had carried out of the hands of its inaugurators and was marching along like a great drama and they were only the spectators" (845). This explanation appears to construct a kind of literary determinism, as the characters act out parts that might have been imagined for them from the stock materials of any dime novel or sentimental romance. This, then, is added to the force of capitalist enterprise that seems to be directing the larger historical momentum that the story dramatizes.

The framing of the group portraits in the would-be hanging scene, together with the panoramic freeze framing of the scene as a whole, concoct miniature versions of the framing of War Post generally; that is, the fencing in of the town by cultural difference and by its own anachronistic economic habits, so that it becomes a kind of remnant, interesting and surprising to the Easterners who witness it.

"Moonlight on the Snow" concludes with the arrival of Jack Potter and Scratchy Wilson, now his deputy, who have a warrant for Larpent's arrest, not for the murder in question but for grand larceny in another case. The closing comment issues from the bartender, who dismisses this charge with the question, "what in hell does grand larceny amount to?" Thus this newly installed spokesman for the town indicates that its attitude toward law and justice has not changed. It is still a vigilante society and will determine its own law. But the story's conclusion underscores the anachronisms in traditional War Post behavior and identity, and the refusal of adaptation that will spell out its demise.

In spite of Crane's vivid pictures of the domestication of the frontier, the West is still presumed to be a field where an individual character can exercise his desires and shape the environment to suit them. The content of those desires seems to produce the sort of anarchy that comes with capitalist competition and with the changes in behavior and character design that foster success in that particular kind of contest. The violence of old War Post is in the process of being supplanted by this alternate social and economic system, the heart of which is as designed and performed as the types and systems of the Swede's literary imagination. Thus, in Crane's rendering of the tension between these two lifestyles, he maintains some degree of affection for the old West at the same time as he demonstrates its absurdity; and the schemes that replace it are made to appear rank substitutes, perhaps more inauthentic than the scenes they overtake but not profoundly different.

To some extent the naturalist polemics about the pressures of social development and environment on character and culture fulfills the "settlement" half of the archetypal Boone story in all of Crane's Westerns. But it is important to note that, as much as the environment is cast as the governing element in these works, it is clear that the relationships Crane draws among landscapes, economies, communities, and persons are in several ways mutual—even as these relations are played out under the banner of the closed frontier. Thus the pressures of social evolution as Crane conceives of them and as Turner had charted them in the figure of the historical palimpsest make the end of the West an ethical reality. But the new forms of behavior begin to revise not only the communal environment, as in "The Bride Comes to Yellow Sky"; they effect as well the meanings and dispositions of landscape itself, as evidenced in the real-estate logic that operates in "Moonlight on the Snow."

THE LACK OF AN edge of difference in Crane's fictional Nebraska and Texas is somewhat counterbalanced in some of the earlier stories that emerged from the 1895 journey and were set south of the border in an exotic and mysterious Mexico. Mexico is a desert wasteland where shadows and hidden forms work on and are produced in the minds of his American protagonists. The danger level is high, and it is real, unlike the dregs of violent living that provide the central problems for the Westerns set in the U.S. proper. Here the types of Scratchy Wilson and Tom Larpent, as well as those imagined by the Swede, are active and, according to Crane's fictional account of Mexican culture, appropriately placed. In this sense, Crane manages to revise the old story formula so that what emerges are very contained studies of a North-South tension that has replaced the defunct East-West opposition. For if the sort of wildness that the Mexican stories exhibit is the stuff of which dreams of the lost West to the north are made, it is a wildness that still has a future.

Crane's images of Mexicans appear to follow familiar patterns of representation of Indians by Euro-Americans in the north since the seventeenth century. The locals of "One Dash—Horses" seem too primitive to adapt, develop, or survive in partnership with their more advanced neighbors; and they are cast as either gentle, in some cases noble, servants, or unregenerate savages. The lack of particularities in these portraits would suggest a palpable insensitivity on Crane's part toward cultural difference; but such images are of a piece with the scarce attention to preliminary detail in the construction of any of his literary characters. Although the Mexicans, unlike their northern counterparts, acquire no complexity or self-consciousness through the course of events, and although their coarseness is presented as a matter of primitiveness, Crane does not assume this is a necessary, inevitable lack of development. The Mexicans have as much opportunity to make decisions and control events as do any of Crane's characters, but that, of course, is not saying much. As in his other works, environment is all, and that includes the environments produced by entrenched hierarchies of racial and class difference.

The North American protagonists of "One Dash—Horses," like those of the other Mexican stories, are as trapped as the local characters are in the dramatic situations that contain them. These situations are constructed as the likely products of social relations between members of different cultural groups, that is between Mexicans and whites. But finally, the white protagonists have more opportunity to get in and out of the situations they visit, as Crane does in his own literary tourism. The adventure that remains in Mexico is, for them, exhilarating and elucidating; bearing a close resemblance to entertainment, it offers them a chance to run the test of the wilderness at a moment when no such thing is possible in *el Norte*.

Differences of class, race, and culture are palpable in this adventure; and a hair's breadth of difference separates racist, Anglocentric representation from a realist's respect for the exigencies of social fact in Crane's writing. The result is a nearly liminal tone, which seems caught between one inclination to produce social commentary and another to indulge an aesthetic impulse, as if the two could not work together. Unlike the northern stories, these resist commenting on issues of social relations and manners in the dramas of cultural difference in Mexico. Such meditations are reserved for Crane's journalism, where they are spelled out in explicit terms, such that U.S. travelers appear snobbish, ignorant, and exploitative of the culture they visit. But in the fiction, Mexican characters are marginal and servile, either toward the northern protagonists themselves or toward the narrative economies that wind the adventures around those protagonists' interests and destinies.

"One Dash—Horses," which Crane wrote shortly after he returned to New York in the summer of 1895, features a traveling New Yorker named Richardson, his faithful servant José, and a fat Mexican with his band of five or six drunken, violent friends. The action consists simply of two hostile encounters between the American and the Mexicans; and between these events Crane stages a chase. Both encounters involve a good deal of intense staring and very little language. The parties are armed, but no shooting occurs; no one is killed or even wounded. The intensity of the first encounter is deflated by the arrival of a group of women who distract the bandits from their apparent intentions to either rob or kill Richardson and José. The spell is broken in the second encounter by the authority of the Mexican army, which intercedes in the exchange on Richardson's behalf under the illusion that he is an influential and wealthy gringo. The space between the threat of gunfire and actual gunfire, which is commonly crossed in a moment in dime novel Westerns, is not crossed at all in these exchanges. The prolonged threat of violence is never relieved by the catharsis of shooting, and in the end the bad guys simply turn away.

In a sense, these two encounters seem to stage the drama, seen in "The Bride Comes to Yellow Sky" and "Moonlight on the Snow," of the influence of feminine power and civil authority on the wildness of outlaw characters. Indeed, these stories as well as "The Blue Hotel" are to a certain degree studies of what happens when nothing happens. "The Five White Mice," another Mexican tale in which the prelude to a showdown is extended over what appears to the protagonist a "silence of years," concludes in the same way, with the situation defused and not a single shot fired. In the strange moment that follows, voice tones and postures are hesitant and changeful, with characters suspended in perplexity. The story concludes with a spare summary of what is already evident: "Nothing had happened."

Richardson's first encounter with the Mexicans in "One Dash—Horses" leaves him sleepless and highly sensitive to sounds and shadows. The retreat of the Mexicans from the second encounter and from what might have been a deadly exchange of ammunition leaves a trail of ambiguity, reminiscent of the after-battle tones of *The Red Badge of Courage*. With the sudden appearance of the *rurales*, Richardson is as surprised as his enemies are to see that the expected clash will not occur.

The strangely inconclusive conclusions of "One Dash—Horses" and "The Five White Mice" crowd the details of the narratives into self-conscious moments; these moments serve to analyze as well as critique the conventions of frontier violence staged in the dime novels and still current in the culture at large through mythic notions of the dangers of the wilderness. In a sense, Crane's distended time mimics real time more accurately than does the generic textual version, and the fear of impending violence is plausibly rendered in large part by not being cleanly resolved, by the unanswered questions and ambiguous airs that saturate the stories' scenes at the moments of closure.

But this realism is strongly countered by the stories' immensely self-conscious language style. Richardson's perspective, for instance, fixes on images instead of events: "the crimson serape of his servant flamed amid the dusk of the mesquite"; "a beam of firelight fell across the trail"; "the houses . . . were for the most part like tombs in their white silence." Even in the moments of high fear during the first encounter with the bandits, Richardson's attention is drawn to the shape and texture of the blanket that hangs in the doorway of his room: "It was a vague form, black and unmoving. . . . As grim white sheets, the black and silver of coffins, all the panoply of death, affect us because of that which they hide, so this blanket . . . was to Richardson a horrible emblem, and a horrible thing in itself" (732, 737). The blanket has the same effect as the blank surface of the bride who comes to Yellow Sky, in that the meaning of what is behind it cannot quite be read. Richardson's own staring face, as he first views the Mexicans in the doorway, once again presents this opaque and blank image, its emptiness meticulously defined.

These are just a few of the many painterly images that Crane allows to collect through the course of the story, and their general effect is to coat the representation of the Mexican plains with an aesthetic patina and a distinctly gothic tone. They appear not to offer themselves up to metaphorical translation any more than the strange fixedness of Richardson's own gaze, which Crane insists is "not anything that could be interpreted" (735). These writerly constructions drain the element of realism and ironize the roughness of the setting by taking it into account in terms of Crane's signature impressionist aesthetics—in effect bringing the raw Mexican provinciality into the modernity of his artistic mode. But more than that, the literary self-consciousness of the text draws attention, as might be expected, to its status as representation, and this reflexivity of the rhetoric seems to meet that of the self-consciousness of Crane's Easterner sojourning in the West. Indeed it intensifies the performative qualities of character and action in his fictional account of the West and Mexico generally.

Crane's travels in Mexico may have provided authentic source material for these short stories, but his narrating perception in all of them has much in common with the point of view of the Swede in "The Blue Hotel": he orientalizes Mexican savagery to the same degree that the Swede "occidentalizes" the scene at Fort Romper. But for Crane to import an orientalist discourse into his representation of Mexican life is as much a matter of his drawing nostalgic and gothic westernism south of the border as it is of his practicing the habits of an ethnocentric imagination.

The Mexican characters here and in other stories are accorded the predictable panoply of evil attributes: they have snaky eyes, are called "greasers," and have a great talent for sneaking. Richardson's servant José "shadowed the master along the dimming trail in the fashion of an assassin." But the central trope of darkness in their images contributes to the difficulty of seeing and knowing that Crane finds so important to the psychology of danger with which his Westerns are often concerned. The "vibrating and threatening gloom" of "One Dash—Horses" is in many ways a Hawthornian gloom that exploits the ambiguity of spectral evidence in the construction of romantic character. Thus Crane's aesthetics of racism work to reconstruct a mysterious West in the southland and, in this effort at reenchantment, extend the desires of the U.S. frontier to a world where culture and character can be conceivably represented as unknown. The desires and problems of this kind of romance are multiple, and they are not confined to Crane.[12]

THE NEW WOMAN OF Yellow Sky and the trouble in the blue hotel, like the confusion at War Post and the fact that nothing happens in "One Dash—Horses," indicate the difficulty of fin-de-siècle polemics evident in the many questions concerning the status of representation itself in the United States and its relation to the historically or psychologically real. The regional categories of Crane's stories are sustained at the same time that their value for upholding difference is put into question, and the effect of Crane's critique is to emphasize not only the rhetoric in which these categories exist but to concoct an oddly gothic aesthetics in the scope of fin-de-siècle realism.

If things have become so mixed up in the relations of East to West and West to East that the once predictable signifiers no longer work to keep the two categories separate, then the recognition of the frontier as a product of culture—as the "beyond civilization" that civilization itself creates—is unavoidable. Representations of the West come to outline a scene whose face and texture are self-consciously composed from a store of conventional images, metaphors, and motifs. And yet this trend is itself part of the nostalgia and the romantic memorialization that Crane's Western conventions finally produced.

Chapter 8

Willa Cather and the Enchantment of Difference

Romance is the highest form of fiction, and it will never desert us. The sun, sea, God himself are romanticists. Ibsens and Zolas are great, but they are temporary.
—WILLA CATHER, *The World and the Parish*

WILLA CATHER'S WEST WAS in many ways less dramatic and far less glamorous than the West of her contemporaries Norris, London, and Crane. Nebraska in 1883, when her family moved there, was a dusty plain where immigrants from the Eastern states and Europe worked hard to make a minimally comfortable living. Almost half of the population had either been born in Europe or were the children of European parents, and most of them were engaged in agricultural labor of some form. Population densities a few years later ranged from over three hundred people per square mile in eastern counties to less than one in the Western part of the state.[1] Cather's biographer James Woodress recounts that Cather's aunt, uncle, and grandparents had homesteaded in south-central Nebraska ten years before her immediate family arrived; and they experienced many of the severe physical and financial difficulties described in stories of Western settlement, as well as some of the successes. They lived in sod-covered dugouts and had to deal with grasshopper plagues and prairie fires during their first years. They survived all of this and eventually led the organization of the area's scattered population into a township, Catherton. In this relatively brief phase of their lives, Cather's closest relatives participated in the transformation of isolated, colonial settlements to a reasonably well-composed civil life that promised a certain amount of social and economic security.[2]

When they first arrived, her own parents took up farming; but in less than two years, they moved to the town of Red Cloud, where her father became an insurance and real estate agent. Even though the family was no longer breaking sod on the prairie or trying to grow corn and livestock, their life in "town" was still fairly rough. Red Cloud was a hamlet on the Burlington Railroad line and was thus connected to other towns and commercial centers; but it had only one main street and about a dozen cross streets. There was little housing, and although a public school system was in place that seemed to serve Cather well, it was tiny. Her graduating class of three people was only the second group ever to finish Red Cloud High School.

Lincoln, when Cather moved there in 1890, "had a raw look about it" (64), as James Woodress describes it. Some of its population was still housed in dugouts. But it was developing quickly into a significant metropolis, with theaters, good restaurants, two important populist newspapers and the University of Nebraska, where Cather studied.[3] Like the University of California, the University of Nebraska was still quite small in 1890, with construction work underway that contrasted with the stateliness of its few finished buildings. It was only as old as Lincoln itself, dating from the late 1860s. According to Woodress, the student population was about three hundred. Life at the University was rich for Cather, full of stimulating professors and classmates; it served in the chronology of her career as a bridge between the harsher rural environment of Red Cloud and the metropolitan culture of the United States at the end of the century.

Cather did not describe herself as being deeply interested in the rural experience of frontier life, though that experience would become the central focus of much of her fiction. She liked life in the city, and it began for her with Lincoln. Later, moving to Pittsburgh and then to New York, she developed a distinctly urban identity. But the West as a landscape was a rich stimulant to Cather's imagination. Recollections of her first impressions of Nebraska, given from the vantage point of adulthood, are strange and compelling. They describe an encounter between subjectivity and landscape that seems overwhelming: "The

land was open range and there was almost no fencing. As we drove further and further out into the country I felt a good deal as if we had
come to the end of everything—it was a kind of erasure of personality."
Later she related, "I was little and homesick and lonely and my mother
was homesick and nobody paid any attention to us. So the country and
I had it out together and by the end of the first autumn the shaggy grass
country had gripped me with a passion that I have never been able to
shake. It has been the happiness and the curse of my life."[4]

The dichotomies introduced here between persona and terrain are
central to much of Cather's fiction, but the overpowering effects of
material environment are not of the sort projected by her contemporary naturalists. Cather's landscapes *move* her fictional personnel and
stimulate far more openly lyrical responses in them than Norris's,
London's, or Crane's generally do. Her narrators rarely treat these ven-
tures into romanticism with the critical irony we find in Norris and
London; they are themselves often as enraptured by prairie sunsets and
southwestern canyons as are the characters. As the passages above suggest, Cather's imaginative geographies are virtually characters themselves—hostile, challenging, seductive, even openly affectionate beings
who recognize in some fashion the presence of their witnesses.

Cather's experiences of life in Nebraska did not seem to generate
efforts on her part to establish or to articulate a particular, quintessential real of the West in fiction. And this point speaks to one of the great
differences between her work and that of her male contemporaries.
Cather's westernism is not shy about its romantic inclinations. One
finds in her work little of the anxiety that Norris, London, and Crane
betray over the return of a repressed lyricism. Cather is, on the contrary, overtly interested in the needs, desires, and memories that go into
the shaping and painting of landscapes. She does not hesitate to recognize the constitutive powers of romanticism, claiming at one point that
the "sun, sea, God himself are romanticists."[5] What Susan Rosowski
refers to as Cather's sense of the "dark mysteries" of human experience,
"inexplicable by ordinary rules of logic," are inscribed in her purple
fields and mountain sunsets.[6]

Although her terrains are given as entities that precede and stand
apart from their human witnesses, the very process of granting them
some kind of dialogic agency suggests the extent to which Cather

thought about landscapes as metaphors of human experience. Her anthropomorphisms strongly imply that what is important about nature is not that it is a force in its own right, but that it serves as a record for human subjects of their own histories with it, of their own entanglements with its textures and contours. The dominating role "Nebraska" takes in Cather's recollection of her first impressions only elicits an intention for her in some sense to overtake it, a process both frustrating and exhilarating. Thus she can read the remembered scene as inspiring and demonic at the same time, since its power to stimulate lies to a great extent in its status as record of the whole history of her engagement with it.

In all of these ways, Cather's understanding of her experience as a Westerner as well as her literary westernism differ from the other writers discussed in this book. To a certain degree, the differences point up the irony in that Cather's writing, given her particular life in the West, was so romantic. The temptation to theorize a substitution formation at work, in which the long and compelling literary traditions of a lyrical West stand in for a much more banal experience, is almost overwhelming. Norris, London, and Crane, each of whom as young men actually did enjoy a more adventuresome and aesthetically appealing engagement with the West, were much more invested in shaping their interpretations to a determinist framework.

But such a reading would push the dichotomy perhaps a bit too far, since Cather's work throughout her career invokes, tests, and measures naturalist concepts and respectfully exploits determinist limitations in the process of elaborating a surviving romance of the West. Simply put, her fiction, too, takes up many of the intellectual questions addressed in the stories of her male colleagues. Questions about the relative values of science and art as ways of knowing and representing experience; about the engines of biological, psychological, and particularly cultural development; and about the terms of U.S. and especially Western identity after the closing of the frontier constitute some of her novels' central concerns.

As a very young woman, Cather's intellectual interests had been directed mostly toward the sciences. In a lengthy and ambitious address given at her high school graduation, she defended "science and scientific investigation" as "the hope of our age." The speech relies extensively on a Spencerian vocabulary, referring to "all human history" as "an exodus from barbarism to civilization," with "superstition and investigation . . . contending for mastery." The competitions she describes here indicate that her reading had been somewhat conventional for her generation and social class, but it is already evident in the rich and exotic turns of language she uses to describe them that the "mystical and metaphysical" epistemologies she attributes to earlier ages and cultures are powerfully attractive to her.[7]

Eventually, as Woodress describes it, she came in fact to distrust science altogether as a way of knowing. At the University of Nebraska, she changed her program from medical studies to humanities early on. The set of questions surrounding the whole issue gets voiced in the thoughts of Godfrey St. Peter in *The Professor's House* as he speculates on the uses and abuses of Tom Outland's scientific legacy. In a classroom discussion, Cather has him lecture to a student: "No, Miller, I don't myself think much of science as a phase of human development. It has given us a lot of ingenious toys . . . but the fact is, the human mind, the individual mind has always been made more interesting by dwelling on the old riddles, even if it makes nothing of them."[8]

At the University of Nebraska, Cather spent much of her time studying literature, including French realism and American romanticism. Her tastes in literary language, evidenced by her own practice and critical commentary, actually sound very much like those of Howells and Norris when they declare the values of a realist literary style. As editor of the *Hesperian*, a campus literary journal, she favored, in her own words, "plain, unornamented language which anyone can interpret without the aid of a handbook of mythology or a dictionary of similes."[9] Cather's own fiction, of course, follows these principles faithfully. But her plain style is intended more as a democratic invitation to read than a vehicle, as in Howells and Norris, for gaining access to some stable, uncomplicated reality.

Her tastes for the psychology of literature, in consumption as well as production, are closer to Emerson's, as he articulated them in "The American Scholar" and "The Poet." At Lincoln she spent a year studying Emerson, Hawthorne, Ruskin, and Tennyson, and these seem to have left the greater impressions on her. Woodress writes that "Cather agreed perfectly with Hawthorne's view that a romance 'sins unpardon-

ably so far as it may swerve aside from the truth of the human heart' "
(108). The truth of the human heart for Cather would not be a still,
essential entity, but a movable, changeful thing. Indeed, her remarks
about the task of criticism echo the sensibility of Walter Pater: "A
critic's first instincts are the best because they are the truest."[10]

Cather's love of romance gets outrageous expression in her famous
statement that "romance is the highest form of fiction, and it will never
desert us. . . . Ibsens and Zolas are great, but they are temporary."[11] As
Woodress puts it, "She seldom had anything good to say about the work
of William Dean Howells, who led the battle for realism against the
romancers of the 1890's" (107). Although she was dismissive of the
work of Howells, Mark Twain, Hamlin Garland, Ambrose Bierce, and
other realists of her generation, she thought well of Norris's *McTeague*
and *Blix*[12] and devoted a great deal of thought to the fiction and poetry
of Stephen Crane, whom she met when he visited Nebraska in 1897.
"When I Knew Stephen Crane," written on the occasion of his death in
1902, recalls this visit in fictional form. In the piece Crane is a character who reads Edgar Allan Poe much of the time and appears about as
moody and mysterious. He is "a dark and silent figure, somber as Poe
himself."[13]

If Cather has romanticized Crane here, she was deeply critical of
his coarse realism in *War Is Kind* and *Active Service*. For the most part,
though, she found Crane and his work appealing and marked him as
"one of the first post-impressionists," particularly in his use of detail:
"He estimated it at its true worth—made it serve his purpose and felt
no further responsibility about it. . . . If he saw one thing in a landscape
that thrilled him, he put it on paper, but he never tried to make a faithful report of everything else in his field of vision, as if he were a consci-
entious salesman making out his expense account.[14] This comment,
offered as support for the idea that Crane was a postimpressionist *avant
la lettre*, evokes Cather's pleasure in the spin of perception at its first,
instinctive moment and in Crane's ability to play with this virtually
visual energy to his own ends. Cather's choice to find in the details of
his work a dedication to the aesthetics of perception rather than to the
literary ideology of naturalism and the idea of experience as having an
ineluctably material base reflects her own writerly inclinations.
Whether she was right is a question that Crane scholars have long

debated, but there is no reason to think that he was only a romanticist, or that realism and naturalism were his only media, any more than that Cather herself was only a romanticist of the American West. Hermione Lee notes that "Cather's writing would always arbitrate between realism and romance,"[15] and indeed her interests in the turns of perception and in the relations between subjectivity and landscape take her to the fonts of all three genres, even as the element of mystery emerges and reemerges as a chief feature of her work, particularly in the later novels.

A crucial feature of plot and character development in all of Cather's Western fiction is the moment at which a central figure not only sees and hears the landscape in an especially acute perception, but understands his or her own position within its contours. In these moments Cather is able to pay tribute both to the determining influences of local material environments and at the same time to the aesthetics of place as they take shape in the eye of the single viewer. In this way, she allows herself to enact both the romantic and naturalistic modes; but ultimately this simultaneity works to ensure that the value of place, in a poetic as well as social and material sense, is set by the human figure, who interprets both in relation to their desires. Thus the facticities of geography, class, and ethnicity, for instance, serve largely as stages—theatrical as well as chronological—for acting out the processes of overcoming limitation. The light pressure of determinism in Cather's work heralds the broader outcome of naturalism's encounter with Western romance, in which the romantic is inflected in important ways by the limiting effects of the other genre but nevertheless continues its seemingly endless career in American narrative.

Virtually all of Cather's novels give special emphasis to the dynamics of subjectivity and Western landscape; these relations are particularly telling in *The Professor's House* of 1925 and *Death Comes for the Archbishop* of 1927. In these novels, Cather produces certain characteristically—and at times problematically—natural, even supernatural, processes of identification and appropriation between environment and protagonists. The mystery of place in Norris's and London's work is connected with barely scrutable material forces, indifferent to human interests but understood in the framework of naturalist theory and its scientific orientations. Cather, on the other hand, enchants her landscapes with romantic mystery even as she evokes a fixed set of determined cultural and material facticities. In the end, her Western places image the aspirations for regeneration and self-fashioning that send her expeditionary and missionary characters to the West in the first place.

The displacement of indigenous communities that came with this process seems not to have registered much in the life of the family or, indeed, in Willa Cather's own range of concerns as an adult writer. Several Native and Mexican American figures turn up in her later fiction who serve as mediators between settlers and exotic landscapes in what Cather projects as dialogic processes of encounter. But although these "dialogues" demand an appealingly pragmatic address on the part of expeditionary and missionary figures toward the Other, they do not, after all, substantially recognize, or give representation to, the responses. Perhaps this lack instances one of Cather's central comments about communication between native and immigrant Americans: that it can be very difficult, if at all possible. This difficulty and the cultural differences it sustains are key to Cather's oddly simultaneous determinism and romanticism.

THE FIRST SENTENCE OF *The Professor's House* suggests that the story's trajectory will be toward the future rather than retrospective: "The moving was over and done." "The moving" refers, in the most local sense, to the St. Peter family's relocation to a newer, more modern residence in the town of Hamilton. In a more distant sense, it implies the whole history of Euro-American immigration and resettlement in the trans-Mississippi West. In fact, rather than looking ahead, the statement initiates the novel's profound preoccupation with the pasts that both forms of movement create. Professor St. Peter shapes the pasts as containable entities, stored in a vault of personal and cultural memory. His accounts of them, in the sense of both retellings and records of their value, are supplied by the material contents of memory, but their values multiply with every recollection, with each reinvestment of narrative meaning that the professor's reflections produce.

The house figures from the beginning of the novel as a central trope that Cather uses to picture what she imagines as the shifting terms of Western culture in the early twentieth century. A familiar westernist dichotomy is set up between home—as a circumscribed, interior place permeated by social ethics—and a particular kind of male

imagination—associated with individualistic, adventuring inclinations. But a key difference is sustained by St. Peter's identity as a professor, as academic interpreter of historical exploration and adventure
rather than actor in that drama. His armchair status is crucial to
Cather's portrait of him, even as his incessant desire to imaginatively
reconstruct the history of adventure virtually defines his subjectivity.

The old house, now abandoned except for the professor's study,
serves as vantage point for his musings on earlier explorations and
expeditions that are known to him largely through imagination and
interpretation. The adventures of his own life are few—his student
years in France, sabbaticals in Spain, trips to the Southwest and Mexico "on the trail of his adventurers" (16). But St. Peter's intellectual
and aesthetic sensibilities grant him a distanced understanding of the
Spanish conquistadors and a capacity to narrate their movements as
coherent chronologies.

The old house in all its disrepair is, in the professor's mind, infi-
nitely preferable to the family's sleek new residence. More than for any
substantial appeal of its own, the old place is better simply because he is
used to it and, at the moment, because everyone else has already abandoned it. At the point where the story opens, it has virtually no fur-
nishings; its only function is to provide the professor with a study. His
resistance to the new house is patently a resistance to the bourgeois,
middle-class banality that he and the narrator relentlessly associate
with his wife and daughters. Their interests and preoccupations are
understood as utterly representative of an urbane, Midwestern society
that indeed looks to the future for its promises of sophistication and
modernity. As the location of the family community, the new house—
and the downstairs of the older one in former days—prompts St. Peter
to think of the endless round of rituals, conversations, and social gestures in which he is obligated to participate. The systematic invasion of
his privacy by the tedium of the feminine domestic schedule is put in
direct contrast to what the professor construes as his "own," more idiosyncratic activities of researching and writing about the expeditions of
the Spaniards and Outland. Resonantly empty, the old house is a place
of refuge from the daily domestic scene and serves as a more or less
unencumbered vantage point from which St. Peter, in his welcome

aloneness, can engage in imaginative retrospection on his personal past and on continental history.

St. Peter's ambiguous attitude vis-à-vis domestic life is thus evident from the start. Cather intensifies his reactions to it in the curious metaphor of the female sewing forms that occupy his study and that are, emphatically, only forms. Referring to them with humor and fondness as "my ladies" and "my women" in conversation with the sewing woman Augusta, who finds his affection for them odd and inappropriate, St. Peter strongly implies that he likes them better than the more substantial women for whom they seem to substitute—the women in his family. The mute figures have been comfortable company for the obvious reasons that they do not talk back and they absorb whatever imaginary characteristics he projects onto their surfaces.

The feminine forms are rather too representative, however. The female characters with whom readers are strongly invited to associate them are pictured as almost equally wooden or empty. Although his daughter Kathleen has a certain vivacious, innocent appeal, she, like her more designing sister Rosamond, is swept up in the momentum of fashion and social life in the city of Hamilton. Their abysmally small-minded world reduces women to consumers and men to camp followers of feminine interests.

A key figure in St. Peter's memory is the late Tom Outland, a former student and a very romantic adventurer. As a perhaps too influential memory in the old house, Tom's absent presence keeps the professor emotionally and intellectually attached to activities and conversations of the past—to the mentoring relationship that holds the book's ethical and moral center, particularly in comparison with the banal and supercilious relationships associated with the St. Peter women. Tom's project had been field researches at the Cliff City, through which he connected himself powerfully with the ancient Anasazi civilization of the Southwest that passed into oblivion before the arrival of the Spaniards. With this project, Outland complicated the professor's colonialist historical sensibility and put himself in the position of mentor to his mentor.

The antique cliff village becomes one of the most important memory productions to emerge from St. Peter's study, as he edits Tom's diary and simultaneously recalls his student's almost secretive act of telling about it years ago: "It was on one of those rainy nights, before the fire in the dining-room, that Tom at last told the story he had always kept back" (155). In the privacy of the old house and with the professor as his sole company, Tom related the story of his stumbling upon the village and of its long-hidden, perfect form. The professor's house and the houses of the ancient pueblo share an exquisite privacy, a secret separateness that for a time preserves them from the comings and goings of society and history. In this remembered exchange, the two men enjoy their own domestic scene in the privileged comfort of the old house dining room, perhaps all the more so because that scene would not persist beyond the summer.

The pueblo's domestic order vanished ages ago and is only readable in the traces of archaeological evidence. Tom attempted, through his researches and experiences there, to reimagine and restore its strange vitality; but like the effort to recall and record those experiences in his diary, the effort to recall that past requires a good deal of creative interpretation and a composition, so to speak, that willfully leaves gaps and absences of information in place that will suggest that there is something more to know, something the belated imagination cannot reach. Like the old pueblo's domestic order, that of St. Peter and Outland will survive only in the traces of memory that later reconstruct it.

Outland is himself a vehicle to that ancient world, having maintained a closer personal connection to it than the professor does to the culture and events of the Spanish explorers. As Walter Benn Michaels argues in *Our America*, Outland claimed a curious kinship to the Cliff Dwellers.[16] He assumed an imaginative, spiritual affinity that, like the connections Whitman's speaker assumes with citizens of later generations in "Crossing Brooklyn Ferry," obliterates the differences of time and space that produce common history and identity. Recalling the time he approached the Cliff City on his return from Washington to report his findings and after discovering that Roddy Blake had sold the artifacts, Tom meditates on his relationship to the place and its former inhabitants:

> This was the first time I ever saw it as a whole. It all came
> together in my understanding, as a series of experiments do
> when you begin to see where they are leading. Something had

happened in me that made it possible for me to co-ordinate and simplify, and that process, going on in my mind, brought with it great happiness. It was possession. The excitement of my first discovery was a very pale feeling compared to this one. For me the mesa was no longer an adventure, but a religious emotion. I had read of filial piety in the Latin poets, and I knew that was what I felt for this place. It had formerly been mixed up with other motifs; but now that they were gone, I had my happiness unalloyed. (226–227)

Using a scientific method to arrive at a spiritual conclusion, Tom takes "possession" of the scene in ways that far surpass the short-sighted commercialism of Blake and the German collector Fechtig, and, by implication, the imperialist aggressions of the Spanish conquistadors. Possession, as Outland frames it here, is a matter of recognizing affinities, of finding a nonblood relationship that makes the Cliff Dwellers his spiritual ancestors.

Cather focuses Outland's attention closely on the elegance of the Cliff City's design. Its formal perfection and stillness make it appear to him first as a sculpture: "It all hung together, seemed to have a kind of composition. . . . It was beautifully proportioned. . . . There was something symmetrical and powerful about the swell of the masonry. . . . It was more like sculpture than anything else" (179–180). The perfection of these lines and the comfort they afforded the Cliff Dwellers appeal to St. Peter's aesthetic sensibilities as well as to Tom's more rational ones. As Father Duchene, Tom's earlier teacher, interprets the culture of the Cliff to Roddy and Tom, he notes: "There is evidence on every hand that they lived for something more than food and shelter. They had an appreciation of comfort, and went even further than that. Their life, compared to that of our roving Navajos, must have been quite complex." Later he adds, "Wherever humanity has made that hardest of all starts and lifted itself out of mere brutality, is a sacred spot. Your people were cut off here without the influence of example or emulation, with no incentive but some natural yearning for order and security. They built themselves into this mesa and humanized it" (197, 199).

Isolated from trading, war, migration, and other activities that brought different, contemporary communities into close contact with one another, "your people," as Duchene refers to the Cliff Dwellers, developed their own comforts and domestic designs, concentrating on aesthetic effects so much as to produce a comprehensive, rich spiritual life. These qualities invite comparison once again to the domestic order, aesthetic pleasures and imaginative inclinations of Professor St. Peter. Through Outland, he recognizes and finds affinity with the ancient people and their city. All of them are connected to each other by a kinship of the spirit, as Christopher Nealon has argued.[17] What they share is a special, cultivated civility that Cather sets against the homogeneity and dull materialism of Washington and of the St. Peter women, Fechtig, and even Blake, all of whom distance themselves from primitiveness in lurching toward future gains, operating as if there were no deep past or wilderness to remember.

The modernity these individuals represent, Cather seems to suggest, can be equated with consumerism and greed; but most important, it lacks the dimension of memory. The intelligence and retrospection of St. Peter, Outland, and the Anasazi, by contrast, allows them to interpret, influence, and in some sense manage the primitiveness and savagery still associated in European America with the West—even perhaps to be somewhat affected by it, particularly in the area of spirituality and romantic imagining of self. Thus St. Peter has interpretive power over the coarseness, roughness, lack of comfort, and wildness, so to speak, of the Spanish explorers and adventurers, just as he and Outland have over the Cliff Dwellers.

As emblems of very early American culture, the Cliff Dwellers appeal to St. Peter's affections for "culture" in the highbrow sense of the term. But in their status as spiritual ancestors, the indigenous people double as the primitive originators of his and Outland's own cultivation. The refinement of both men allows them to recognize and interpret the Anasazi, who in their time were able to recognize and interpret what was primitive and "hardest of all" in their environment through their own cultivated, aesthetic perceptiveness. Just as the Cliff Dwellers managed savagery and primitiveness with reason and beauty, Outland managed their relative primitiveness by studying it and by implicitly comparing the "composition" of their city to the Aeneid. In this gesture, he claimed the Cliff City as a text, an epic of his own national origins.

Such intelligent domesticity can both connect itself to and distance itself from the primitive. In his writings on his visionary experience at the Cliff City, in which he realizes the power of his feeling of possession, Outland contrasts himself to the explorers. Nevertheless, we are strongly invited to understand him, as St. Peter does, as a kind of modern version of the continental adventurer. Outland's modern difference from the Spaniards, as from the Anasazi, is of course crucial. It is not precisely an identification but a nonblood heredity that allows for difference and for the possibility of interpretation. At the farthest point in time, Professor St. Peter, in his robe and his pipe, interprets the now dead Tom. Again the claim of sophistication is important: without St. Peter's learned status, he would simply identify with Tom and thus lose his ability to "read" him.

What ambivalences lie in these complex relationships of difference and affinity, of reading and being read? Can the professor's imagination, intellect, and research make up for this life he desires to share with Tom and the Spanish adventurers? Can the power of interpretation substitute adequately for the action of being with them? The newhouse, the banal moment in cultural history, the awful family, all certainly figure in the book as influences to avoid—perhaps, to the extent possible, to escape from. Early in the novel we are told that St. Peter believes "a man can do anything if he wishes to enough." In his view "desire is creation, is the magical element in that process. If there were an instrument by which to measure desire, one could foretell achievement. He had once been able to measure it, roughly, just once, in his student Tom Outland—and he had foretold" (19–20).

If St. Peter had been able to measure Tom's desire, he had thereby foretold Tom's creation. Is creation, then, the product of desire so much so that the two become identical? If so, then does Cather, in creating this image of an imaginative intellectual who can recall the wild in such measuring, interpreting, narratizing ways produce a desire, an engine of desire, and an image of that engine, that can continuously recall the West, over and over again?

Perhaps, but this is apparently not enough, as the professor's brush with suicide near the end of the novel seems to imply. The last paragraph continues this ambivalent response to the present and to the banality of the middle-class scene in which his life is situated: "His temporary release from consciousness seemed to have been beneficial. He had let something go—and it was gone: something very precious, that he could not consciously have relinquished, probably. He doubted whether his family would ever realize that he was not the same man they had said good-bye to" (258). In representing him as having "let something go" during his moment of unconsciousness, Cather presumably cuts any attachment he might have to the family. With his distanced posture, he can "face with fortitude the Berengaria," the ship on which his family is returning from Europe, "and the future"—cut off from that present and living primarily in his interpretive recollections of the various primitive states he has "known."

Two years after publishing *The Professor's House*, Cather turned her attention once again to the Southwest. In *Death Comes for the Archbishop*,[18] her backward glance goes to the colonial frontier of mid-nineteenth-century New Mexico. Again "history" becomes a companion narrative to the fiction; and the fiction, as distanced, cultivated form, emerges as a reading and a reimagining of a once chaotic negotiation of differing beliefs, practices, and ideologies. As James Woodress explains in his biography of Cather, the material for the novel came from her researches into the life of Father Joseph Machebeuf, vicar general of the diocese of New Mexico in the mid-nineteenth century and assistant to Archbishop Jean Baptiste Lamy, who becomes the titular figure in her story. The process of interpreting this phase in the history of New Mexico is recapitulated in brief by the strategic narration of stories and anecdotes out of the Spanish and Pueblo past by the priests' various hosts and parishioners.

Like *The Professor's House*, this is the story of an earlier West the plot of which is generated by a dichotomy, in psychological, cultural, and geographical space, between comfort, civility, and cultivation and discomfort, roughness, and primitiveness. The blandness of social ambition and middle-class consumerism that contrast so starkly with aestheticism and high culture in the earlier novel is largely absent from *Death Comes for the Archbishop*. If that sensibility has any avatar here, it is in the shape of the Roman prelates of the Prologue, whose interests and activities revolve, we are subtly informed, around the accumulation and securing of power within the papal hierarchy.

The novel opens with a gathering in Rome of Vatican officials. But apart from the vague aura of decadent medieval Catholicism, the scene serves to introduce religion as a crucially influential concept in the novel. Cather will play with belief as a feature of character, of imperial and regional new world culture, and as a factor in the turns of individual and communal fates. Religion thus becomes the means of articulating relationships between subjects and places, as domestic architecture does in *The Professor's House*; and, likewise, it becomes the measuring discipline of civility and cultivation.

Again, aestheticism is closely associated with a fine, thoughtful, spiritual sensibility. Whatever counts for Cather as good art, music, and literature, like religion, is necessary fuel for cultivated civility, perhaps even constitutes it. These influences strengthen perceptions for the interpretation and management of coarser, more primitive styles of being. The boundaries become porous as the perceptions and criteria of self for those who do the interpreting come into intimate contact with those whom they read, but Cather sustains an exoticizing aura of difference even in these contacts. The narrative is elaborately interested in the methods, effects, and styles of hybridization between the highly cultivated and the primitive; but in the end Cather presents us with an imaginative projection of cultural identities that continue to be incomprehensible and "wild" to each other.

Cather takes her interests in the cultivated imagination to further limits in *Death Comes for the Archbishop* than she does in *The Professor's House*. Here she studies the various directions that such civility can take. The opening scene in the Sabine Hills shapes the cardinals' sophistication as a form of high-styled ignorance, at least of the geographical and cultural realities of the New World regions over which they have so much influence. And the series of decadent Spanish missionaries confirms this suspicion: Father Gallegos and Fray Balthazar represent the worst of the worst of Spanish colonial exploitation and personal decadence. But the novel turns its attention again and again to the elegance, balance, and comfort of Father Latour's domestic life in the still rough environment of Santa Fe, as if his household were not only a practical but an artistic achievement.

The story proposes, however, that aesthetic integrity is yet more than the harmony of rationalist form. In it reside the mysteries of human perception and imagination. To the extent that any of his parishioners is productive of such domestic beauty and harmony, they are more or less reflections of Latour's missionary success—not because

they imitate him, but because their quotidian styles, under his nurturing influence, bespeak their own imaginations, more richly self-
conscious than under previous cultural regimes.

Although Cather draws a line between decadent and productive
aestheticism, both are of enormous interest to her and absorb the
novel's attention with almost equal weight. Their distinct dimensions
emerge in contrast to each other. The privileged form for Cather's
investigations of the varieties of aestheticism is the garden. Virtually
every one of the religious figures has his own private garden that reflects
his persona. The elegant and highly landscaped terraces of the Spanish
cardinal's residence in the Sabine Hills is simply an extension of the
cardinal's high tastes and privileged access to beauty. Fray Balthazar's
garden exhibits his exploitation of the people of Acoma, its exotic
species brought in and maintained by their labor and its fruits reserved
for his private use. Father Jesus's garden, on the other hand, is a reflection of his modesty and sweetness, "full of domesticated cactus plants of
many varieties and great size (it seemed the Padre loved them)" (84)
and parrots, an affection for which he shares with the local Indians.

Bishop Latour's garden, laid out in a symmetrical pattern in hard-
baked, rough ground, is blooming and fruitful, connected by lines of
poplars and tamarisks to the church and school. His fruit trees, the
healthy products of cuttings brought from St. Louis by the nuns, are
reproduced in local Mexican gardens. The bishop's garden thus bears
the marks of his character in its beauty, its rational design and produc-
tivity, and in the way it mimics the missionary reach by extending from
his private space to the church and other gardens of the diocese.
Latour's cultivated self is extended to his garden and his diocese, where
the missionary project is to cultivate a lively, orthodox Christian faith
among the local population.

The work of gardening is thus a trope for "cultivating" New Mexico. The work of transforming the religions of the region overlaps with
the work of transforming aesthetics and work habits. Ways of thinking
and imagining are themselves at stake, and indeed missionary work is,
to some degree at least, aimed at the transformation of culture. Where
the Western missionary perceives that religious difference means there
is no culture, the trope of cultivation becomes more appropriate than

that of transformation. In either case, though, religious influence is a part of the larger umbrella of empire, which seeks to alter politics, language, even soil, in the project of transplanting European ways of being and knowing to North America.

But missionary "gardening" is not treated as a univocal practice in *Death Comes for the Archbishop.* The novel presents several different ways of conducting this work, and the gardens, reflecting their attendants, figure as opportunities for indulgence and exploitation as much as for inspiration and regeneration. How one gardens, to what ends, and for whose benefit are crucial questions. Thus the garden has the power of the house in *The Professor's House* to resonate far beyond its location in a given scene and to accumulate a sweeping range of literary values. The domestic world of Godfrey St. Peter functions not only as a safe haven for reflection and recollection; at times it seems potentially destructive of self and environment, since it signals the bourgeois suburbanization of the West, and since it invites too much reproduction of self, too much privacy and decadence. The gardens of *Death Comes for the Archbishop* present opportunities for the cultivation of beneficent but also of destructive and decadent lifestyles; they also recapitulate one of the oldest metaphors of the new world as a paradise for old Europe—the place that produces "Mother Eve."

The kind of garden one has measures one's ability, as a cultivated, civilized, relatively comfortable aesthete, to measure, interpret, and manage the primitive. As Father Latour approaches death, he directs the attention of the young priests who come to learn from him toward the difficulties endured by the early missionaries.

> A European could scarcely imagine such hardships. The old
> countries were worn to the shape of human life, made into an
> investiture, a sort of second body, for man. There the wild
> herbs and the wild fruits and the forest fungi were edible. The
> streams were sweet water, the trees afforded shade and shelter.
> But in the alkali deserts the water holes were poisonous, and
> the vegetation offered nothing to a starving man. Everything
> was dry, prickly, sharp; Spanish bayonet, juniper, greasewood,
> cactus; the lizard, the rattlesnake,—and man made cruel by a
> cruel life. (275–276)

The novel puts these obstructions and hardships in the way of the cultivated man from the start, when Father Latour finds his way through the harsh desert to Durango and back again to Santa Fe. He and his colleague are constantly in contact with what Cather constructs as primitiveness. But Cather takes several turns from the traditional Western narrative motif of individual against the wilderness, particularly, as Susan Rosowski argues in her 1986 *The Voyage Perilous*, in the shift of emphasis from a rationalist, Enlightenment mode of tracking and conquering physical space to a spiritual and symbolic one. Latour finds his way through the desert by praying and by keeping faith in the rectitude of his mission. In the first chapter, for instance, after getting lost in the desert's "geometrical nightmare," he locates himself, so to speak, by recognizing the cruciform shape of a juniper tree. He is still in his God's world, and with half an hour of devotion before the cruciform tree, Latour is refreshed. As Rosowski writes, "His actions contradict rational calculations"—the latter being central means for conquering the wilderness in iconic North American expeditionary narratives.[19]

But if it is true that, as Rosowski argues, Latour and Vaillant neglect worldly concerns, their pursuits of spiritual interests are conducted by means of an intense focus on the shapes, textures, and dimensions of the material world—of landscapes as well as domestic space. Latour's sensitivity to form accounts for a good deal of his delirium in the desert, as the multitude of triangular sand-hills and narrow cracks in the dry ground fill his eyes and overwhelm his consciousness. At the other end of the spectrum, Latour is capable of being powerfully moved by the prospect of beautiful mountain scenes and by the symmetries of his home and garden in Santa Fe.

Latour and Vaillant even gauge the successes and failures of their missionary project by the forms in which the tasks of daily life, including religious belief and ritual, are conducted. These forms at times satisfy and calm the priests' desires to convert, but just as often they are shockingly alien, even after the communities have long been exposed to Christian influence. Rather than demoralizing the missionaries, such arresting sights and stories stimulate their intellectual and aesthetic curiosities. In such presumably unscheduled interests, the novel proposes, lie the seeds of dialogue.

Latour and Vaillant are both pragmatists, ready to negotiate religious as well as cultural principles. And so they are treated as sympathetic converters who recognize the ineluctable differences of Indian lives and cultures. They recognize that they will not be able to transform these cultures with any degree of promise. To do so would require some basic, mutual comprehension between them and the local population; but Latour is convinced that "neither the white men nor the Mexicans in Santa Fe understood anything about Indian beliefs or the workings of the Indian mind" (133). The trader Zeb Orchard affirms this attitude for Latour, advising him that "The things they value most are worth nothing to us. They've got their own round of superstitions, and their minds will go round and round in the same old ruts till Judgment Day." Latour, the narrator tells us, "remarked that their veneration of old customs was a quality he liked in the Indians, and that it played a large part in his own religion." Orchard insists, however, that although the priest "might make good Catholics among the Indians . . . he would never separate them from their own beliefs" (135).

Earlier, Latour himself meditates on what to him is the virtually prehistoric state of the people of Acoma Pueblo: "Through all the centuries that his own part of the world had been changing like the sky at daybreak, this people had been fixed, increasing neither in numbers nor desires, rock-turtles on their rock. Something reptilian here, something that had endured by immobility, a kind of life out of reach, like the crustaceans in their armour" (103). The narrator carefully avoids confirming or denying such observations. Instead, the perception of ineluctable difference is simply displayed, as if, even in projecting a certain heroism in these missionary efforts, Cather were more acutely interested in imagining the impossibility of conversion. Latour's image of an unchangeable, entrenched aboriginality in the people and landscape of the West in a sense secures a reserve of difference from European influence, and, in doing so, implies an enduring difference between the Euro-American West and its eastern Other.

Father Latour and the narrator share a view of the local people as exotic and unadapting heathens, even when they are Catholic. Arriving at Los Ranchos de Taos, Latour is met by the boisterous and decadent Padre Martinez, who accompanies him to the church where the people of the village present an elaborate reception: "In his own

country all this would have been highly distasteful to Jean Marie
Latour. Here, these demonstrations seemed a part of the high colour
that was in the landscape and gardens, in the flaming cactus and the
gaudily decorated altars,—in the agonized Christs and dolorous Virgins
and the very human figures of the saints. He had already learned that
with this people religion was necessarily theatrical" (142). Local representations of saints, Christ, and the Virgin draw on a traditional Pueblo
pantheon as well as the passionate fanaticism of the *Penitentes*. The
results are just barely recognizable to Latour as the marks of his own
religion; in fact, the narrator's account of his gaze on scenes of local
Christianity strongly imply that the references of these performances,
the concepts and beliefs they celebrate, are indeed beyond his grasp.

Visiting the countryside outside of Taos with Padre Martinez, Latour
observes the mountainside that served as Popé's hideout during the
Pueblo uprising and which the narrator describes as "painted" by the
designs of aspen groves set against a dark, evergreen background, "like
symbols; serpentine, crescent, half-circles": "The mountain and its
ravines had been the seat of old religious ceremonies, honeycombed
with noiseless Indian life, the repository of Indian secrets, for many
centuries, the Padre remarked" (151). "The Padre remarked" comes as
something of a surprise, since the scene has been set more or less from
Latour's point of view, with the narrator describing things as if through
his eyes. But Martinez is in the role of guide here, so the logic of the
story would have him giving the commentary that actually sounds more
like the voice of a third-person authority. The point is that the narrator
seems to sanction this exoticizing interpretation of the mountainside as
a mysterious place, made so by the inscrutable practices of generations
of Indian life.

Pecos Pueblo too "had more than its share of dark legends." The
narrator introduces a series of rumors about ancient, exotic practices
with the phrase "It was said that": "It was said that this people had from
time immemorial kept a ceremonial fire burning in some cave in the
mountain, a fire that had never been allowed to go out, and had never
been revealed to white men. The story was that the service of this fire
sapped the strength of the young men appointed to serve it,—always
the best of the tribe." And: "There was also the snake story, reported by
the early explorers, both Spanish and American, and believed ever

since: that this tribe was peculiarly addicted to snake worship, that they kept rattlesnakes concealed in their houses, and somewhere in the mountain guarded an enormous serpent which they brought to the pueblo for certain feasts. It was said that they sacrificed young babies to the great snake" (122). The phrase "It was said that" allows the speaker to keep a distance from the stories related, and Father Latour's reflections on them express his amazement—not, of course, at the possibilities of their being true, but at the fact that anybody might believe them. Nevertheless, like any good gossip, the narrator of *Death Comes for the Archbishop* keeps these stories alive by passing them along, even as nothing is admitted about their viability or their sources. Rather, it seems the narrator's interest lies mostly in maintaining an element of exoticizing in order to enchant the landscape and culture of the place, as Father Latour reflects on them in the dark of night, by a campfire with a very inaccessible guide, Jacinto, by his side.

The "remote black past" of Pueblo life thus continues to resonate in the story's present, since Spanish exploitation and native "superstition" still influence local culture and character. Latour's missionary intention is to alter all of this by substituting a more rationalist form of piety and a presumably less ensnared consciousness. Insofar as their work might get done, it would cancel the differences, make the Southwest ready to be "American," and create a need to remember the complications of difference. At the end of the novel, we get a replay, given quite nostalgically, of Father Latour's own New Mexican past and the past of his mission now that his work is done, but "done" only in the sense that death is coming. The resonant essentialisms of earlier statements about native consciousness and cultural practice still reverberate in the background.

If one's method of cultivation allows for dialogue and exchange—mutual influence to some extent, or at least not the excessive extension and reproduction of oneself onto the colonized scene that utterly oppresses otherness—then, the novel suggests, one will reap the fruits of success. Ultimately the natural and the indigenous in *Death Comes for the Archbishop*, as in *The Professor's House*, serve to stimulate the modern and the immigrant to new levels of consciousness and to new powers of conversion. What gets privileged overtly is not the old or the new, but some mixture, with a cultural frontier still running through it that obviates assimilation. If St. Peter can "know" Tom Outland and the Spanish adventurers, in all their differences from him, it is not through utter identification but through the learned sophistication that allows him to interpret them well. They remain as familiar to and yet as distinct from him as he is in relation to his own family: close, even perhaps related in some sense—St. Peter has researched the lives of all of them so thoroughly that he has come to look like a Spaniard and clearly has constructed a kinship with Outland—but with the crucial differences between their experiences and his in place. And if Outland could know the Cliff Dwellers, it is by virtue of a privileged, indeed mystical communication with people he imagines as ancestors, but a communication that depends, finally, on their differences from him to be worth trying to comprehend at all.

Although the earlier novel suggests that such comprehension of indigenous life is possible, even at a great temporal remove, the later one calls this understanding into question. Latour and Vaillant can only cultivate and alter the forms of daily life, of domesticity and devotion. Native ways of being and knowing finally remain secret and unavailable to them, outside the epistemological frameworks of their church. In both novels, Cather projects a stronger interest in not settling than in settling the conceptual and aesthetic debates that come with these differences; her desire is to leave frontiers of ineluctable difference in place.

Rather than joining her contemporaries in imagining the mythic moment of the end of the West, Cather reshapes regional culture and geography such that the familiar and the exotic and the differences between them are sustained. Her stories find the given, unbridgeable gaps between cultures, characters, and their perceptions of landscape to be the brute facts of modern as well as colonial life in North America. Acute powers of intellect and perception can help one to understand and even to manage the form of the indigenous or ancient other, but finally interpretation is the product of one's own vision and of one's cultural training. These impermeable limitations obstruct conventionally romantic efforts to extend the self "as far as the eye can see," as Meriwether Lewis does. At the same time, though, they affirm the surviving fault lines of difference that ensure the future of enchantment.

The Strangeness
of Closure

Chapter 9

We tried to think of anything we had seen or heard of
that did not have some stealthy, shadowy sort of
explanation sneaking after it and hunting it down.
—FRANK NORRIS, *"The Strangest Thing" (1902)*

THE FRAMES OF NATURALISM and the apparent closures brought by the depletion of free land did not substantially alter the conceptual base of American wilderness romanticism. The naturalist Westerns considered in this study construct images to preserve as well as to analyze wildness. The designs of realism, inflected with the evolutionary ideology of naturalism, produced memorials to primitivity at the same time that their theoretical assumptions were affirmed by "natural" processes.

As Donna Haraway suggests in her biographical sketch of the adventurer and scientific naturalist Carl Akeley, perhaps best known for his dioramas at the Museum of Natural History in New York, much of the cult of Anglo-Saxon manhood of the 1890s both derived from and fostered a form of biological determinism that assigned to the manly type the status of "fittest" in the long run of human survival.[1] At the same time, this cult announced an anxiety about the disappearance of a purer masculine world in the face of modernity's technological imposition of the grid and settling of the imperial space of the unknown.[2] The realism of Akeley's taxidermy and nature photography, Haraway argues, are mechanisms for conserving the dead by giving fixed and lifelike form to what is "captured." As Akeley and his col-

187

leagues saw it, photography and taxidermy were clear, undesigning forms of representation, the execution of which preserved not only the object captured but, for the moment, protected the hunters and scientists responsible for them from technological consumption by modernity. The unmediated relation that was meant to be suggested between these images and their real referents allowed for an authority in the scientific artist who could perform his work without self-consciousness. This authority was assumed to ensure a stay against the distortions of romantic representation, as well as against the decaying of vigorous masculinity in, as Haraway puts it, "unruly and primitive excess."

The realist practices of taxidermy and photography preserve nature, the vital antidote to modernist emasculation, and, in the process, clearly construct nature as a saving and rehabilitating field. Thus nature in Haraway's argument is a machine for preservation of those who construct it and who attribute agency not to themselves and their usually unseen desiring practices but to natural determinism. The latter, like technological determinism, is the concept that men like Akeley used to foster the illusion that things simply happen, beyond their control, in a kind of religiously articulated force.

The extensive efforts to block deterioration that Haraway sees in Akeley's Museum of Natural History dioramas are perhaps less analytic in their determinist views of frontier vigor than those found in the writers considered in this study. But the mixture of naturalist mechanics with Western nostalgia in their work produces a similarly hard-line representation of a much-loved mode of being, dead in its literary containment. The natural world of the West is appropriated by the "science" of naturalist literature, its vigor given over to the energetic controls of determinist thinking.

The call of the wild is the more difficult to resist and to control, though, in that it emits not from a zone that is truly separate from that of the writing subject but from within the same cultural-biographical scope. In the desire to encounter what is truly other, the frontier personnel—the hunters, miners, trackers, and scientists—of Akeley's projects and of Western naturalist fiction continuously project new areas of unarticulated experience that have yet no "shadowy sort of explanation sneaking after [them] and hunting [them] down," to quote from Norris's story "The Strangest Thing." But the process for Akeley, Norris, and the others seems again and again to mean recalling and reproducing familiar images and situations that shape what is strange in terms of what for them are older cultural forms. Rather than supposing that some situation might not be translatable into such terms, the subjects of such narratives can only imagine true otherness existing across the frontier of actual life, in death.

IN JULY 1897, five years before his death, Norris published "The Strangest Thing," which exemplifies the preoccupation with reference in fin-de-siècle American imaginative work considered in the preceding chapters. Like Joseph Conrad's narratives within narratives, this one presents a tale within a tale of a group of men sitting in a boat, attempting to recollect the strangest things they have ever encountered. The problem is to "think of anything we had seen or heard of that did not have some stealthy, shadowy sort of explanation sneaking after it and hunting it down."[3] "The Strangest Thing" seems to experiment with storytelling in order to find a narrative that cannot be explained outside of its own terms, that does not connect to a logic that precedes or is larger than itself; in short, a story that does not refer to anything tangibly or conceptually real.

The story within the story that comes to be presented as satisfactorily strange to the men in the boat tells of a Harvard man whose affairs have not gone well and who takes a job as caretaker and grave digger at a burying ground for the poor. In the climax of the tale, an unknown man visits the graveyard one night, reads through all of the markers, and, arriving at one, digs it up, takes something from a baby's coffin, and flees. The caretaker has been watching from the distance of his shed, not concerned to stop or question the man. Here "The Strangest Thing" ends, and the question remains: what has the stranger taken from the coffin? Although the story of the grave digger himself is far more interesting than this rather conventional mystery, the fact that the mystery is left unexplained means that the initial project of "The Strangest Thing" has been fulfilled. But the demonstrably incomplete tale, left open-ended in this awkward manner, rather than evoking something truly mysterious, experiments with traditional form by violating it. A story without closure is no story at all; by denying an answer to the mystery, Norris forces the satisfaction of the initial purpose established in the frame narrative but begs the question of reference, of explanation, anyway.

A central interest of "The Strangest Thing," in spite of its ultimately formal concern with strangeness, seems to lie in the representation of death, indeed *the* mystery that eludes humanistic if not logical accounts. In another series of yet smaller stories within the scope of "The Strangest Thing," the caretaker paints names, dates, and epitaphs, as his fancy dictates, upon the blank gravestones. The names are suggested by the epitaphs and the epitaphs by the names to construct a series of minimal fictions across the face of the cemetery.

Although the opening narrator's purpose is only falsely fulfilled in the ending of the story, it is fulfilled in the inexplicable desire on the part of the caretaker to inscribe these little tales on the tombstones. Norris's preoccupation is with the vitality of the signifier, in that it does not root itself in a respectable source but rather comes from "nowhere"—the fancy of the ex-Harvard man—and has no relationship to the ground or the granite marker on which it is inscribed. The cementing of language that the image of gravestone writing seems to provide is as misleading as the names and dates of the inscription. Indeed, the play of reference is rampant in this case, as the "writer's" articulations refer to anything his fancy or the fancy of a potential reader might suggest; in a sense, his effort is a waste of signification.

The strangest thing in Norris's story is not the inexplicable theft, but the gravedigger's pleasure in mixing writing with death, one of the many expressions of waste with which the story is preoccupied. The digger's education is not being used; his time is wasted sitting around the burial ground such that he "diverts" himself by writing epitaphs; he uses up the paint that is supplied for the simple marking of grave numbers to create unnecessary rhymes and jingles for the unknown dead.

Connected to these attributes of waste in the central character is the image of the men in the outermost frame of the story sitting around trying to think of something that makes no sense; the forced absence of an explanation at the closure of the story, underscoring its status as a sketch and an experiment, also suggests a sense of waste—as if this were the type of work that in many hands would end up crumpled and in the garbage. And of course the looming referent here, death, is itself the

capital image of waste, in the literal, if not actual, sense of not participating in any system of exchange—economic, social, or narrative.

All of this waste exuded by the story suggests a resistance to narrative accounting and to the linearity of explanatory logic. It is as if
Norris is trying to tell a story here that resists being a story. If waste
means unexchangeable material, then a waste of a story is one that does
not "work"—does not tell, and thus does not do well on the market.
We might argue that the desire of the initial project within "The
Strangest Thing" is satisfied in this abundance of waste, except that
waste itself would then be understood as the *explanation* of the narrative
mode and the wasted ending.

In "The Strangest Thing," Norris attempts to exploit the difficulties of reference and representation with which he was so often preoccupied by evading reference altogether; but in spite of these efforts the
story makes sense, that is, it has its referents. The waste suggested in
virtually every term of the story also helps to do the telling. The words
on the gravestones create characters—representations of once human
beings; but the conditions of such characters as dead cannot be
accounted for in these tiny narratives, even if they were true. In this
sense, death stands quite distinctly as the thing that has no "stealthy,
shadowy sort of explanation sneaking after it," as the mark that exists as
if for its own sake.

Norris's considerable probe of the value of marks, words, photographs, paintings, coins, and other forms of representation seems in his
work to press ever closer to this major hoax behind which lies empty
space. Norris's imagination had always imbibed a good amount of
death; his earlier chivalric romances depended heavily upon it, and the
early installments of *McTeague* and *Vandover* had begun with the effects
of death on fictional family structures. In many ways the dominant
attributes of the frontier in his fiction, its disappearance and death,
seem to provide its most compelling mystery, perhaps its major attraction. The intense emphasis on the material constitution of character
and culture in Norris's naturalist discourse provides a peculiar contrast
to the language and imagery of dematerialization and disappearance
that are central to his motif of the end of the frontier and of what he
imagines as authentic Western culture.

London, more than other writers of his time, was concerned with representing the physical dimensions and the materiality of the West and of frontier culture. But his vitalism was most intensely exercised at the brink of civility, safety, and the regions of the known. The wildness that activated the desires of his central characters and drew them to the edges of control was an operative factor in his life. His famous recklessness, still a major attraction, particularly for male readers, often brought him into contact with danger: in oyster pirating, tramping, prospecting in the Klondike, researching London's East End disguised as a bum, sailing to Tahiti and Australia, and many other adventures. At home, as away, he drank heavily and regularly took opium, heroine, morphine, strychnine, belladonna, and other strong drugs to treat his many physical disorders.[4] His death at the age of forty has been explained as the result of an "acute 'gastro-intestinal type of uremia and possibly a self-induced drug overdose.' "[5] The latter is still a matter of debate; but even if it were found untrue, much of London's life and work seems to suggest that he was drawn to death as the most impassable challenge to material existence and bodily strength.

In pushing his body to its limits, he became even more intensely conscious of its parts, and of himself as a physical being, than he had been as a healthy man. Close-up images of frozen fingers, hands, legs, and feet are common features in the Klondike stories, in which the narrative problematic is provided by nature's constant threat to survival. One of the immediate effects of these momentarily fetishized body parts is to reduce human beings to collections of limbs. But as London articulates the mental conditions of these characters, a peculiar separation begins to take place, in which the body becomes a weak but monstrous, parasitic creature that drains the life of its far superior host.

In these moments, a clarity of mind, expressed as the lucid understanding of some intellectual idea but verging on a spiritual perception, announces the onset of death. It is as if the mind remains to analyze the implications of the succumbing of the body, and in the process demonstrates the discreet and privileged place occupied by the mind, cut from its material body, in London's imagination. Rather than dwelling on the loss and pain of the moment, this meditation typically evolves into a kind of rapture on mortality and a fascination with death, motifs long evident in London's life and work.

Perhaps one of the most palpable demonstrations of this attraction appears in one of London's South Pacific stories, "The Red One," which he wrote a few months before he died. The explorer Bassett, trapped by illness in the jungles of Guadalcanal, is drawn progressively farther into the heart of the island by the lure of a strange sound emitting from somewhere in the hinterland. Its source turns out to be an enormous meteor being struck by a gong. The islanders worship the great object, known as the Red One, and only certain men are permitted to approach it. Bassett's wish to look closely at the Red One, an act that is strictly taboo for him, combined with the progression of his illness, drives him to make a deal with Ngurn, the deity's chief priest. If Ngurn's attendants will carry Bassett to the Red One so he can observe its sound and surface, Bassett will give the old priest an opportunity he has long sought by permitting him to cut off his head and smoke it. The encounter with the Red One proceeds, and as Basset bends his head under Ngurn's tomahawk, he introduces himself to death:

> He knew, without seeing, when the razor-edged hatchet rose in
> the air behind him. And for that instant, ere the end, there fell
> upon Bassett the shadow of the Unknown, a sense of
> impending marvel of the rending of walls before the
> imaginable. Almost, when he knew the blow had started and
> just ere the edge of steel bit the flesh and nerves, it seemed
> that he gazed upon the serene face of the Medusa, Truth—and
> simultaneous with the bite of the steel on the onrush of the
> dark, in a flashing instant of fancy, he saw the vision of his
> head turning slowly, always turning, in [Ngurn's] house beside
> the breadfruit tree.[6]

The image of his own head, dried and hanging like a work of art on display in Ngurn's gallery of heads, is a ghastly sight, and symptomatic of the savagery that London ascribes to the Solomon Islanders. But for all its horror, it is not the most impressive aspect of Bassett's last, flashing thought. The "onrush of the dark" is the central moment of the paragraph, since it marks the onset of death. The preceding moment when he feels the bite of steel sets up the key instant of darkness; death is still impending, and only its shadow is present. Just before it occurs, the truth appears to him in the "serene face of Medusa." The truth is not death itself, but a benefit of it beforehand; the Unknown, Spencer's well-known category for the realm beyond the edge of recognized phenomenal reality, is death itself. That is where Bassett is drawn, and its image here is precisely the image of the frontier of known and unknown worlds that London's naturalist Westerns explore.

THE SPANISH-AMERICAN WAR submitted the Philippines, Guam, and the Solomon Islands to United States occupation and made them more familiar in U.S. popular culture than they had previously been. As Amy Kaplan has argued, the exploration and exploitation of these islands in the aftermath of the closed continental frontier satisfied some important aspects of the culture of U.S. nationalism, particularly of the changing formations of masculinity in the 1890s.[7] If classic Western narrative was centered most intensely on the representation of desire for the frontier and on the mysteries of its depths, the fin-de-siècle version of that narrative would largely be played out without a temporary historical referent, but it could—and did—reach out to the Pacific as a watery extension where the old stories could be exercised in "new" settings.

The naturalist account of the post-Turner frontier, wherever it was located, emphasized the mysteries of the wilderness in the mind of the human subject and the fated terms of human life. Naturalist discourse, for all of its modernity and efforts to scientifically observe human social and psychological phenomena, is equally enraptured with the unknown in the form of inarticulate "brutish" levels of consciousness and with the spontaneous action of experimentalism. But the attention to the unpredictable in human behavior converts it into an empirically measurable entity; and the resistance to prescribed theory in experimental writing commonly provokes a textual self-consciousness productive of anything but spontaneous expression.

Earlier nineteenth-century Western representations typically sought to designate the space of the wild in order to celebrate its powers in the regeneration of romantic human will; and the overt efforts of naturalist portraiture were to delineate the degenerate effects of such will. The antithetical progressive and regressive "forces" in these mechanisms become much less evident in the postfrontier 1890s, when serious

Western fiction turns to a naturalist ethos as one alternative to the sheer repetition of traditional form. In this fiction, irony and self-consciousness load representation of the wild with ambiguity, so that it appears simultaneously anachronistic, degenerate, and romantic.

In their efforts at recalling the wild, naturalism and Westernism attempted to construct an emptiness activated before, or beyond, cultural form. It was designed, with all the ingenuity available in the 1890s, to stand as a real Other to civil experience. This simulated aboriginal condition might be a way to match death in literature; more pressingly, it expresses the anxiety of Western and naturalist representations to frame significant differences from the civil status quo of what this generation of writers saw as fin-de-siècle modernity.

Notes

Introduction

1. Some of the earliest Spanish and French expedition texts celebrated "new world" landscapes in terms that suggested openness and plenty (such as the writings of Fray Marcos de Niza, Gaspar Perez de Villagra, and Samuel de Champlain). More often, however, they concentrated on the specifics of movement, struggle, and accomplishment in a given area without giving extensive attention to landscape for its own sake, or to the exploring subject's relation to it beyond projecting a sense of confinement or deprivation. Sixteenth- and seventeenth-century accounts by English settlers of what was considered the "West" in North America generally did not tend to celebrate open space as an emblem of "new world" possibility as much as their descendants in the eighteenth and nineteenth centuries did. North American space was more often constructed as dark and mysterious, the realm of a threatening, if nevertheless potentially valuable, unknown. Michael Wigglesworth's famous reference in "God's Controversy with New England" to the forest beyond the settlements as "a howling wilderness" and Mary Rowlandson's complex images of the Native American world as a field of temptation and sin are emblematic of sixteenth-century English attitudes toward the "West." John Smith and others who wrote about Virginia, like Thomas Morton on New England, were often optimistic in their descriptions of the "wilderness" and the indigenous people; but such descriptions were generally attentive to the immediate advantages available for entrepreneurial activities as well as for mere survival. Even Morton's rhapsodic accounts of the beauties of the forest and of indigenous culture are constructed in relatively close focus and proceed in the manner of an elaborate and well-decorated list or "chorography"—a favorite sixteenth-century term for verbal delineations of particular regions or districts. Thus, his attention is largely devoted to the details of culture and ecology in a very specific location. See William Cronon's *Changes in the Land: Indians, Colonists and the Ecology of New England* (New York: Hill and Wang, 1983) for further discussion of Morton's environmental writing on New England. Henry Nash Smith argues in *Virgin Land: The American West as Symbol and Myth* (Cambridge, Mass.: Harvard University Press, 1950) that, until the later eighteenth century, English-speaking colonists generally had little knowledge of the "interior of the continent," and their references to it commonly construed it as a place of danger and darkness without the regenerative qualities it would acquire in the myths and symbols,

to use Smith's terms, of later generations of European Americans. Smith seems to associate this lack of knowledge with a lack of interest, or at least less than would follow in subsequent eras.

In the essay "Reinventing Common Nature: Yosemite and Mount Rushmore—A Meandering Tale of a Double Nature," in *Uncommon Ground: Rethinking the Human Place in Nature*, ed. William Cronon (New York: Norton, 1996), Kenneth Olwig notes: "In the period between Jefferson and [Theodore] Roosevelt a sea change occurred in prevailing ideas about the natural. Though this change had been brewing since the Renaissance, it is during the nineteenth century that we see a virtual reversal in the symbolism of the natural. The wild, which had once been the epitome of the unnatural, now becomes a natural ideal" (399).

Indeed, late eighteenth- and nineteenth-century North American expedition accounts commonly projected romantic and celebratory images of the West, precisely by focusing on its unknown and mysterious contents, even when those contents had already been mapped, or at least explored, by other whites. Thus it seems important to note that U.S. imaging of the frontier beginning in the eighteenth century featured the open, horizontal format that invited interpretation in terms of the hegemonic ideas of national identity at the time; that is, by the romance of the democratic revolution.

2. In his introductory essay to Timothy Flint's *Biographical Memoire of Daniel Boone* (New Haven, Conn.: College and University Press, 1967), James K. Folsom uses this term to describe Flint's attraction to the West. Folsom argues that Flint is celebrating the cultivation of a once-wild zone and that his interest in the frontier area is an expression of his own will to cultivate.

3. The concept of wilderness in Western historiography and in contemporary environmentalist discourse has been comprehensively investigated in several recent discussions. Rather than rehearse or add to these arguments, I assume throughout this book that the term refers to an idea and a way of imaging nature in European and Euro-American thinking rather than a specific material phenomenon. For some particularly useful analyses of the problems inherent in the concept, see William Cronon, "The Trouble with Wilderness; or, Getting Back to the Wrong Nature," in *Uncommon Ground*, 69–90, as well as the other essays in Cronon's collection; and Edward S. Casey, *Getting Back Into Place: Toward a Renewed Understanding of the Place-World* (Bloomington: Indiana University Press, 1993), 188–190 and 233–238.

4. Frank Norris associated with this group during his early years as a writer for the San Francisco *Wave*. See Franklin Walker, *Frank Norris: A Biography* (New York: Doubleday, Duran, 1932), 134.

5. For an original and well-informed discussion of the relations between decadence, or dandyism, and Western romanticism, see Perry Meisel's *The Cowboy and the Dandy* (New York: Oxford University Press, 1999).

6. See Patrick Morrow, "Bret Harte, Mark Twain and the San Francisco Circle" in *A Literary History of the American West*, ed. Thomas Lyon (Fort Worth: Texas Christian University Press, 1987), for a discussion of local-color humor and some of its Western descendants.

7. The enigma of cultural identity at the end of the nineteenth century and the military, financial, commercial, and gender issues implicit in it have been analyzed by several critics and historians of U.S. culture, among them June Howard, *Form and History in American Literary Naturalism* (Chapel Hill: University of North Carolina Press, 1985); Amy Kaplan, *The Social Construction of*

American Realism (Chicago: University of Chicago Press, 1988) and "Romancing the Empire: The Embodiment of American Masculinity in the Popular Historical Novel of the 1890s," *American Literary History* 2 (Winter 1990): 659–680; T. J. Jackson Lears, *No Place of Grace: Antimodernism and the Transformation of American Culture* (New York: Pantheon, 1981); and Walter Benn Michaels, *The Gold Standard and the Logic of Naturalism* (Berkeley: University of California Press, 1987) and *Our America: Nativism, Modernism and Pluralism* (Durham, N.C.: Duke University Press, 1995). Howard writes: "Any study of late nineteenth-century and early twentieth-century America encounters not just a vague discomfort but the sense, widely articulated by contemporaries and uniformly reflected by historians, that there is an immediate threat to social order, a sense that the very foundations of American life are endangered" (75). Howard is concerned here with economic and politic dynamics, specifically the momentum of the money economy replacing more traditional modes of exchange; and with the development of populism. Michaels and Kaplan have addressed the contributions of these and other changes in arts and literature to a pervasive sense in Euro-American culture that national identity and the standards of what constituted the real were very much in question.

8. Leo Marx, *The Machine in the Garden* (New York: Oxford University Press, 1964). Shannon Applegate writes in "The Literature of Loneliness: Understanding the Letters and Diaries of the American West," in *Reading the West: New Essays on the Literature of the American West,* ed. Michael Kowalewski (New York: Cambridge University Press, 1996) that "late in his career, Henry Nash Smith . . . conceded that his seminal work, *Virgin Land*, had failed to underscore the 'tragic dimensions of the Westward movement.' 'I took over from Turner,' he said. . . . Smith expressed regret that his work virtually ignored the role of indigenous cultures" (69) as well as the role of violence, racism, and environmental abuse. Applegate quotes from Smith's "Symbol and Idea in *Virgin Land*," in *Ideology and Classic American Literature*, eds. Sacvan Bercovitch and Myra Jehlen (New York: Cambridge University Press, 1986).

9. Annette Kolodny, *The Lay of the Land: Metaphor as Experience and History in American Life and Letters* (Chapel Hill: University of North Carolina Press, 1976); Slotkin, *Regeneration Through Violence: The Mythology of the American Frontier, 1600–1860* (Middletown, Conn.: Wesleyan University Press, 1973).

10. Some of the influential works along these lines are Howard Lamar and Leonard Thompson, eds., *The Frontier in History* (New Haven: Yale University Press, 1981); William Cronon, *Nature's Metropolis* (New York: Norton, 1991); Patricia Nelson Limerick, *Legacy* (New York: Norton, 1987); Jane Tompkins, *West of Everything* (New York: Oxford University Press, 1992); William Cronon, George Miles, and Jay Gitlin, eds., *Under an Open Sky* (New York: Norton, 1992); Richard White, *It's Your Misfortune and None of My Own: A New History of the American West* (Norman: University of Oklahoma Press, 1992) and *The Middle Ground: Indians, Empires and Republics in the Great Lakes Region, 1650–1815* (Cambridge, U.K.: Cambridge University Press, 1991); and Donald Worster, *Rivers of Empire: Water, Aridity, and the Growth of the American West* (New York: Pantheon, 1985) and *Under Western Skies: Nature and History in the American West* (New York: Oxford University Press, 1992).

11. In "New City, New Frontier: The Lower East Side as Wild, Wild West," in *Variations on a Theme Park: The New American City and the End of Public Space*, ed. Michael Sorkin (New York: Hill and Wang, 1992), Neil Smith contends that myth, in addition to "wrenching meaning from its historical contexts," must

"be transportable over space: the loss of the geographical quality of things is . . . central to the making of myth." He finds this transportability in the U.S. frontier and traces it—in space as well as time—to contemporary New York City, as manifested in real estate and advertising imagery.

Chapter 1 **Romantic Westernism and the Example of Daniel Boone**

1. Frank Norris, "The Frontier Gone at Last," and "The Literature of the West," in *Novels and Essays* (New York: Library of America, 1986).
2. For more comprehensive discussions of Western literature, see John Cawelti, *The Six-Gun Mystique*, 2nd ed. (Bowling Green, Ohio.: Bowling Green State University Popular Press, 1984); Stephen Fender, *Plotting the Golden West: American Literature and the Rhetoric of the California Trail* (Cambridge, U.K.: Cambridge University Press, 1981); James K. Folsom, ed. *The Western: A Collection of Critical Essays* (Englewood Cliffs, N.J.: Prentice-Hall, 1979); Lucy Lockwood Hazard, *The Frontier in American Literature* (New York: Crowell Publishers, 1927); Annette Kolodny, *The Land Before Her: Fantasy and Experience of the American Frontiers* (Chapel Hill: University of North Carolina Press, 1984) and *The Lay of the Land: Metaphor as Experience and History in American Life and Letters* (Chapel Hill: University of North Carolina Press, 1976); Thomas Lyon, ed., *A Literary History of the American West* (Fort Worth: Texas Christian University Press, 1987); Roderick Nash, *Wilderness and the American Mind* (New Haven, Conn.: Yale University Press, 1982); Henry Nash Smith, *Virgin Land: The American West as Symbol and Myth* (Cambridge, Mass.: Harvard University Press, 1970); and Jane Tompkins, *West of Everything: The Inner Life of Westerns* (New York: Oxford University Press, 1992).
3. For an account of the role of violence in the conquest of the American West, the standard text is still Richard Slotkin, *Regeneration Through Violence: The Mythology of the American Frontier, 1600–1860* (Middletown, Conn.: Wesleyan University Press, 1973).
4. The dynamics of exploration and empire outlined in the texts of late-eighteenth- and early-nineteenth-century Euro-American expeditions recall some of the earliest and what may appear to be more overtly imaginative geographies of the new world. These representations themselves invoke older myths of European civilization concerning the very concept of the West. Speaking of Renaissance images and interpretations of the Western hemisphere, Slotkin writes in *Regeneration Through Violence*: "Within the body of European myths about America were two antagonistic pre-Columbian conceptions of the West: the primitive belief in the West as the land of the sea, the sunset, death, darkness, passion, and dreams; and the counterbelief in the West as the Blessed Isles, the land of life's renewal, of rebirth, of reason and a higher reality" (27). In Slotkin's argument, the tension is productive of ideological conflicts between conserving, reactionary thought and behavior on the one hand, and progressivism on the other, that continue to alternate with each other in the rhetorics of Euro-American frontier culture and politics. But it is easy enough to see that, like the apparently antithetical modes of settlement and expansion, these two orientations work hand-in-hand in the European acquisition of the North American continent to its end. For a more recent discussion of the continuation and revision of older myths in the earliest American discovery texts, including those of Columbus, see Stephen Greenblatt, *Marvelous Possessions* (Chicago: University of Chicago Press, 1992).

5. I refer in this chapter to John Mack Faragher, *Daniel Boone: The Life and Legend of an American Pioneer* (New York: Henry Holt, 1992). From 1998 to 2000, five new biographical studies of Boone appeared in print: Stephen Aron, *How the West Was Lost: The Transformation of Kentucky from Daniel Boone to Henry Clay* (Baltimore: Johns Hopkins University Press, 1999); Lyman Draper, *Life of Daniel Boone* (Kiowa, Colo.: Kitchen Keepsakes, 1998); Neal Hammon, ed., *My Father Daniel Boone: The Draper Interviews with Nathan Boone* (Lexington: University of Kentucky Press, 1999); Richard Kozar, *Daniel Boone* (Broomall, Penn.: Chelsea House, 1999); and Pat McCarthy, *Daniel Boone: Frontier Legend* (Springfield, N. J.: Enslow, 2000).
6. John Filson, *The Discovery, Settlement and Present State of Kentucke, with the Life of Colonel Daniel Boone* (Wilmington, Del., 1784; rep. Ann Arbor, Mich.: University Microfilms, 1966), 50.
7. Faragher also notes that Boone himself presumably had nothing but praise for Filson's narrative. After reading the text aloud on one occasion Boone reportedly declared, "All true! Every word true! Not a lie in it!" (7).
8. Richard Drinnon notes in *Facing West: The Metaphysics of Indian Hating and Empire Building* (New York: New American Library, 1980) that in a later Boone biography that drew heavily on Filson's, William Gilmore Simms "denounced [Filson's] clumsy attempts at eloquence and poetry, the flourishes and 'marks of ambitious composition quite unlike our hunter,' but proceeded to follow his emphasis on the discovery of Kentucky, quoted him extensively, and revealed his own enchantment over what the writer had made of Boone" (134).
9. For an extended discussion of these dynamics in several Boone biographies, see my essay, "The Fictions of Daniel Boone," in *Desert, Garden, Margin, Range: The Frontiers of American Literature*, ed. Eric Heyne (New York: Macmillan, 1992), 29–43.
10. Timothy Flint, *Biographical Memoire of Daniel Boone* [1833], ed. James K. Folsom (New Haven, Conn.: College and University Press, 1967).
11. Slotkin, *Regeneration Through Violence*, 420.
12. See Smith, *Virgin Land*, 59. According to Smith, this was "perhaps the most widely read book about a Western character during the first half of the nineteenth century."
13. Faragher recounts this story as well in his *Daniel Boone*. His explanation is interesting and to the point: "The story of the hunter who falls in love with his prey is, in fact, common in the folklore of many hunting peoples; the sexual union of hunter and deer-woman was a recurrent motif in the oral culture of American Indians" (44). Faragher cites the incident not for its biographical accuracy, but because it has important metaphorical value in demonstrating the "tensions between frontier men and women" (44). While Rebecca Bryan is in danger, she is "saved by the restraint of [Boone's] passion" (44). Daniel Boone, however, has to give up his autonomous life style in order to become her partner. Faragher's analysis of the tale emphasizes the way it stages "certain discontinuities of gender and suggests that men must forsake certain freedoms to achieve union with women" (44).
14. Reading this portion of Flint's narrative in *The Land Before Her*, Annette Kolodny draws an interesting comparison to medieval allegories of the hunt:

> If the fire-hunt legend calls to mind medieval allegories in which the hunting of the hart plays out a lover's pursuit of his dear it does so with a difference. In medieval allegories, the hunt begins with the wounding of the hart and terminates with its capture, the symbolic uniting of the lovers thus dis-

placing the prior pursuit. In Flint's *Biographical Memoir of Daniel Boone*, however, the hunting never ceases. The imputed consummation that closes the story does not, in fact, bind Daniel to Rebecca's side. For Boone's 'darling pursuit of hunting' is not metaphorical: it is his controlling 'passion' (Flint 227). The 'unexplored paradise of the hunter's imagination' (Flint 48) is the forest here, not the marriage bed. As a result, the Rebecca Bryan of the fire-hunt legend emerges not as a person beloved in her own right but, instead, as a human cipher who has managed, if only briefly, to take on the erotic appeal of the wilderness that defined her husband's meaning (87).

15. See my discussion, in "The Fictions of Daniel Boone," 33–37, of James Hall's characterization of Boone in his *Letters From the West, Containing Sketches of Scenery, Manners, and Customs; and Anecdotes Connected with the First Settlements of the Western Sections of the United States*, ed. John T. Flanagan (Gainesville, Fla.: Scholars' Facsimiles and Reprints, 1967).

16. Ralph Waldo Emerson, *Selected Essays*, ed. Larzer Ziff (New York: Penguin, 1982), 190.

Chapter 2   Scenes of Visionary Enchantment: The Lewis and Clark Narratives and the Leatherstocking Novels

1. Richard Slotkin, *Regeneration Through Violence: The Mythology of the American Frontier, 1600–1860* (Middletown, Conn.: Wesleyan University Press, 1973), 23.

2. See John Cawelti, *The Six-Gun Mystique*, 2nd ed. (Bowling Green, Ohio: Bowling Green State University Press, 1984), 107; Stephen Railton, *Fenimore Cooper: A Study of His Life and Imagination* (Princeton, N. J.: Princeton University Press, 1978), 90–91; and Slotkin, *Gunfighter Nation: The Myth of the Frontier in Twentieth-Century America* (New York: Harper Perennial, 1992), 16. Richard Drinnon, in *Facing West: The Metaphysics of Indian Hating and Empire Building* (New York: New American Library, 1980), writes that "Natty Bumppo was Boone II, the hunter and fugitive from the 'settlements' " (161); Annette Kolodny, in *The Land Before Her: Fantasy and Experience of the American Frontiers* (Chapel Hill, N.C.: University of North Carolina Press, 1984), draws a somewhat less direct line of influence between the two figures in describing the isolated, male hunter figure of frontier literature as "[d]erived from Daniel Boone [and] reified by Cooper's Leatherstocking" (224).

3. Lewis referred to Boone in his journal during the winter of 1804–1805, when the expedition approached the mouth of the Osage River: "this part of the contry is generally called Boon's settlement, having derived its name from its first inhabitant Colo. Daniel Boon, a gentleman well known in the early settlement of the state of Kentucky." See Gary Moulton, ed., *The Journals of Lewis and Clark*, vol. 3 (Lincoln: University of Nebraska Press, 1987), 338. Lewis was clearly impressed by Boone's reputation, for in 1808, when he was Governor of Upper Louisiana Territory, he confirmed Boone as Justice of the Peace of Femme Osage. See Richard Dillon, *Meriwether Lewis: A Biography* (New York: Coward-McCann, 1965), 299. In 1804, when Lewis and Clark arrived with the expedition crew at La Charette, on the Missouri River, the seventy-year-old Boone had already been living nearby for several years; but apparently neither of the explorers was aware of his presence. See Dillon, 103, and Bernard DeVoto, ed., *The Journals of Lewis and Clark* (Boston: Houghton Mifflin, 1953), 5n.

Narrating his version of the expedition in *Lewis and Clark, Partners in Discovery* (New York: Morrow, 1947), John Bakeless finds several connections between Boone and the explorers. He writes that, in preparing for the journey in Missouri Territory, Clark "paid frequent visits to the village of St. Charles, [where] he probably met and talked with the aged but vigorous Daniel Boone, who had long been collecting all the information he could regarding the country to the West" (110); and that "Old Daniel Boone and his family came calling" at Clark's house well after the expedition, when Clark was Indian Superintendent in Missouri Territory. "The Boones knew Clark simply as Will," writes Bakeless (445). Gary Moulton notes that another member of the expedition, Private John Shields, "trapped in Missouri for a time with Daniel Boone, a kinsman." See Moulton, ed., *Journals of Lewis and Clark*, vol. 2 (1986), 522.

4. Elliott Coues, *History of the Expedition Under the Command of Lewis and Clark to the Sources of the Missouri River*, 3 vols. (New York: Dover, 1964; reprint of the 4-vol. edition, New York: F. P. Harper, 1893). Citations from Coues's edition are taken from volume I. Coues writes in his "Preface to the New Edition" that "It is singular that this History, which has held its own for nearly a century as a standard work of reference, has never before been republished in full, nor ever until now been subjected to searching and systematic criticism"(vi). Other references to Lewis's and Clark's journals which were not included in Coues's edition of the *History* are taken from DeVoto's.

5. References to Jefferson's "Memoir of Lewis" are taken from the Coues edition of 1893 rather than the original Paul Allen edition of 1814, *History of the Expedition Under the Command of Captains Lewis and Clark, to the Sources of the Missouri, Thence Across the Rocky Mountains and Down the River Columbia to the Pacific Ocean* (Philadelphia: Bradford and Inskeep, 1814). Coues's annotations provide a great deal of information not included in the Allen text, and his "Supplement to Jefferson's Memoir of Meriwether Lewis" presents additional research on the mystery of Lewis's apparent suicide in 1809. Lewis and Clark ostensibly shared the leadership of the expedition, although Jefferson's directions and other communications with the explorers tended to be directed more often toward Lewis.

6. Donald Jackson, ed., *Letters of the Lewis and Clark Expedition, with Related Documents, 1783–1854* (Urbana: University of Illinois Press, 1962), v.

7. Stephen Ambrose surmises in *Undaunted Courage: Meriwether Lewis, Thomas Jefferson, and the Opening of the American West* (New York: Simon and Schuster, 1996) that it is indeed through Jefferson that Lewis "learned how to write." Ambrose is referring not to basic literacy but to the development of Lewis's prose style. During his employment as the president's secretary from 1801 to 1802, according to Ambrose, "Lewis's sense of pace, his timing, his word choice, his rhythm, his similes and analogies all improved. He sharpened his descriptive powers. He learned how to catch a reader up in his own response to events and places, to express his emotions naturally and effectively" (67). If we understand Lewis's style to have been not simply the transparent vehicle of disinterested accounts, but, like many other things in his life, a product of Jefferson's teaching and a crafted means for shaping images of the continent, Lewis's self-generated characterization as a natural intellect becomes part of the stylistic machinery of his narrative.

8. Emile Zola, "Naturalism in the Theatre," in *Documents of Modern Literary Realism*, ed. George J. Becker (Princeton, N.J.: Princeton University Press, 1963), 199.

9. DeVoto, 163. In this and the following citations from DeVoto's edition, I have amended Lewis's and Clark's spelling to suit contemporary standards.

10. Stephen Ambrose quotes Charles MacKenzie, a British trader who visited the Corps of Discovery at Fort Mandan in the late fall of 1804, to demonstrate the difficulty of these translation processes between expedition personnel and residents of the country: "Sacagawea spoke a little Hidatsa, in which she had to converse with her husband, who was a Canadian and did not understand English. A mulatto, who spoke bad French and worse English, served as interpreter to the Captains, so that a single word to be understood by the party required to pass from the natives to the woman, from the woman to the husband, from the husband to the mulatto, from the mulatto to the captains" (187).

    MacKenzie's description illustrates the instability of communication and the enormous potential for incomprehension, misunderstanding, and the play of meaning in a more general sense in the pastiche of language per se in the West.

11. In *Imperial Eyes: Travel Writing and Transculturation* (London: Routledge, 1994), Mary Louise Pratt offers similar observations on the figure of the New World explorer-scientist and the discipline of natural history in the late eighteenth century. Natural history in this period, employing Linnaeus's classification system, "conceived of the world as a chaos out of which the scientist produced an order. It is not, then, simply a question of depicting the planet as it was" (30–31). Further, "natural history extracts all things of the world and redeploys them into a knowledge formation whose value lies precisely in its difference from the chaotic original" (33).

12. See Annette Kolodny, *The Lay of the Land: Metaphor as Experience and History in American Life and Letters* (Chapel Hill: University of North Carolina Press, 1976), 46, 90, and *The Land Before Her*, 5; Slotkin, *Regeneration Through Violence*, 21, *The Fatal Environment: The Myth of the Frontier in the Age of Industrialism 1800–1890* (New York: Atheneum, 1985), 81–82, and *Gunfighter Nation*, 15–16; Cawelti, *The Six-Gun Mystique*, 14; Drinnon, *Facing West*, 123–124; and Henry Nash Smith, *Virgin Land: The American West as Symbol and Myth* (Cambridge, Mass.: Harvard University Press, 1950), 61. Kolodny uses the term "pastoral" rather than "Western" to designate the generic category of Cooper's work and of the models he set, but her discussion in general relates to the same body of American frontier literature that I address.

13. In *Plotting America's Past: Fenimore Cooper and the Leatherstocking Tales* (Carbondale: Southern Illinois University Press, 1983), William P. Kelly writes that "Cooper based some of his characters, incidents, and settings on contemporary accounts of the New West—most particularly those of the Lewis and Clark and the [Steven] Long expeditions . . ." (91n).

14. James Fenimore Cooper, *The Deerslayer: Or, the First Warpath*, vol. 2 of *The Leatherstocking Tales*, ed. Blake Nevius (New York: Library of America, 1985), 525.

15. Frederick Jackson Turner, *The Significance of the Frontier in American History*, ed. Harold P. Simonson (New York: Ungar), 27, 58.

Chapter 3 Frederick Jackson Turner, Edward S. Curtis, and the Romance of Disappearing

1. Frederick Jackson Turner, *The Significance of the Frontier in American History*, ed. Harold P. Simonson (New York: Frederick Ungar, 1963), 2.

2. This holds true in spite of, indeed perhaps because of, the many recent revisionist histories of the American West that cite Turner's thesis as a position

against which to construct new interpretations of U. S. expansionism. As Alan Brinkley wrote concerning several newer histories of the West in *The New York Times Book Review* (September 20, 1992), "Central to almost all descriptions of the new history is an obligatory, almost ritualistic repudiation of Frederick Jackson Turner. The 'frontier thesis' may long ago have lost its allure in other areas of American history, but it retains a perverse hold on students of the West" (22). Among the texts described by Brinkley are William Cronon, George Miles, and Jay Gitlin, eds., *Under an Open Sky: Rethinking America's Western Past* (New York: Norton, 1992); Patricia Nelson Limerick, Clyde A. Milner, and Charles E. Rankin, eds., *Trails: Toward a New Western History* (Lawrence: University Press of Kansas, 1992); Richard White, *"It's Your Misfortune and None of My Own": A New History of the American West* (Norman: University of Oklahoma Press, 1992); Donald Worster, *Under Western Skies: Nature and History in the American West* (New York: Oxford University Press, 1992); and William Cronon, *Nature's Metropolis: Chicago and the Great West* (New York: Norton, 1991).

In "The Return of the Native: The Politics of Identity in American Indian Fiction of the West," in *Reading the West: New Essays on the Literature of the American West* (New York: Cambridge University Press, 1996), Philip Burnham writes: "Radically qualified, if not rejected, by revisionist historians today, the Turner theory still has a hold on the public imagination. From supermarket fiction to big-budget Hollywood westerns, Indian people seem tied to the West of buffalo, wide open plains, and the obligatory setting sun" (199).

3. Two years after the deletion of the frontier category from the 1890 Census, this fact was noted unceremoniously in a four-page pamphlet entitled "Extra Census Bulletin No. 2., Distribution of Population According to Density: 1890." See Ray Allen Billington, *Frederick Jackson Turner: Historian, Scholar, Teacher* (New York: Oxford University Press), 117.

4. In *Turner and Beard: American Historical Writing Reconsidered* (New York: Free Press, 1960), Lee Benson offers the persuasive argument that Turner's thesis was influenced not so much by the census data but, however indirectly, by the economist Achille Loria, whose ideas "concerning the role of land in the social process profoundly influenced both European and American thought" in Turner's time (1). Benson's first two chapters, "Achille Loria's Influence on American Economic Thought: Including His Contributions to the Frontier Hypothesis" and "The Historical Background of Turner's Frontier Essay," are crucial for an understanding of the atmosphere in which Turner's thesis emerged.

5. Much important work in Native American studies in the 1980s and 1990s by Vine Deloria, Dee Brown, Ward Churchill, Annette Jaimes, Patricia Nelson Limerick, William Cronon, and others has focused scholarly attention on the perspectives of indigenous historiography; these perspectives offer substantial counter-narratives to the stories that might be said to derive from Turner and that are subscribed to even today in most textbooks of U.S. history.

6. Quoted in Mick Gidley, *Edward S. Curtis and the North American Indian, Incorporated* (New York: Cambridge University Press, 1998), 180.

7. Quoted in Christopher Lyman, *The Vanishing Race and Other Illusions: Photographs of Indians by Edward S. Curtis* (Washington, D.C.: Smithsonian Institution Press, 1982), 79.

8. Quoted in Christopher Cardozo, ed., *Native Nations: First Americans as Seen by Edward S. Curtis* (Boston: Little, Brown, 1993), 122.

9. Gidley, *Edward S. Curtis and the North American Indian, Incorporated*, 6. See also James Clifford, *The Predicament of Culture: Twentieth-Century Ethnography, Literature and Art* (Cambridge, Mass.: Harvard University Press, 1988), 284.

10. Quoted in Cardozo, 20–21.
11. Quoted in Cardozo, 11.
12. Gidley, 43.

Chapter 4   Importing Naturalism to the American West

1. Quoted in Naomi Schor, *Zola's Crowds* (Baltimore: Johns Hopkins University Press, 1978), 181.
2. William Cronon, *Nature's Metropolis: Chicago and the Great West* (New York, Norton: 1991), xvii.
3. In this understanding of literary character as a textual figure that has the capacity of self-analysis, I am assuming the definitions of character that Harold Bloom charts in his essay "The Analysis of Character," in his edition of *Ahab* (Broomhall, Penn.: Chelsea House, Major Literary Characters Series, 1991), ix–xiv. Bloom's idea is that self-analysis emerges in moments when, through the ironies of narrative situations, a literary figure overhears or oversees his or her own being; and this is precisely the kind of character formation I am referring to in the dynamics of naturalist Westerns.
4. Donald Pizer, "Evolutionary Ethical Dualism in *McTeague* and *Vandover and the Brute*," *PMLA* (December 1961): 552–560.
5. See, for example, the theories of LeConte and Fiske as discussed by Pizer in "Evolutionary Ethical Dualism" and in *The Novels of Frank Norris* (Bloomington: Indiana University Press, 1966). Spencer's ideas of the relations between the baser and the higher human propensities are articulated in several of his works; a sufficient introductory account is provided in his 1862 *First Principles* (New York: Dewitt Revolving Fund, 1958).
6. Freud's and Breuer's earliest psychical theories were expressed in their "Preliminary Communication," which was translated into English in 1893 and published in the British *Proceedings of the Society for Psychical Research* (June 1893). See James Strachey's introduction to the *Standard Edition of the Complete Psychological Works, Volume II: Studies on Hysteria* (London: Hogarth Press, 1955), xv. Like the spiritualist and spirit communication movements that were popular in the U.S. and Britain throughout the later decades of the nineteenth century, psychoanalysis posited a "second" mode of the human self to which hypnotism and other forms of trance gave access. Although Freud would later dispense with hypnotism as a vehicle for psychoanalysis, his and Breuer's concept of the unconscious is obviously the most important of these ideas of the divided human subject that appeared in the late nineteenth century.
7. Brian Nelson comments on this contradiction as it applies to Zola's broader social vision in his *Zola and the Bourgeoisie: A Study of Themes and Techniques in "Les Rougon Macquarts"* (Lanham, Md.: Barnes and Noble Books-Imports, 1983):

> An element of ambiguity arises from the contrast between Zola's positivist ideology, which leads to an optimistic vision of a well-ordered society based on science, and his detailed observation of the anarchic nature of a society based on the survival of the fittest. Zola's scientific faith, in other words, is at odds with his Darwinian view of humanity. Moreover, his commitment to social justice might seem to be in conflict with his own dogmatic temperament and with his admiration of those forceful characters who succeed in imposing their will on others. (24)

Chapter 5   *Frank Norris and the Fiction of the Lost West*

1. Verne A. Stadtman, *The University of California, 1868–1968* (New York: McGraw Hill, 1970).
2. See *University of California Annual Report for the Year Ending June 30, 1890*, 46–49. Courtesy, University Archives, The Bancroft Library, University of California, Berkeley.
3. William Carey Jones, *Illustrated History of the University of California, 1886–1895* (San Francisco: Frank H. Kukesmith, 1895), 70.
4. *U. C. Annual Report* . . . 1889, 89. Courtesy Bancroft Library.
5. *U. C. Annual Report* . . . 1885, 55; 1886, 29; 1889, 89. Courtesy Bancroft Library.
6. *U.C. Annual Report* . . . 1885, 52; *The Berkeleyan* (Oct. 14, 1885):14, 18. Courtesy Bancroft Library
7. For a detailed discussion of San Francisco architecture during this period, see Kevin Starr, "Arthur Page Brown and the Dream of San Francisco," in his *Inventing the Dream: California Through the Progressive Era* (New York: Oxford University Press, 1985).
8. A comprehensive and useful account of the sources and circulation of the "germ theory" in the American academy and its implications in Norris's work appears in Donald Pizer's "Frank Norris and the Frontier as Popular Idea in America," *Amerikastudien* 13 (1978): 230–239. See also Pizer's sources, Howard Mumford Jones, *The Theory of American Literature* (Ithaca, N.Y.: Cornell University Press, 1948); and Edward N. Saveth "Race and Nationalism in American Historiography," *Political Science Quarterly* LIV (September 1939): 421–441.
9. Kevin Starr, *America and the California Dream* (New York: Oxford University Press, 1973), 50.
10. For San Francisco population statistics by ethnic groups, see Department of the Interior, *Report on the Population of the United States at the Eleventh Census: 1890* (Washington, D.C.: Government Printing Office, 1892), table 22, 491.
11. Department of the Interior census statistics indicate an increase in the 1880 female population of San Francisco County over 1860 and 1870. By 1890 the population of women in San Francisco county was 43.2 percent of the total, about the same percentage as the census indicated for 1880, which was 43.3 percent. See the Department's *Statistics of the Population of the United States at the Tenth Census (June 1, 1880)* (Washington, D.C.: Government Printing Office, 1883), table 23, 649; *A Compendium of the Ninth Census (June 1, 1870)* (Washington, D.C.: Government Printing Office, 1872), table 57, 557; and *Population of the United States in 1860; Compiled from the Original Returns of the Eighth Census* (Washington, D.C.: Government Printing Office, 1864), 22–27. In spite of this apparent leveling off of the male-female ratio, the 1880 census offers a gender analysis of the population at large as follows: "the preponderance of females is in the Atlantic Region. . . . The most marked cases of the excess of males are in the territories and newer states of the West, where settlement is recent, where immigration is still active and where the luxuries and the comforts of life are greatly abridged by the necessities of frontier existence" (xxxv). This condition holds true for all states and territories "in which the number of females is 50 to 80 per cent of the number of males." Whereas the population of women in the state of California was calculated at 66,872 to every 100,000 men, the figures for San Francisco show a closer parity between the sexes.

12. Patricia Nelson Limerick argues in *The Legacy of Conquest: The Unbroken Past of the American West* (New York: Norton, 1987) that "the American West is a preeminent case study in conquest and its consequences" in a national history that has conquest as its "bedrock" (28). Such a claim, however, might be made for any region of the continent at any moment of the Euro-American presence, from the seventeenth through the nineteenth centuries, precisely because conquest has indeed been one of its central principles, if not an overtly expressed intention, from the beginning. But where Western history does seem to have preeminence is in its emblematic, symbolic capacity to image and recall the narrative of conquest throughout Euro-American history. Although Limerick argues convincingly and usefully for "removing Western history from the domain of myth and symbol and restoring it to actuality" (52), it should be remembered that the momentum of myth and symbol in what might be termed the reception history of the West has done a great deal to fuel the staying power of the paradigms and practices that Limerick so powerfully addresses.

13. Starr, *America and the California Dream*, 262.

14. Norris, *Novels and Essays* (New York: Library of America, 1986), 1165. In *Reading for Realism: The History of a U.S. Literary Institution, 1850–1910* (Durham, N.C.: Duke University Press, 1997), Nancy Glazener writes that Norris's "protest against the previous literary establishment was made in the name of "romance"; some other early twentieth-century writers and critics protested against Howellsian realism in the name of a deeper realism, which subsequent literary historians often called 'naturalism'. . . . What most of these . . . rebels shared was an animus against not only or even primarily a kind of writing, but against the infrastructure of publishing and class hierarchy that had enculturated and promoted it" (235). Glazener thus sees Norris's identification with "romance" as not so much a literary issue as the expression of a political position vis-a-vis Howells and the powers of the current literary establishment. Her point is well taken, since Norris's fiction most often appears invested in pursuing a plain style of realist language and the "deeper realism" of French naturalism, while its romanticisms seem to be more inadvertent and anxious. So for Norris to claim to identify with romantic writing, as he does, for instance, in "Zola as a Romantic Writer" and "A Plea for Romantic Writing," is for him to preach a position that he does not overtly practice. The term "naturalism" did not only emerge later as a critical category but was used by Norris and others of his generation to designate a current literary phenomenon; and Norris overtly identified with it.

15. In 1893 Norris studied the history of literary criticism and aesthetics with Gayley, who was one of the more well-known academic critics in the United States during the 1890s. In 1898 Gayley published *An Introduction to the Methods and Materials of Literary Criticism: The Bases in Aesthetics and Poetics* (Boston: Ginn and Co., 1898), in collaboration with his colleague Fred Newton Scott. This extensive bibliographic essay presents the arguments about literary aesthetics and analysis outlined in rougher form in Gayley's class notes (on file at the Bancroft Library, University of California, Berkeley.) The relationship posed in *Methods and Materials* between Pater and Matthew Arnold actually frames the book's dominant concerns and situates Gayley's intellectual habits as a critic and teacher. Arnold's famous comment in *Essays in Criticism* (London: Macmillan, 1916) that the role of the critic is to see "the object as in itself it really is"

(1) appears to be the central statement in relation to which others are placed. Nevertheless, Gayley's attitude toward Arnold's position is peculiarly ambivalent:

"Concerning his definition of criticism, we may ask whether, philosophically speaking, it is possible to see anything as in itself it really is. Things are understood only as they are seen in relation to other things. More than that, we always see them as colored by our personal views and tendencies; the same thing has different meanings for different persons" (10–11). This explanation seems to be informed by Pater's response to Arnold in the preface to *The Renaissance: Studies in Art and Poetry* (London: Macmillan, 1900), where Pater writes that "the first step toward seeing one's object as it really is, is to know one's impression as it really is, to discriminate it, to realize it distinctly" (viii). Gayley and Scott simply note that Pater's argument "approves of Arnold's definition of criticism. The first step in aesthetic criticism is to realize one's own impressions clearly" (30). In *The Renaissance*, Pater challenges Arnold's model by celebrating expressiveness and the exquisite moments of the writer's temperament as the manifest focus of his vision of art. The Paterian position implied in Gayley's and Scott's questions suggests an ambivalence on their part about the values of subject- as opposed to object-oriented critical theory. The dichotomies that arise in consideration of such questions, and of others that emerge in the debate between Pater and Arnold, repeat a typically Victorian one between impressionism and science that in contemporary literature of the American West was suggested in the opposition between allusive, metaphorical language and the simple, straightforward realism that deals in facts and objects. In many ways, these oppositions address the anxious wish in Norris's writing, as in much Western prose and fiction, to be new and different in relation to a dominant tradition and to have access to the precultural state to which Arnold aspires. Norris's relinquishing of the wish to represent what is real never quite expires, but it continually expresses an awareness of the necessarily secondary quality of any literary or artistic composition.

16. Donald Pizer, ed., *The Literary Criticism of Frank Norris* (Austin, Tex.: University of Texas Press, 1964), xv.
17. William Dillingham, *Frank Norris: Instinct and Art* (Lincoln: University of Nebraska Press, 1969), 59.
18. Larzer Ziff, *The American 1890s: Life and Times of a Lost Generation* (New York: Viking, 1966), 253.
19. "An Opening for Novelists: Great Opportunities for Fiction Writers in San Francisco," in Norris, *Novels and Essays*, 1113.
20. In *Literary Criticism of Frank Norris*, ed. Pizer.
21. In *Literary Criticism of Frank Norris*, ed. Pizer.
22. In *Literary Criticism of Frank Norris*, ed. Pizer.
23. In *Novels and Essays*, 1183, 1185.
24. Kenneth Lynn, *Mark Twain and Southwestern Humor* (Boston: Little Brown, 1960).
25. In *A Deal in Wheat: Collected Stories* (New York: Doubleday, Page, 1903). Page citations for quotations from the stories discussed refer to this volume.
26. James Clifford, "Of Other Peoples: Beyond the "'Salvage' Paradigm," *DIA Art Foundation Discussions in Contemporary Culture*, ed. Hal Foster (Seattle: Bay Press, 1987), 121–130.
27. In *Novels and Essays*.

28. Walter Benn Michaels, *The Gold Standard and the Logic of Naturalism* (Berkeley: University of California Press, 1987). Michaels presents an interesting and by now quite influential discussion of the question of value in several fields of representation during the 1890s, particularly in relation to gold and money.
29. For a similar discussion of gold as the incarnation of the "economic principle of substitution and replacement" and its gender-inflected ways of producing meaning in Balzac, see Shoshana Felman, "Rereading Femininity," *Yale French Studies* 62 (1981): 37–39.
30. This discussion has some things in common with Felman's reading of Balzac's "The Girl with the Golden Eyes," but there gold's double function of signifier and signified is understood as ultimately representative of male desire.
31. Norris, *McTeague* (New York: Norton, 1977).

Chapter 6   *Jack London and the Politics of Evolution*

1. Andrew Sinclair notes in *Jack: A Biography of Jack London* (New York: Harper and Row, 1977) that "he always would exaggerate the hardships of his childhood to dramatize his great leap forward from his origins" (5). But the record shows that, in spite of periods of relative comfort, the London family was never really financially viable, and Jack had to start working at a very young age to help the family to meet its needs. Working kept him from finishing school at the standard pace. For further discussion of London's mythologizing of himself for the public, see Jonathan Auerbach, *Male Call: Becoming Jack London* (Durham, N.C.: Duke University Press, 1996); Joan D. Hedrick, *Solitary Comrade: Jack London and His Work* (Chapel Hill: University of North Carolina Press, 1982); Alex Kershaw, *Jack London: A Life* (New York: St. Martin's, 1997); and John Perry, *Jack London, An American Myth* (Chicago: Nelson-Hall, 1981).
2. Sinclair, 14. For further discussion of Oakland's origins, see "The Beginning of Oakland and Other East Bay Communities," in Lawrence Kinnaird, *History of the Greater San Francisco Bay Region*, vol.1 (New York: Lewis Historical Publication Co., 1966).
3. Quoted in Sal Noto, *Jack London's California* (New York: Beaufort Books, 1986), 147.
4. See Perry, 47, Sinclair, 35, and David Starr Jordan, *The Days of a Man: Being Memories of a Naturalist Teacher and Minor Prophet of Democracy*, vol. 1 (Yonkers on Hudson, N.Y.: World Book Co., 1922), 460.
5. Letter to Cloudsley Johns, July 29, 1899, in *The Letters of Jack London*, Vol. 1: *1896–1905*, eds. Earle Labor, Robert C. Leitz, III, and I. Milo Shepard (Stanford, Calif.: Stanford University Press, 1988), 99.
6. See David Mike Hamilton, *"The Tools of My Trade": The Annotated Books in Jack London's Library* (Seattle: University of Washington Press, 1986), 175. Hamilton notes that, "although London's early correspondence with Anna Strunsky and Cloudsley Johns indicated an affinity with Jordan's philosophy, he later rejected Jordan's writings as bourgeois."
7. David Starr Jordan, "California and the Californians," *Atlantic Monthly* 82 (December 1898): 793–801.
8. For a more detailed discussion of Jordan's ideas, see Kevin Starr, *Inventing the Dream: California Through the Progressive Era* (New York: Oxford University Press, 1985), 224–226, 245, and 247.
9. It should be noted that, as Kevin Starr explains in *Inventing the Dream*, Jordan "knew and respected Japanese culture from his travels there and fostered the

coming of Japanese exchange students to Stanford" (260). This admiration stood in contrast to the attitudes of many Californians who felt that Asians could never assimilate to the culture of the United States and that immigration for them should be very strictly limited. Nevertheless, Jordan's comments about Catholics and people from certain non-Anglo-European cultures clearly mark him as an ethnocentric thinker.

10. Herbert Spencer, *First Principles* (New York: P. F. Collier and Son, 1902), 329–359.

11. *The Letters of Jack London*, ed. Labor et al., 92.

12. Like Norris's McTeague, London's characters of this sort dramatized his understanding of the "blonde beast" as Nietzsche conceptualized it in *The Genealogy of Morals*, trans. Walter Kaufmann (New York: Vintage, 1967), 40.

13. In London, *Novels and Stories* (New York: Library of America, 1982). Page citations for quotations from London's stories and *The Call of the Wild* refer to this volume.

14. For a discussion of these debates and of the public figures who conducted them at the turn of the century, see Robert L. Beisner, *Twelve Against Empire: The Anti-Imperialists, 1898–1900* (New York: McGraw-Hill, 1968).

15. See Donna Haraway, "Teddy Bear Patriarchy: Taxidermy in the Garden of Eden, New York City, 1908–1936," in *Primate Visions: Gender, Race and Nature in the World of Modern Science* (New York: Routledge, 1989); Mark Seltzer, *Bodies and Machines* (New York: Routledge, 1992); and Amy Kaplan, "Romancing the Empire: The Embodiment of American Masculinity in the Popular Historical Novel of the 1890's," *American Literary History* 2 (winter 1990).

16. In Frantz Fanon, *The Wretched of the Earth*, trans. Constance Farrington (New York: Grove Press, 1968), 148–205.

17. Sinclair explains that London supported women's suffrage in 1911 because he was in favor of the prohibitionist stance that the feminists typically took. Even though he was a notorious drinker himself, he claimed to like the idea of women working to keep men dry and thus to help with the "preservation of the white race." While this may be so, London also expressed admiration for stronger women who could keep up with the pace and the risk of adventure. The compelling characteristics of this "Mate Woman"—for example, Ruth Mason of "The White Silence," Maud Brewster of *The Sea Wolf*, as well as London's wife Charmian Kittredge—is that she takes great physical risks and manages to survive the dangers of wilderness experience along with the central male characters. Often more male than female, these women are not so much arguments for feminist politics as they are for the desirability of masculine being. The narratives in which they appear attempt to dramatize the idea that their physical and psychological strengths are equal to those of their male companions, but this equality is based on a kind of macho strength rather than on a balance of power between different, male and female experiences.

18. See Earle Labor, Robert C. Leitz, and I. Milo Shepard, eds., *Short Stories of Jack London* (New York: Macmillan, 1990), xxiii.

19. In *Form and History in American Literary Naturalism* (Chapel Hill: University of North Carolina Press, 1985), June Howard describes *The Call of the Wild* as "the story of a dog that becomes a wolf," in contrast to *White Fang*, where "a wolf becomes a dog." This dog-wolf, she argues, is "the most characteristic and distinctive figure of London's effort to grasp and resolve" the central dichotomy between nature and culture in much of London's Northland fiction. Howard complicates this binary relationship, however, by adding that "each story

develops a network of oppositions that makes it possible for the animal protagonist to cross the boundary between nature and culture and thus makes it possible to envision their reconciliation" (51). Her reading of the novel attempts
to deconstruct these oppositions and show the instability of the arbitrary structures that they tentatively provide. I would agree with this argument, insofar as
it depicts these two terms as continuously implying each other; but I do not see
that they and the world views they suggest are ultimately resolved by the instability of the opposition. If nature is associated with a romantic mode of being
and culture with a deterministic one, the terms are certainly necessary to the
mutual construction of meaning between them; but this does not mean that
the competition between them as principles for representing the fin-de-siècle
West ceases.

20. See, for instance, Sinclair, 37, and Labor et al., xiv.
21. Auerbach makes the case that the frozen landscape of *The Call of the Wild*
    works as a surface to image the writing with which London is preoccupied. He
    writes, "toiling in the traces that leave their own marks on the white landscape,
    both Buck and Jack fulfill their calling" (98). Auerbach is interested in show-
    ing how London's writing articulates a concern with writing itself, not so much
    as an artistic or intellectual issue as a matter of the dynamics of publishing and
    having a career as a writer. In my view, the landscape illustrates an argument
    London is trying to sustain about evolutionary theory, however confused or
    contradictory the argument may be.
22. In London, *Novels and Social Writings* (New York: Library of America, 1982),
    665. Page citations for quotations from *Martin Eden* refer to this volume.
23. For a stimulating account of these more ominous dimensions of the poet's pre-
    sumably egalitarian poetics, see David Simpson, "Destiny Made Manifest: The
    Styles of Whitman's Poetry," in *Nation and Narration*, ed. Homi Bhabha (New
    York: Routledge, 1990).
24. Henry Noble Day, *The Science of Aesthetics; or the nature, kinds, laws and uses of
    beauty* (New Haven, Conn.: Chatfield, 1872).

Chapter 7   Stephen Crane's Literary Tourism

1. Sculley Bradley, Richard C. Beatty et al., eds., *The American Tradition in Literature*, vol. 2 (New York: Grosset and Dunlap, 1956), 787.
2. For useful discussions of the religious context of the Crane household when
   Stephen was young, see Christopher Benfey, *The Double Life of Stephen Crane:
   A Biography* (New York: Knopf, 1992), 21–38; and R. W. Stallman, *Stephen
   Crane: A Biography* (New York: Braziller, 1968), 1–17.
3. Stanley Wertheim and Paul Sorrentino, eds., *The Correspondence of Stephen
   Crane, vol. 1 (New York: Columbia University Press, 1988), 42.
4. Stephen Crane, "The Mexican Lower Classes," in *Prose and Poetry* (New York:
   Library of America, 1984), 731. Page citations for quotations from Crane's fiction refer to this volume.
5. I agree with Frank Bergon, writing in *Stephen Crane's Artistry* (New York:
   Columbia University Press, 1975), that "it is difficult . . . to accept parody as
   the main intention of [Crane's Western] stories" (106); yet it is clear that
   Crane uses parody to underscore the sense of self-consciousness and awkwardness that his Western stories project. Bergon's book includes an extended discussion of Crane's Westerns that centers on his impressionistic treatment of
   incommensurate perceptions. Bergon addresses the mixture of irony and affir-

mation in Crane's representations of the West, although he ultimately seems to read them as indications of the writer's affection "for the great honest West" as opposed to the "false East." In my view Crane's impressionism complicates the picture of the West and of Western culture too much for such a dichotomous view to be considered representative of his thoughts on the matter.

6. In *Realism, Writing, Disfiguration: On Thomas Eakins and Stephen Crane* (Chicago: University of Chicago Press, 1987), Michael Fried considers Crane's "upturned faces" in *The Red Badge of Courage*, "The Monster," and several of the 1894 New York City sketches to be indicators of an apparently involuntary preoccupation with the writing process itself. Fried's approach traces the metaphors for writing and drawing in Crane's fiction that subvert the distancing effect of the journalistic-realist pose of the narrator. These images seem indeed to disrupt the illusion of reportorial objectivity, but my comments on Crane focus on character and subjectivity rather than on the reflexivity of the "scene of writing" that concerns Fried.

7. In the conclusion of "The Blue Hotel," the Easterner offers the theory that events proceed from the "collaboration" of all persons involved in them. His way of explaining the Swede's death is thus to distribute responsibility for it among all of the characters, himself included. The philosophical implications of this idea have been debated extensively, particularly as they relate to naturalist theories of determinism. Some representative essays include Alan H. Wycherly, "Crane's 'The Blue Hotel': How Many Collaborators?" *American Notes and Queries* (February 1966): 88; James T. Cox, "Stephen Crane as Symbolic Naturalist: An Analysis of 'The Blue Hotel,' " *Modern Fiction Studies* (summer 1957): 147–158; and Bruce L. Greenberg, "Metaphysics of Despair: Stephen Crane's 'The Blue Hotel,' " *Modern Fiction Studies* (summer 1968): 203–213. I would add to this discussion only that, assuming every word, character, and step of plot contributes to the effects of a literary text and to the ways that it produces meaning, this idea of collaboration cannot be denied. Considered as a principle of actuality, it becomes more difficult to test. Crane's notion that perception and experience are too complex to account for univocally would seem to suggest that any one person's causal responsibility for a particular event would be difficult to establish by any method other than consensus. But to say that everyone is responsible for everything is not to say much at all.

8. These structures are explicitly and succinctly described by John Cawelti in *The Six-Gun Mystique* (Bowling Green, Ohio: Bowling Green State University Popular Press), 59–60, 98–100.

9. R. P. Blackmur uses this phrase in *Language as Gesture* (New York: Harcourt Brace, 1952). James D. Bloom writes in *The Stock of Available Reality* (Lewisburg, Pa.: Bucknell University Press, 1984) of "Blackmur's demand that poets [of his generation] develop distinctive 'idioms' which 'add to the stock of available reality' and deploy 'language as gesture' " (10).

10. Zola, "The Experimental Novel," in *Documents of Modern Literary Realism*, ed. George Becker (Princeton, N. J.: Princeton University Press, 1963), 168.

11. Crane's seemingly deterministic attitude toward the schemes of capitalist development in the story should be understood in the context of naturalist politics. That is, he assumed not that no alternative was possible to such development but that, as long as its momentum was as active as it was in his time, it would determine the economic and social factors of life for most people. Crane's New York City sketches, as well as much of his more socially focused journalism, give evidence of his assumption that other modes of development

might be possible and preferable for the United States. Without offering a picture as to what those modes might be, his portraits of urban development generally express his sense that it was often socially divisive, that it neglected
poverty and simply repressed violence between and within the social classes.

One of his most well known stories, the 1894 "An Experiment in Misery,"
concludes with the central character ruminating on the ethics of the nation's
corporate powers, among the products of which are the indigence and depres-
sion that he has just witnessed during his "experiment" in misery among the
downtown bums: "In the background a multitude of buildings, of pitiless hues
and sternly high, were to him emblematic of a nation forcing its regal head into
the clouds, throwing no downward glances; in the sublimity of its aspirations
ignoring the wretches who may flounder at its feet. The roar of the city in his
ear was to him the confusion of strange tongues, babbling heedlessly; it was the
clink of coin, the voice of the city's hopes which were to him no hopes" (*Prose
and Poetry*, 548). The politics of "An Experiment in Misery" may be said to
reflect Crane's own indigence and sense of failure at the time he wrote it, but
his continued interest in urban degradation, expressed in the publication of
George's Mother and the revised version of *Maggie, A Girl of the Streets* in 1896,
indicate that the tone of the earlier city sketches had not diminished. The passage from "An Experiment in Misery" converts the harsh expression of urban
corporate wealth into an image of national romanticism reminiscent in certain
ways of Emerson's "Nature." The problem with this transcendental blindness,
Crane suggests, is not just its isolation and vanity but its ignorance.

Crane casts the loftiness of its aspirations in the nearly religious terms that
speakers for the "national interest," like those who spoke for corporate interests, often used to represent their destinies. But this by no means suggests that
Crane perceived any sort of necessity in such progresses; on the contrary, the
passage from "An Experiment in Misery," like the rest of the story, presents a
critique of the unnatural power that U.S. corporate capitalism has acquired, as
well as of the national destiny the corporate world presumes to represent. The
critique assumes the possibility of change, of a "downward glance" being drawn,
if by no other means than by writing like Crane's.

12. For an interesting and useful account of this dynamic in later twentieth-
century U.S. fiction, see John McClure, *Late Imperial Romance* (London: Verso,
1993).

Chapter 8   *Willa Cather and the Enchantment of Difference*

1. Robert W. Cherny, *Populism, Progressivism and the Transformation of Nebraska
Politics, 1885–1915* (Lincoln: University of Nebraska Press, 1981), xv–xvi, 1,
4.

2. James Woodress, *Willa Cather: A Literary Life* (Lincoln: University of Nebraska
Press, 1987).

3. The newspapers were *The Alliance Independent*, which Cherny describes as "the
Populist state organ" (41). The rise of populism made for a very lively political
scene during Cather's years as a college student in Lincoln. But neither the
vociferousness of Nebraska's electoral politics nor the ideologies of the parties
seem to have engaged Cather's imagination very extensively. The one great
exception was her interest in William Jennings Bryan, whom she met in Lincoln and wrote about in "The Personal Side of William Jennings Bryan." As
Woodress notes, "The political and economic issues that produced the Populist

party in the nineties interested her very little, but the personality of Bryan was fascinating" (100–101).

4. Quoted in Woodress, 36.
5. Ibid., 107.
6. Susan Rosowski, *The Voyage Perilous: Willa Cather's Romanticism* (Lincoln: University of Nebraska Press, 1986), 209.
7. For the entire address, see Woodress, pp. 60–62.
8. *The Professor's House* (New York: Random House, 1990), 54–55.
9. Quoted in Woodress, 75–76.
10. William M. Curtin, ed., *The World and the Parish: Willa Cather's Articles and Reviews, 1893–1902* (Lincoln: University of Nebraska Press, 1970), 70.
11. Quoted in Woodress, 107.
12. See her comments on these writers in "Selected Reviews and Essays, 1895–1940," in *Cather: Stories, Poems and Other Writings* (New York: Library of America, 1992).
13. In *Cather: Stories, Poems and Other Writings*, 938.
14. "Introduction to Stephen Crane's 'Wounds in the Rain,' " ibid., 954–955.
15. Hermione Lee, *Willa Cather: Double Lives* (New York: Pantheon, 1989), 37.
16. Walter Benn Michaels, *Our America: Nativism, Modernism and Pluralism* (Durham, N. C.: Duke University Press).
17. Christopher Nealon, "Affect-Genealogy: Feeling and Affiliation in Willa Cather," *American Literature* 69 (March 1997): 29–31.
18. *Death Comes for the Archbishop* (New York: Random House, 1990), 84.
19. Rosowski, *The Voyage Perilous*, 162–163.

Chapter 9   *The Strangeness of Closure*

1. Donna Haraway, "Teddy Bear Patriarchy: Taxidermy in the Garden of Eden." In her *Primate Visions: Gender, Race and Nature in the World of Modern Science* (New York: Routledge, 1989).
2. For an extensive reading of English and American literary efforts from the late nineteenth century to the present to retain a realm of unmapped mystery and enchantment beyond the pale of home, see John McClure's *Late Imperial Romance* (London: Verso, 1993).
3. Norris, *The Third Circle* (New York: John Lane, 1909), 76.
4. See Andrew Sinclair, *Jack: A Biography of Jack London* (New York: Harper and Row, 1977).
5. Donald Pizer, "Chronology," in London, *Novels and Stories* (New York: Library of America, 1982), 994.
6. London, *Novels and Stories* (New York: Library of America, 1982), 990.
7. Amy Kaplan, "Romancing the Empire: The Embodiment of American Masculinity in the Popular Historical Novel of the 1890s," *American Literary History* 2 (winter 1990).

Index

Académie Julian, 77, 89
Acoma Pueblo, 183
Agua Caliente Reservation, 55
Akeley, Carl, 187–188
Allen, Paul, 203n. 5
Ambrose, Stephen, 203n. 7, 204n. 10
Applegate, Shannon, 199n. 8
Arnold, Matthew, 87, 109, 208n. 15, 209n. 15
Aron, Stephen, 201n. 5
Auerbach, Jonathan, 210n. 1, 212n. 21

Bakeless, John, 203n. 3
Becker, George, 203n. 8, 213n. 10
Beisner, Robert L., 211n. 14
Benfey, Christopher, 212n. 2
Benson, Lee, 205n. 4
Bergon, Frank, 212n. 5
Bercovitch, Sacvan, 199n. 8
Bhabha, Homi, 212n. 23
Bierce, Ambrose, 5, 85, 169
Bierstadt, Albert, 2
Billington, Ray Allen, 205n. 3
Blackmur, R.P., 213n. 9
Bloom, Harold, 86, 206n. 3
Bloom, James D., 213n. 9
Bonté, John H.C., 75, 76, 77
Boone, Daniel: as colonialist, 28; and Rebecca Bryan Boone, 24–26, 201n. 13, 202n. 14; and William Clark, 203n. 3; elusiveness of, 23–24, 103; John Filson biography of, 7, 19–24, 28, 29, 37, 38, 39, 60; Timothy Flint biography of, 7, 24–27, 28, 37, 39; as

Indian, 21; innocence of, 22; language of, 23; violence of, 26; reading of Western landscape, 26–27, 30; similarities to Leatherstocking, 36, 37; similarities to Lewis and Clark, 28–29, 31, 36, 132; and Frederick Jackson Turner, 40; as Western character model, 15, 17, 72, 132; and ideal West, 19.
Boone, Rebecca Bryan, 24–26, 201n. 13, 202n. 14
Bowie, Jim, 15
Breuer, Josef, 67, 206n. 6
Brown, Dee, 205n. 5
Brinkley, Alan, 205n. 2
Brown, Arthur Page, 207n. 7
Bryan, William Jennings, 214n. 3 , 215n. 3
Bureau of Indian Affairs, 47
Burgess, Gelette, 5
Burnham, Philip, 205n. 2
Burns, Ken, 8

California: as model of U.S. development, 114; Native Americans in, 57, 82; "personality" of, 80; State Constitution of, 72; University of at Berkeley, 8, 72–77, 81, 165, 207n. 2
Cardozo, Christopher, 205n. 8, 206nn. 10, 11
Casey, Edward S., 198n. 3
Cather, Willa: aesthetics of place in fiction of, 170; character compositions of, 76; cities in novels of, 64; on

About the Author

Mary Lawlor is associate professor of English and American Studies at Muhlenberg College, where she teaches courses in nineteenth-century U.S. and Native American literature.

DATE DUE
